The Study of Public Law

THE STUDY OF

 Random House New York

PUBLIC LAW

WALTER F. MURPHY
Princeton University

JOSEPH TANENHAUS
State University of New York at Stony Brook

Copyright © 1972 by Random House, Inc.
All rights reserved under International and Pan-
American Copyright Conventions.
Published in the United States by Random House,
Inc., New York, and simultaneously in Canada by
Random House of Canada Limited, Toronto.

ISBN: 0-394-31633-9

Library of Congress Catalog Card Number: 78-152856

The epigraph is from Ezra Pound, "A Pact," *Personae*.
Copyright 1926 by Ezra Pound. Reprinted by
permission of New Directions Publishing Corporation
and Faber and Faber Limited.

Manufactured in the United States of America
Printed and bound by Halliday Lithograph, Inc., West Hanover, Mass.

Text Design by Mel Haber

First Edition
98765432

To ROBERT E. CUSHMAN, 1889–1969, and C. HERMAN PRITCHETT

It was you that broke the new wood,
Now is a time for carving.
                                    —EZRA POUND

Preface

This book has its origins in a seminar we conducted during the summer of 1963 for the Inter-University Consortium for Political Research. The participants in that program may find that the long gestation has removed any resemblance between the working papers we prepared for those sessions and the contents of this book. In this instance, we suspect that the shock of nonrecognition is preferable to that of recognition.

This is the first volume in what we plan as a trilogy. The second will focus on a cluster of problems of public policy that judges in a number of countries have faced—such as federalism, political rights, and criminal justice—and its core will consist of cases and materials bearing on those problems. The third volume will present a more systematic, more detailed, and, we hope, a more sophisticated analysis of the roles of courts and judges in modern democratic nations. It will be based not only on the more extensive research into comparative politics that is now in progress but also on a series of opinion surveys of national samples and elite groups. We want to be able to show not only how courts and judges can function, do function, and should function, but also how the people who have to live with judicial rulings see courts as functioning and want courts to function.

A word about the title of this volume: One noted scholar* has said that the study of judicial behavior is replacing the study of public law. Although we chose the older characterization for descriptive rather than ideological reasons, we think that political scientists who study courts and judges are concerned with much more than how judges vote and write opinions or how they make up their minds. We believe that most of our colleagues who call themselves behavioralists would agree with that judgment. In our view the study of judicial behavior is only one segment, although a major segment, of the larger study of public law.

Any book so long in gestation must have depended for nourishment on many people other than its putative authors. Our wives and children put up with all the inconveniences and annoyances of research with their usual good grace. We are also grateful to Dr. Warren E. Miller, organizer and sometime Director of the Inter-University Consortium for Political Research, for inviting us to come to Ann Arbor in 1963; to his wife, Kip, for her warm hospitality; and to his most able assistant, Miss Ann Robinson, for taking care of such basic arrangements as salary. The National Science Foundation financed the surveys of public opinion to which we refer at scattered places throughout the book. We shall soon publish a monograph based on more systematic analyses of these survey data than we could present here. During the final stages of manuscript preparation, the Center of International Studies of Princeton University provided much needed financial support. We are obliged to several teams of computer specialists who worked so hard to program and process the data we required: Mrs. Shirley Gilbert of the Office of Survey Research and Statistical Studies, Princeton University, Mr. Gary Soverow of the Princeton Class of 1968, Mr. Lawrence Kegeles of the Princeton Class of 1969, Mr. Daniel L. Kastner of the Princeton Class of 1973; Professor Alonzo Mackelprang of American University, Professor Harrell R. Rodgers of the University of Georgia, Professor Kenneth A. Wagner of Los Angeles State College; Mr. Steven Roth of the Class of 1970 of the State University of New York at Stony Brook, and Mr. Gauri Srivastava of the State University of New York at Stony Brook. For services above and beyond the call of duty in editing, typing, and reproducing the manuscript we are indebted to Mrs. Judith Anderson, Mrs. Rosalie Bergen, and Mr. Fred Gordon, all of the State

* Glendon A. Schubert, "Introduction: From Public Law to Judicial Behavior," in his *Judicial Decision-Making* (New York: Free Press, 1963).

University of New York at Stony Brook; Mrs. Janet Bloor, Mrs. Lynn Waters, Mrs. Jane G. McDowall, Mrs. Mary Merrick, and Mrs. Meri Lea Scott, all of Princeton University; Mrs. Margaret Trott of Charlotte, N. C.; and Mrs. Mary June Forsythe of Atlanta, Georgia.

Miss Anne Dyer Murphy first persuaded us to undertake this book; her successor at Random House, Mr. Barry Rossinoff, succeeded in prying the manuscript out of our filing cabinets. At the moment we are inclined to be grateful to them, at least for their friendship and encouragement. Miss Jane Cullen and Mrs. Stefanie Gold performed yeoman service in translating our writings into English. All readers should share our appreciation.

We begged, bribed, or blackmailed a host of colleagues into reading all or portions of the manuscript in various draft forms. In alphabetical order our victims were:

David W. Adamany, Wesleyan University
David J. Danelski, Cornell University
Irving Faber, Colgate University
Rosalie Feltenstein, Ronda, Málaga
George H. Gadbois, Jr., University of Kentucky
Gerald Garvey, Princeton University
Takeo Hayakawa, University of Kobe
Donald P. Kommers, University of Notre Dame
W. Duane Lockard, Princeton University
Alpheus T. Mason, Princeton University
Charles A. Miller, Princeton University
Edward R. Tufte, Princeton University
Rudolph Wildenmann, State University of New York at Stony
    Brook and University of Mannheim

We thank these people for their help and want to say publicly that we forgive them for causing us many headaches of rethinking, rewriting, and reediting. If any errors remain after all these careful analyses, we must, of course, take full blame. We shall do so, however, with sullen reluctance and shall forever hold it against whoever among our friends was supposed to protect us from those particular aspects of our incompetence.

Princeton, N.J.
Stony Brook, N.Y.

March 17, 1971

Contents

Preface vii

Introduction 3

1 The Development of the Study of Public Law 7

2 The Question of Relevance: The Political Consequences of Judicial Decisions 30

3 Access and Influence 65

4 Judicial Recruitment, Training, and Tenure 92

5 Judicial Decision Making: The Individual Phase 116

6 The Group Phase of Decision Making 150

7 Statistical Methods in the Study of Public Law 179

8 The Future of Public Law 215

Indices 229

The Study of Public Law

Introduction

For many years the study of public law was central to the discipline of political science in the United States. In the 1950s and early 1960s, however, it seemed to many observers that public law had drifted out of the mainstream of American political science.[1] As do many of our professional colleagues, we find public law to be an exciting and important area of political inquiry, and we sense that a renaissance of interest in the judicial field is under way. Thus we believe that the time is ripe for a reiteration of the reasons—if not for formulation of new reasons—why political scientists should concern themselves with courts, judges, lawyers, and that nebulous concept, the law.

In this book we concentrate on the work of American scholars, but not on American courts. Many of the intellectual justifications for judicial review were known in Europe before the Revolution of 1775, but it was in the United States that the process matured in a viable government setting. The American Supreme Court was the first major national tribunal to function as a constitutional court,* that is, as a court exercising authority to declare acts of the national legislature and executive invalid. And that tribunal is still the most important constitutional court. Yet it is no longer a unique institution. It has been frequently imitated and its analogues grafted onto more than thirty different political systems.[2] In part because of this widespread imitation, in part because American scholars have been broadening their jurisdiction to study courts and judges outside the United States, and in part because of the intrinsic interest of the material, we have drawn illustrations about the functions of constitutional courts from a number of countries. Frequently we cite practices in Australia, Canada, India, Ireland, Japan, and West Germany, although the U.S. Supreme Court remains the central reference point.

Our decision to operate along such a broad spectrum has carried a pair of expensive price tags. First, we have had to neglect the work of trial courts and of intermediate appellate courts. We attempt to bring some discussion of these important tribunals into the text, but we look at them mainly from the perspective of a nation's highest constitutional court. Without a doubt, one could gain many insights by viewing a political system and its judicial subsystem from the perspective of lower courts, and we hope that other scholars will quickly repair our omission.[3]

A second cost has been equally high. The study of public law in the United States has been heavily interdisciplinary. The greatest American scholar in the field, Edward S. Corwin, was trained as a historian, taught in a department of political science, and in writing about constitutional law brought to bear self-taught technical legal knowledge as well as massive learning in history and politics. Both before and after Corwin, anthropologists, economists, historians, journalists, lawyers, philosophers, political scientists, psychologists, and sociologists have contributed to understanding the work of courts and judges. And like Corwin, these writers have themselves often been educated in several intellectual disciplines. In the chapters that follow we concentrate on the interests and writings of political scientists, without, we hope, obscuring either the quality or quantity of scholarship developed by people in other fields.

Our rationalization for paying these high costs is that in a book of this size there are close limits even to what two foolhardy authors can accom-

---

* In discussing federal courts in the United States, analysts have often made a distinction between "constitutional courts," that is, courts established by Congress under Article III, Section 1 of the Constitution, and "legislative courts," tribunals established by Congress under Article I, Section 8. In the context of cross-national research "constitutional court" has taken on a broader meaning to refer to a tribunal possessing the authority to review the legitimacy of acts of coordinate branches of the government, and it is in this broader sense that we use the term throughout this book.

plish. Assigning priorities was imperative, and we chose four objectives, none of them modest: (1) to indicate the relationship of the study of public law to the larger discipline of political science; (2) to suggest some of the basic problems to which political scientists interested in courts and judges orient their research; (3) to explore some—but only some—of that research; and (4) to assess the utility of various approaches and methods in developing answers to important questions. Because of the long, acrid, and sterile methodological debates between "behavioralists" and "traditionalists," we attack the last goal with considerable trepidation. We think the value of any research method or mode of analysis lies in its capacity to help provide answers to interesting questions; and it is on this basis that we look at the writings of traditionalists, behavioralists, and those who identify with neither faction.

In the first chapter we sketch a brief outline of the reasons why social scientists in general and political scientists in particular study public law, how that field has developed in American political science over the past few generations, and what sorts of questions political scientists have been trying to answer. In chapters 2 through 6 we take up some of the more important of these areas of concern: the political consequences of judicial decisions, access to and influence on courts, the selection and training of judges, and the individual and collective processes of judicial decision making.

Chapter 7 is in many ways quite different. It was also quite difficult to write and for many people may be quite difficult to read. There we examine several of the techniques of quantitative analysis used by scholars in public law. We try to explain those techniques in at least an intuitive way and to assess their utility in helping to find solutions to significant problems. It may well be that some readers will want only to sample the subsections of that chapter, which are intended to serve as brief introductions and not as substitutes for a textbook or a course in statistics. Especially in chapter 7 but also in chapters 5 and 6, we used for illustrative purposes data drawn from the work of other scholars. We tried to present material that was already published, so that the reader could easily go to the source and see for himself the context of this scholarship.

Chapter 8 returns to the format of chapters 2 through 6 and examines one set of problems that political scientists have tended to evade: the set concerned with the ends of law and the larger purposes of the judicial process. That chapter also attempts to plot what seems to us to be the future course of the study of public law in its latest reincarnation as an integral and prominent part of political science.

NOTES

1. See Glendon A. Schubert, *Quantitative Analysis of Judicial Behavior* (New York: Free Press, 1959), chap. 1; Schubert, "The Future of Public Law," 34 *George Washington Law Review* 593 (1966); and Albert Somit and Joseph Tanenhaus, *American Political Science: Profile of a Discipline* (New York: Atherton, 1964), chap. 6.

2. For general surveys of the work of constitutional courts, see Julius J. Marke and John G. Lexa (eds.), *International Seminar on Constitutional Review* (New York: New York University School of Law, mimeographed, 1963); Edward McWhinney, *Judicial Review* 4th ed. (Toronto: University of Toronto Press, 1969); Glendon A. Schubert and David J. Danelski (eds.), *Comparative Judicial Behavior* (New York: Oxford University Press, 1969); Thomas M. Franck (ed.), *Comparative Constitutional Process: Cases and Materials* (New York: Praeger, 1968); and Henry J. Abraham, *The Judicial Process* 2d ed. (New York: Oxford University Press, 1968).

3. Although political scientists have tended to give far less attention to trial and intermediate appellate courts than those tribunals deserve, there is a substantial body of literature available.   See, for example, Rodney Mott, "Judicial Influence," 30 *American Political Science Review* 295 (1936); Herbert Jacob, *Justice in America: Courts, Lawyers, and the Judicial Process* (Boston: Little, Brown, 1965); Jacob, *Debtors in Court: The Consumption of Government Services* (Chicago: Rand McNally, 1969); Jacob, "The Effect of Institutional Differences in the Recruitment Process: The Case of State Judges," 13 *Journal of Public Law* 104 (1964); Jacob and Kenneth N. Vines, *Studies in Judicial Politics* (New Orleans: Tulane Studies in Political Science, 1963); Vines, "The Judicial Role in the American States," in Joel Grossman and Joseph Tanenhaus (eds.), *Frontiers of Judicial Research* (New York: Wiley, 1969); Kenneth M. Dolbeare, *Trial Courts in Urban Politics* (New York: Wiley, 1967); Dolbeare, "The Federal District Courts and Urban Public Policy," in Grossman and Tanenhaus; Marvin Schick, *Learned Hand's Court* (Baltimore: The Johns Hopkins Press, 1970); Daryl R. Fair, "An Experimental Application of Scalogram Analysis to State Supreme Court Decisions," 1967 *Wisconsin Law Review* 449; Henry R. Glick, "Judicial Decision-Making and Group Dynamics: A Study of Role Perceptions and Group Behavior on Four State Supreme Courts," a paper presented at the Northeastern Political Science Association Meetings (1969); Walter F. Murphy, "Lower Court Checks on Supreme Court Power," 53 *American Political Science Review* 640 (1959); Murphy, "Chief Justice Taft and the Lower Court Bureaucracy," 24 *Journal of Politics* 453 (1962); Murphy, *Elements of Judicial Strategy* (Chicago: University of Chicago Press, 1964), chap. 4; Jack W. Peltason, *58 Lonely Men: Southern Federal Judges and School Desegregation* (New York: Harcourt, Brace & World, 1961); and Sheldon Goldman and Thomas P. Jahnige, *The Federal Courts as a Political System* (New York: Harper & Row, 1971). See also the literature cited in the sections of chapters 2, 4, and 5 dealing with the impact of court rulings, the relationships between social background and decision making, and judicial role perceptions.

1
The Development
of the
Study of Public Law

Perhaps the question most frequently asked of any social scientist interested in public law is, What are you doing studying law? Unlike the attorney, the social scientist must constantly justify his research in the legal processes, and he often envies his colleagues in the law schools who can do their own thing without having to reiterate its relevance or their own competence. Yet this need for justification is not an unmixed evil, since it serves to remind the social scientist that he is not a lay lawyer but a professional with special interests of his own.[1]

The historic functions of the lawyer in civil and common law countries have been to know the content of that corpus of rules formulated by various governmental bodies to control human behavior and to advise clients of their rights and duties under those rules. The attorney takes a set of legal rules as a starting point and tries to justify his client's conduct under, or to shape his client's conduct to conform to, those rules.   Of course, the lawyer's role in the modern world can be much broader.   At his best, he is a professional problem solver, and the problems on which he works may go far beyond those involving legal technicalities.   He is frequently asked to help resolve basic social, economic, and political difficulties, which is one reason why good lawyers are so often recruited for important positions in business and government.

To a considerable extent, a lawyer's problem solving for his clients is based on his prediction of what a given court—that is, a judge, a judge and jury, or a group of judges—will do if presented with certain kinds of controversy. He predicts what a court will decide are the facts, what rules it will apply, and what judgments will follow.   This is a very complex process. First, the facts are usually in dispute.   Second, there are, typically, several, and perhaps contradictory, sets of rules that appear more or less equally relevant.   Third, because few judges and jurymen reason as dispassionately as computers, a formula like Facts × Rules = Decision will not suffice as an explanation of the adjudicatory process.   Emotional and ideological elements can affect what judges and jurors will perceive to be the "facts" of a case as readily as they can influence choice among competing rules.[2] Further complicating matters, an attorney's predictions, if forcefully and eloquently presented, may persuade judges and jurors—and thus, the law— to take one possible direction rather than another.[3]

With his role sanctioned by tradition and often by constitutional prescription, the lawyer has no difficulty in justifying his study of the law. That is his field of special competence, and many lawyers tend to view all other people, whether laymen or social scientists, who proclaim an interest in law as poachers on a private hunting preserve.   Yet many people other than lawyers have a valid interest in the law.   The layman, after all, is the man at whom most legal rules are aimed.   Aristotle's dictum that the diner is a better judge of a feast than the cook[4] is particularly appropriate here.

Similarly, the practicing politician has a stake in the study of public law and in the actions of judicial officials.   Because court decisions can vitally affect his right to hold office, the powers of his office, and the policies he wants effected, the politician has to know how judges are apt to act. In addition, he may want to affect the way they will act.   To be sure, with his time and energy limited, the government official, party officer, interest-group leader, or even the politically active citizen may rely on his attorney for guidance.   Nevertheless, in most democratic polities no serious political actor whose views are not unanimously shared by his fellow citizens can afford to ignore the courts in planning his program.   His justification for studying the law—and this is an additional reason why in Western nations so many political leaders have been first trained as lawyers[5]—is an instrumental one.　He must concern himself with judicial action to achieve his ambition, whether it be the selfish one of merely getting ahead or the more grandiose one of molding a great society.

Social Scientists and the Study of Law

The social scientist finds himself in a more difficult position than that of the lawyer.　He cannot claim the right to advise clients, because lawyers have a legal monopoly on this function and are quick to harass anyone who practices law without a license.　Nor is the social scientist's stake as a social scientist as evident as that of the professional politician or as it would be in his role as ordinary citizen concerned with the practical consequences of legal decisions.　Yet like the lawyer, the layman, and the politician, the social scientist may be concerned with understanding, predicting, and perhaps even shaping the development of law.　Insofar as he is influenced by the last objective his concern may be as pragmatic as that of a practicing politician or as detached as that of a closet philosopher.

Even when the social scientist restricts himself to the scholarly objectives of understanding the judicial process and explaining it to a public audience he, like the philosophically reflective lawyer or judge, faces a serious obstacle. Over the years some lawyers and judges—sometimes with the passive and sometimes with the active cooperation of other groups in society—have surrounded the judiciary with a series of myths. The most important for our purposes is that of mechanical jurisprudence: Judges only discover "the law"; they neither create legal rules nor do they make public policy.　This myth is powerful not because it is a deliberate sham—for most assuredly it is not— but because judges themselves have often believed that it is a valid explanation of their work.　They have confused a normative prescription with a factual description.　As Chief Justice John Marshall put it:

> Judicial power, as contradistinguished from the power of the laws, has no existence.　Courts are the mere instruments of the law, and can will nothing.... Judicial power is never exercised for the purpose of giving effect to the will of the Judge; always for the purpose of giving effect to the will of the Legislature; or in other words, to the will of the law.[6]

American judges inherited this myth; they share it with their brethren in other countries.　In 1952 Chief Justice Sir Owen Dixon of Australia explained the judicial role in simple, mechanistic terms: "The Court's sole function is to interpret a constitutional description of power or restraint upon power, and say whether a given measure falls on one side of a line consequently drawn or on the other, and that is nothing whatever to do with the merits or demerits of the measure."[7]*

A politician can subscribe to this myth in his public pronouncements at the same time that he is quietly ignoring it in his actions; a lawyer can phrase his advice, given in privileged confidence to his client, so as to avoid the myth altogether; a judge can cloak himself in its covers; and the layman can operate in blissful ignorance of what is orthodox doctrine. The dilemma of scholars, whether they are lawyers, judges, or social scientists, is not so easily resolved if they feel they have a duty not only to understand but also to explain.

The judicial myth is based on two postulates, neither of which is acceptable to most scholars. First, it assumes that a judge has no discretion. Second, it assumes that judges are neutral, that they have no deep concern about the results of their decisions, that they function, as Blackstone said, merely " as the mouth of the law."

As we have already indicated, and as many judges and lawyers have themselves pointed out, legal rules are often imprecise in just those areas where important governmental policies are likely to generate troublesome cases. The American Constitution, for instance, does not forbid all searches and seizures, but only " unreasonable " ones; it does not forbid government to take "life, liberty, or property," but only to do so "without due process of law." Other crucial terms, like "commerce among the several states," "the executive power," "equal protection of the laws," and "freedom of speech," are left conveniently undefined.

Constitutional clauses of other polities abound in similar ambiguities. For instance, Article 40 of the Irish Constitution "guarantees liberty for the exercise " of the rights of citizens "to express freely their convictions and opinions," "to assemble peaceably and without arms," and "to form associations and unions." At the same time Article 40 stipulates that all these rights are "subject to public order and morality." And it specifically hedges these guarantees with qualifications, excluding from the protected area speech that is "blasphemous, seditious, or indecent" and assemblies that are calculated "to cause a breach of the peace or to be a danger or nuisance to the general public."

Article 13 of the Japanese Constitution displays an equal ambivalence:

> All of the people shall be respected as individuals. Their right to life, liberty, and the pursuit of happiness shall, to the extent it does not interfere with the public welfare, be the supreme consideration in legislation and in other governmental affairs.

---

* The chief justice was not so naïve as this statement might indicate. As he wrote five years earlier: " The Constitution is a political instrument. It deals with government and governmental powers . . . ." Melbourne v. Commonwealth, 74 *Commonwealth Law Reports* at 82 (1947).

Nor are all the precepts within a given constitution always easy to reconcile with each other. Article 43 of the Irish Constitution, for example, both giveth and taketh away:

> The State acknowledges that man, in virtue of his rational being, has the natural right, antecedent to positive law, to the private ownership of external goods. . . . The State recognizes, however, that the exercise of the rights mentioned in the foregoing provisions of this Article ought, in civil society, to be regulated by the principles of social justice.

Section 92 of the Australian Constitution provides that "trade, commerce, and intercourse among the States, whether by means of internal carriage or ocean navigation, shall be absolutely free." On the other hand, Section 51 empowers Parliament "to make laws for the peace, order, and good government of the Commonwealth with respect to— (1) Trade and Commerce with other countries, and among the States. . . ."[8]

Controversial statutes are frequently as fraught with vagueness as are constitutional clauses, allowing (at times, even forcing) judges to exercise considerable discretion. To interpret such documents, Felix Frankfurter once said, a judge must read life, not law.[9] On the other hand, most scholars do not assert that judges have unfettered choice. Judicial tradition and ethical norms absorbed through professional training combine with social, institutional, and political checks to set limits on how far a judge can exercise his creativity. He has leeway, not license.

The second postulate of the judicial myth, that of neutrality, confuses two kinds of impartiality: the neutrality of a judge toward the litigants and his neutrality with respect to competing principles of law and underlying assumptions about what constitutes the best political order. In the overwhelming number of cases decided in Western nations, judges probably do not show favoritism toward one or the other of the parties to a suit. This does not mean, however, that a judge is without strong views about general principles of legal or political philosophy or that those views do not influence his decision about what the facts in a case are or what set of rules should be applied.[10] Most scholars would deny that judges can consistently—and many would deny that judges should—ignore the effects likely to accrue to society because of certain types of decisions. Nor does a belief in the judge's neutrality toward the litigants mean that legal rules are themselves neutral.* In most instances the rules punish some kinds of conduct and permit others; they protect only some of what many people consider, or wish, to be their fundamental rights.

* To speak of neutral rules is, of course, to reify. Neutrality is a human quality, and only by analogy can one speak of rules as neutral or not neutral. See Arthur S. Miller and Ronald F. Howell, "The Myth of Neutrality in Constitutional Adjudication," 27 *University of Chicago Law Review* 661 (1960).

Any scholar who publishes his analyses of public law thus faces a serious dilemma.   On the one hand, he is committed to a pursuit of the truth.   On the other hand, as a responsible citizen, he may feel restrained from directly attacking the myths of his own society, for he knows these often serve a worthwhile purpose and that in destroying them, he may only be planting a dangerously negative cynicism rather than nourishing a new and more realistic faith.   To explain that judges have leeway but not license, that they are impartial in one sense, yet are not intellectual eunuchs or robots—not, as Chief Justice Earl Warren remarked, monks[11]—is a delicate task.   All too frequently the social scientist, like his colleagues in the law school and on the bench, has left misleading impressions that because judges often must exercise discretion and because they have intellectual and emotional pre-dilections in matters of jurisprudence or political theory, they merely translate their biases into law.   At other times, when scholars have tried to hedge their descriptions with softening adverbs and adjectives, they have left the impression that they themselves are weasel-worded pedants.   This impression is sometimes wrong.

These difficulties cannot, however, affect the basic fact that social scientists have many, varied, and legitimate interests in studying and explaining public law and judicial behavior.   An economist is forced to recognize court decisions as forming part of the framework within which exchanges of goods and services take place as well as a force helping to determine what roles government or specific agencies of government will play in that process. A historian may be concerned with the judicial past or the impact of court decisions on a given historical era.   A sociologist may see juries or collegial courts as miniature social systems; or he may view the entire court structure as a social subsystem and examine interactions among judicial officials. On a broader plane, a sociologist may be interested in the functions of law in society as a whole, just as an anthropologist may find the development of prototypes of law and lawmakers a key to understanding a primitive society. A psychologist may see judges as providing ideal material for case studies of human beings acting under great stress; he may also be interested in the impact of judges' decisions on the psyches of the people who must live with the results of those rulings; or he may feel obliged to enlighten the judges on such matters as mental illness and individual responsibility.

A political scientist has to be concerned with the activities of judges because the consequences of what judges do may vitally affect both specific policies and the general conditions under which polities operate.   And if judicial decisions do have such effects, how judges make up their minds, how they are selected, and how they can manipulate their power, all become matters of fundamental importance.

Public Law Before Behavioralism

In the decade before the outbreak of World War I, Lord Bryce, A. Lawrence Lowell, Woodrow Wilson, and Charles Beard complained that American political science had become arid and formalistic.[12] Political scientists, they said, appeared more interested in what was supposed to transpire in a political system than concerned with what actually took place. They paid too much attention to purely abstract analysis and superficial descriptions of formal structures of government at the price of ignoring informal structures, processes, and the actual functions performed by political and quasi-political institutions.

This criticism had a sharp, if not immediate, impact. During the period between the two world wars the Realism so strenuously urged by these critics became the dominant mood of American political science in general and public law in particular. In a different way the better law schools also felt the effect of this pervasive mood. Indeed, Legal Realism became and has remained an intellectually powerful movement among judges and academic lawyers.[13] It has served as a far more influential counterweight in the courts to the mechanistic myths than has the work of social scientists. Perhaps these developments were only reflections of the larger cynical reaction that occurred in American society. The leading scholars in public law during this period, Edward S. Corwin, Robert E. Cushman, Charles Grove Haines, and Thomas Reed Powell, were all Realists. They scorned the idea that judges are value-free technicians who do no more than discover "the law."

Charles Grove Haines' essay "General Observations on the Effects of Personal, Political, and Economic Influences in the Decisions of Judges," first published in 1922, is still being cited, read, and reprinted. In it he carefully spells out his conclusions about the effects of such influences, effects that went beyond mere catchwords like "economic bias."

> A complex thing like a judicial decision involves factors, personal and legal, which carry us to the very roots of human nature and human conduct. Political prejudices, the influences of narrow and limited legal training with antiquated legal principles and traditions, or class bias having little or no relation to wealth or property interests, are more likely to affect the decisions of judges than so-called "economic interests."[14]

These factors, Haines felt, may be difficult to trace, but their impact on judicial decisions cannot be ignored.

One can find early touches of Realism in Part III of Haines' first major work, the 1914 edition of *The American Doctrine of Judicial Supremacy*.[15] And after 1922 his substantive writings contain frequent, detailed, and occasionally quantitative evidence that he took his "General Observations" essay seriously. As he repeated in 1944:

> Not only have personal and political factors profoundly affected the decisions of the Supreme Court, but these decisions have also had far-reaching effects on the political and economic life of the people. It is appropriate, therefore, to give special consideration to the work of the Court where it impinges on the field of politics and becomes one of the foremost political agencies.[16]

And this is precisely what Haines did.

The realism of Edward S. Corwin was neatly reflected in his *Twilight of the Supreme Court*, published in 1934. The theme of that volume was that "the Constitution of a progressive society [must] keep pace with that society." Writing on the eve of the great battle between Franklin D. Roosevelt and the Supreme Court over the constitutionality of the New Deal, Corwin insisted that there was nothing that obligated the Court to invalidate the National Industrial Recovery Act.

> Due process of law is no Frankenstein's monster that rides down legislation in defiance of its creator's will—it is the servant of the Court's *legislative* judgment. Were NIRA and her kin to perish at the Court's hands, it would not be by the decree of "some brooding omnipresence in the sky," but of a majority of nine entirely human beings.[17]

One can readily find much earlier indications of Realism in Corwin's writings. If the Court were to play the role intended for it by the framers of the Constitution, he had suggested in a book on John Marshall published in 1919, it had to blend politics with jurisprudence and establish a firm "hold on the imagination of the country."[18] Marshall, Corwin claimed, recognized this fact and acted "with mingled boldness and caution" to provide the Court with "the leadership the circumstances demanded." By doing so, he had made "his Court one of the great political forces of the country."

Robert E. Cushman's early reputation was based on an impressive series of articles that closely analyzed, in a traditional legal way, judicial decisions dealing with the concept of national police power.[19] Nonetheless, by the mid-1920s Cushman's commitment to Realism had been fully documented. In 1925 the first edition of his *Leading Constitutional Decisions*—a small casebook widely used for more than four decades as a supplementary text for introductory courses in American government—was published. In the preface Cushman wrote:

The Supreme Court does not do its work in a vacuum. Its decisions on important constitutional questions can be understood in their full significance only when viewed against the background of history, politics, economics, and personality surrounding them and out of which they grew. It is the purpose of the brief introductory notes to reconstruct this background [and] to suggest the significance of the cases in our constitutional development. . . .[20]

Time and again Cushman's notes stressed that particular litigation before the Court was but a stage in a struggle between contending political forces—Presidents and congressmen, state and federal authorities, political parties, or economic interest groups. He made frequent references to the importance in judicial decision making of the personal values of the justices and, therefore, of changes in Court personnel. Occasionally, he alluded to judicial strategy, as when Marshall apparently delayed a decision in the Dartmouth College case[21] until he could be certain of a majority for his position. Repeatedly, Cushman called attention to adverse reactions to particular decisions, reactions ranging from widespread popular abuse of the Court and even defiance of its rulings to attempts to diminish the Court's authority or tamper with its membership. The justices, he pointed out, sometimes found it expedient to avoid a head-on collision with elected politicians, or even, when severely pressed, to retreat from earlier pronouncements. Nor did Cushman ignore the broader systemic consequences of major decisions. In discussing the *Slaughterhouse Cases*,[22] for example, he wrote:

The importance of the case[s] can hardly be overestimated. By distinguishing between state citizenship and national citizenship, and by emphasizing that the rights and privileges of federal citizenship did not include the protection of ordinary civil rights, such as freedom of speech and press, religion, the right of assembly, etc., but only privileges which one enjoyed by virtue of his federal citizenship, the Court averted the revolution in our constitutional system intended by the framers of the fourteenth amendment, and reserved to the states the control of civil rights generally.[23]

Again, the note to *Gibbons v. Ogden*[24] states: "The economic consequences of it in freeing a developing commerce from the shackles of state monopoly can hardly be overestimated; and it established for all time the supremacy of the national government in all matters affecting interstate and foreign commerce."[25]

The fourth leading American constitutional scholar, Thomas Reed Powell, who was both a political scientist and a lawyer, explicitly acknowledged his debt to Roscoe Pound, the founder of the Sociological School of Jurisprudence, and to John Dewey, one of the leading philosophers of pragmatism. Constitutional law, Powell asserted, is not "an impersonal and

majestic power which moves in some mysterious way its wonders to perform."
It is rather the product of "human beings performing a human task."
The rhetoric of Supreme Court justices

> is not unlike the rhetoric we all use.   And the logic behind the rhetoric is the
> logic with which you and I debate our disagreements. . . .   Many men of
> many minds have sat on our supreme Bench as they have read papers at meet-
> ings of the American Political Science Association or lectured in college class-
> rooms.   Judges argue from undisclosed assumptions, as you and I argue from
> undisclosed assumptions.   Judges seek their premises from facts, as you and I
> strive to do.   Judges have preferences for social policies, as you and I.   They
> form their judgments after the varying fashions in which you and I form ours.
> They have hands, organs, dimensions, senses, affections, passions.[26]

Powell took pains to convey the impression that judges were limited
by the language of the Constitution and by precedent, public opinion,
"existing conditions," and the fear of legislative or executive noncompliance
and reprisal.   Nevertheless, in many cases of great consequence "there are
two or more courses equally open to the Supreme Court."   When alternatives
were available, the justices relied on their common sense, as they had to do.

One could readily show that scholars of the succeeding generation, men
like Robert K. Carr, Charles Fairman, Alpheus T. Mason, and Carl B.
Swisher, viewed the U.S. Supreme Court in an equally Realistic fashion.
But enough has now been said to demonstrate that leading American students
of public law in the period from 1920 to the end of World War II shared the
following assumptions:

☐ **1.** The American Constitution delineates, although often in a vague
   fashion, the fundamental boundaries of authority within the political
   system and between the political system and its environment.   The
   Constitution performs this delineation by granting authority and
   withholding authority from both federal and state political institutions.

2. The Supreme Court is an integral part of the political system because:
   a. To a very large extent the Constitution and federal statutes mean
   what the Supreme Court says they mean.   As a result, many Supreme
   Court decisions have far-reaching effects on the authority and the
   activity of political officials.
   b. What the Court collectively does is, in turn, affected by the
   conduct of other political officials who are in a position to select
   its personnel, restrict its authority, and bring a plethora of other
   sanctions against it.

3. Supreme Court decisions are likely to be a mixture of law, politics,
   and policy.   The background, training, personality, and conscious

as well as unconscious value preferences of individual justices influence the manner in which they decide cases. Judges, however, are not completely free agents. To some extent their choices are restricted by the wording of the Constitution, precedents, fear of sanctions, and systemic and environmental forces.

As good as the work of these scholars was, it was subject to certain important limitations. First of all, they wrote mainly about the Supreme Court of the United States. Insofar as one can tell from their publications, they, with the possible exception of Haines, had only slight interest in state courts or in courts and judges in foreign political systems. Second, their interest in the U.S. Supreme Court was largely confined to two particular aspects: (1) what we might call the boundary-defining decisions of the Supreme Court, that is, its demarcations of the lines of authority among various public officials and (2) the influence of a justice's personal values on his decision making. Explorations of the first question were more thorough—and more intellectually satisfying—than those of the second. In large part this was due to the tools of analysis that were popular among the leading scholars: close examination of the historical context of cases and equally close examination of the reasoning in the opinions the justices handed down and the consequences that logically followed from that reasoning.

An additional limitation on work in public law was that, like political scientists generally, these leading scholars did not take great advantage of techniques of quantitative analysis that had been available since the 1920s. Instead, they basically relied on judicial opinions, on the writings of judges like Oliver Wendell Holmes and Benjamin Cardozo, and on their own informed intuition to demonstrate the influence of personal values.

There were a few significant exceptions. During the National Conferences on the Science of Politics, 1923–1925, the round table devoted to public law gave extended attention to the potentialities of quantification.[27] At the third conference in 1925, Isidore Loeb presented a statistical analysis of Supreme Court decisions from 1914 to 1924. Attention also turned to Rinehart Swenson's analysis of the Supreme Court's interpretation of antitrust legislation and to determining the stability of the "grouping" of judges in nonunanimous decisions. The participants at the round table discussed other ways of discovering whether concepts such as due process are "used merely as available arguments when a judge finds them useful to attain an end deemed to be desirable on other than legal grounds, or are . . . guiding forces that tend to determine the judicial product." There was much interest, for example, in an elaborate plan presented by Rodney Mott. His proposal called, in part, for a systematic attempt to correlate judges' decisions with such data as age, marital status, nationality of parents, political affiliation before appointment, education, training, and religion.

Each member of the 1925 public law round table agreed to attend a subsequent meeting a year later and bring with him the results of his efforts to test some of the methods discussed. For reasons that are not entirely clear, however, the 1925 National Conference on the Science of Politics turned out to be the last, and the public law round table never reconvened. Despite initial hopes for its yield, interest in quantitative legal research more or less evanesced with the demise of the National Conferences. Nevertheless, in the twenty years that followed, a tiny fistful of political scientists carried on some quantitative work in public law. Rodney Mott published his analysis of judicial influence;[28] Haines produced a study of decisions made by workmen's compensation boards;[29] and Cortez Ewing collected a mass of data on the social backgrounds of Supreme Court justices.[30] Harold Lasswell even prepared sophisticated content analyses of newspaper publications for governmental use in several criminal prosecutions during World War II.[31] But all these were exceptions to the prevailing pattern and also only beginnings. For example, although a team of social psychologists headed by Frederick Gaudet sought to relate judicial sentencing behavior to such variables as the type of crime involved, use or nonuse of juries, the length of the judge's service on the bench, and the imminence of his reappointment or reelection,[32] no political scientist actually followed up on Mott's suggestion that judicial decision making might be correlated with social background characteristics.

Recognition of these shortcomings does not at all denigrate the quality of work of the best scholars of the period between the two world wars. What they did, they did superbly. More recent political scientists have tinkered with their concept of courts as a part of the political process and have broadened their focus to include American trial and intermediate appellate courts as well as judicial systems outside the United States, but they have said little that is new about the boundary-defining role of the judiciary. Although the story has not been quite the same in the study of judicial values, later scholars have largely devoted themselves to demonstrating in a more orderly, quantitative way the insights of these earlier students.

The Behavioral Impact on the Study of Public Law

During World War II, C. Herman Pritchett wrote a series of articles on the voting records of contemporary justices of the U.S. Supreme Court.[33] The publication in 1948 of his book *The Roosevelt Court*[34] constituted a benchmark in the study of public law. Pritchett's objective was the long-cherished one of discovering the values that underlie judicial decisions. But if his target was old, his tactics were new. Struck by Lord Kelvin's dictum, "When you cannot measure, your knowledge is meager and unsatisfactory,"* Pritchett imaginatively applied elementary quantitative procedures to analyze systematically the votes of justices in nonunanimous cases over the ten-year period from 1937 to 1947. He was thereby able to demonstrate that members of the Court could be ranked in terms of their support of policies toward organized labor, freedom of speech and religion, criminal justice, and economic regulation.

Somewhat later, Pritchett formulated and tested an intervening variable between a justice's values and his votes: judicial role. A judge's behavior, he hypothesized, was a function not only of his policy predilections but also of his conception of "what is appropriate for him as a judge to do."[35] In addition, Pritchett devised a method for measuring the extent of agreement and disagreement between pairs of justices. He was thus able to outline the composition of blocs of justices and to chart their stability over time.

The Roosevelt Court foreshadowed the interest in both quantification and judicial decision making so characteristic of much of the behaviorally oriented public law literature of the present. We have said "foreshadowed" rather than "caused," not because Pritchett's influence was not widespread and deep, but because other more general influences were at work within public law as well as within the broader discipline. Most important was the mood of behavioralism, a vaguely defined approach that, in political science, has emphasized quantification, empirical theory, and the actual behavior of political actors. This mood had ebbed and flowed through much of the history of American political science,[36] and during the late 1920s and 1930s its capital was the University of Chicago. It was, therefore, fitting that Pritchett, who had received his doctorate from that university and then joined its faculty, laid the foundation of a new behavioral approach to the study of public law.

As great as was the attention attracted by *The Roosevelt Court*—and six years later, by *Civil Liberties and the Vinson Court*[37]—Pritchett's quantitative approach did not immediately begin a new school. Counting and analyzing votes of Supreme Court justices became standard fare in law reviews as well as in newspapers and political science journals.[38] But, although many scholars recognized the merit of Pritchett's work, many others, including an occasional Supreme Court justice, deplored his use of statistics, comparing it to "box scores" in baseball reports—an analogy, incidentally, that could not have been totally displeasing to Pritchett, an avid White Sox fan. But if there was wide imitation and even wider controversy over Pritchett's method, for a decade there was little additional construction on the foundations that

---

* Aristotle, of course, had seen the same problem and had provided a qualification to Kelvin: "[I]t is the mark of an educated man to look for precision in each class of things just so far as the nature of the subject admits. . . ." *Nicomachean Ethics*, Book I.

he built. Those who followed him imitated, rather than added to, his methods.

In the late 1950s, however, a new group of scholars began to take off from the runway that Pritchett had laid. Within a few years behavioralism was well established in public law. Scholars like David J. Danelski, Herbert Jacob, Fred Kort, Stuart Nagel, Harold Spaeth, S. Sidney Ulmer, and most especially Glendon A. Schubert were writing numerous books and articles, pushing out far beyond the statistical techniques that Pritchett pioneered. As Schubert noted in dedicating a book to Pritchett, Pritchett had "blazed a trail" that had become a well-traveled road.[39]

At the time when quantitative analysis was becoming an accepted part of the discipline and taking many diverse forms that Pritchett had never envisioned, other behavioral approaches were also flourishing. Jack Peltason, in particular, stressed the need for more penetrating investigation of the external environment of judicial decision making. His call was answered—in several instances anticipated—by a series of case studies.[40] Some focused on the activities of pressure groups in fostering their interests by sponsoring law suits, while others investigated the actual impact of Supreme Court decisions on specific facets of public policy and the feedback from those decisions into Congress, the presidency, state politics, and again into the judicial process. Other scholars were expanding their jurisdiction to include at least portions of a far wider range of problems than had men like Corwin and Cushman and were using as laboratories state, local, foreign, and lower federal courts.

Whither Do We Tend?

The questions to which political scientists in public law are seeking answers are tightly interrelated, but for analytical purposes we can arrange them on three levels: (1) How *can* the judiciary operate? What are the possible courses of action open to judges and what are the potential consequences of their choices? (2) How *does* the judiciary operate? What is it that judges actually do? What factors influence these actions? What effects do those actions have on the political order? (3) How *should* the judiciary operate? What are the proper ends to which judges should be working, and what are the proper means for them to use?

The Operational Level

It is on the second, or operational, level—how courts in fact function and with what effects—that most American political scientists have been working; and it is on the problems raised by this kind of research that the major portion of this book will focus. If judicial decisions do have significant political consequences and if judges have some discretion in their decision making, then a plethora of issues demand scholarly attention.   How judges are chosen, for instance, becomes a vital matter.   It is not enough to know the constitutional mechanics of judicial selection; one also has to understand the criteria that appointing officials consider and the points at which different kinds of pressure can be applied to influence their choices.   The social and political backgrounds of the men who are selected become critical if it can be demonstrated that such factors make real differences in actual decisions.

If judges have discretion in fostering one policy rather than another, the personal values the individual jurist brings to his work and the manner in which he feels a judge in his role as judge is obligated to behave may be critical in the way he both perceives and selects alternatives.   Thus a whole series of questions political scientists ask cluster around the place of judges' personal values and role perceptions in their decisions and conduct.

Closely related are questions about the influence of judges on one another—of lower court judges on higher court judges, of higher court judges on lower courts, and of judges of the same court on each other.   Not only are there major policy areas in which lower court judges generally have the last word,[41] but even in those areas dominated by higher courts, trial judges are not automatons who slavishly apply the directions of appellate jurists. Lower court judges have room for discretion.   Moreover, they frequently have experience, respect, and intellectual acumen equal or superior to those of their seniors, and their views can influence members of higher courts. What is more, even if they do nothing else, trial judges may shape the issues that upper court judges decide.   And when a case reaches a higher court, the judges who staff that bench typically have an opportunity to persuade and lead each other.

Formal decision-making procedures may also structure judicial choices. Some constitutional courts rely basically on oral argument, others principally on written briefs; some, like the U.S. Supreme Court, allow both.   On some courts, before a case is heard, one judge is assigned responsibility for preparing a memorandum for his colleagues summarizing the facts, outlining the issues, and recommending a decision.   Custom also affects the nature of discussion among the judges.   On the Australian constitutional court, or High Court, for example, each judge typically functions very much alone, whereas in the United States formal conferences are long and frequent, and informal discussions go on continually.   In some courts each judge normally writes his own opinion; in others opinions are issued only in the name of the court. The American practice* of having the opinion of the Court signed by its

---

* The formal decision-making procedures of the U.S. Supreme Court are by no means universally followed by all collegial courts in this country. See the two studies by the Institute of Judicial Administration, "Appellate Court, Internal Operating Procedures" (mimeographed, 1957 and 1959), and the Report by a Committee of the Section of Judicial Administration of the American Bar Association, "Internal Operating Procedures of Appellate Courts" (1961).

author and allowing separate dissenting and concurring views to be published is not universal.

One could multiply almost endlessly examples of widely varying kinds of formal procedures. The important question is what effect these institutional arrangements have on decision making and, thus, on the political system. Does it make any difference that a judge does not see the opposing lawyers or does not read a written brief or does not consult with his colleagues? If it does not, why not? If it does, how does it? And how great is the effect of his doing or not doing so? Does a rule against separate opinions move the majority to compromise with the minority? Is it the character of individual judges or the nature of group interaction that is crucial?

Other lines of inquiry at the operational level concern output. Judicial behavior may, to be sure, have an immediate impact in selecting and achieving societal goals as well as in the distribution of things valued in the community. What a judge says and does in particular circumstances may affect not only the litigants but also the subsequent conduct of other judges and of lawyers, legislators, bureaucrats, executives, and leaders of social, economic, patriotic, religious, and other organizations. On occasion even large segments of the general public may be reached and their support for the judicial and political systems augmented or diminished. The longer-run impact may become even more consequential as output feeds back into the judicial process and other processes of government and politics and perhaps returns to the courts a third or fourth time. Thus research in these areas must take into consideration the dimension of time: immediate versus delayed effect, short-run impact versus long-run influence. Such problems follow the circular course of the political processes. Decision makers attempt to fit policies to real and supposed concerns. Sometimes these policies settle the problems. Often they please only some persons. Those who are displeased may press new demands or intensify old ones; those who are pleased may go over to the defensive. Each side is apt to resort to any avenue of access to power that seems particularly useful, whether these avenues run through formal political institutions or informal structures of authority. At times it seems that successful governments tend to outlive as much as solve their problems.

The Level of Capability

Analytically prior to the operational level of inquiry is what may be termed the "level of capability": the potential, on the one hand, of courts and judges to influence the political system and, on the other hand, of other actors in that system to influence the judicial processes. In examining Western democratic systems, scholars have tended, at least subconsciously, to modify the verb "influence" by the adverb "legitimately," since, although political violence is more frequent than most people like to admit,[42] attempted revolutions or even coups d'état are uncommon in nations like Australia, Canada, Ireland, Norway, the United States, Germany, and Japan. In those countries and many others, judicial honesty is more or less taken for granted, although specific instances of the corrupt judge[43] are easy to find.

In contrast to the peaceful transfer of power in most industrial democracies, *Putsch*s in Argentina have been rather frequent and have hit hard at that country's constitutional court. After Perón, Aramburu, and Ongania seized power, each removed judges from the Supreme Court and replaced them with more sympathetic men. Thus in studying political systems, especially in regions still in the throes of modernization or undergoing radical transition from one kind of political culture to another, it would be imprudent for a scholar to assume that violence, intimidation, and fraud are not used to influence judges.

In any event, even where such "illegitimate" techniques are not used, a judge finds himself in many ways very much like other government officials, and an understanding of the alternatives open to him as well as of the costs and benefits each alternative carries is as important to the study of the judicial branch of government as it is to any other phase of politics. Just as one cannot even pretend to understand international relations without a rather precise notion of the power potential of individual nations, or to understand executive-legislative relations without knowing a great deal about the sanctions and rewards that each can bring to bear against the other, so one cannot truly understand the way judges operate without understanding the sources of their power, the instruments they may use, and the formal and informal restrictions to which they are subject. Many periods of American constitutional history, for instance, make little sense unless one keeps in mind not only that the Supreme Court can declare acts of the President or Congress unconstitutional, but also, as Corwin, Cushman, and others stressed, that the President can refuse to enforce judicial decisions and that the Congress can increase the number of justices, remove the Court's jurisdiction to hear certain kinds of cases, and propose constitutional amendments to reverse particular decisions or even to curb judicial power itself.

In short, capability analysis is concerned with power, with what judges— or, more broadly, any political actors—can do, how they can maximize their ability to influence their political environment. Scattered throughout the literature of political science are many sentences, paragraphs, and even chapters on judicial power, at least the power of the U.S. Supreme Court. Dicta about the Court's power being the power of public opinion are commonplace,[44] just as are the linkages of judicial authority to particular institutional arrangements. But systematic mappings of the power relations between judges and the rest of the political system are rare. We are aware of only two, and neither is complete. One focused more on the U.S.

Supreme Court as a governmental institution.[45]   The other took as its point
of departure the individual Supreme Court justice and tried to show how,
given his power as one of nine judges and operating within a web of institutional and ideological restraints, he could maximize his influence on public
policy.[46]

Despite the paucity of elaborate capability analyses, most scholars who
have written about courts have had at least a rough model* of how judges
can influence their respective polities.   It takes only a moment's reflection to
understand why few full-blown capability studies are published.   Explaining
a model of this kind is extremely difficult because of the complex network of
formal and informal relations that must be outlined, along with lines of
change and development.   To speak intelligently of the political potential
of judges, one has to be prepared to describe the environment of the entire
political system, to chart its anatomy and physiology, and to sketch its
psychology as well as its pathology.   Describing only what a constitution
allows would not be enough.   One would also have to be explicit about
what can be done practically, not only in terms of power politics but in terms
of political culture as well, since in most societies some actions are taboo,
even though apparently perfectly legitimate in terms of statutory or constitutional law.

The Ethical Level

At the third level of analysis are the "should ' questions.   What are the
ultimate goals that judges should use as criteria in selecting the principles
to guide their own decisions and those of other policy makers?   To what
extent should judges in democratic countries influence the choice of goals
for society or even the selection of means to achieve whatever goals are being
pursued?   Questions about fundamental political purposes and permissible
means to achieve those ends constitute, of course, some of the most basic
concerns of political philosophy.

Reflective constitutional court judges are sensitive to these questions.
John Marshall, for example, believed that the Constitution of the United

---

* One can, of course, construct models to help account for many processes, and scholars in
public law have done a fair share of model building, although only recently of a mathematical
kind.   For a general discussion, see Joel Grossman, " Social Backgrounds and Judicial Decisions:
Notes for a Theory," 29 *Journal of Politics* 334 (1967).   For pioneering efforts to construct
mathematical models of judicial decision making, see Edward J. Weissman, " Mathematical
Theory and Dynamic Models," in Glendon A. Schubert and David J. Danelski (eds.), *Comparative
Judicial Behavior* (New York: Oxford University Press, 1969); Werner F. Grunbaum, "Analytical
and Simulation Models for Explaining Judicial Decision-Making," in Joel Grossman and Joseph
Tanenhaus (eds.), *Frontiers of Judicial Research* (New York: Wiley, 1969), chap. 10; Alan M.
Sager, " The Use of Simulation in the Study of Judicial Processes," mimeographed (1970), 38 pp.;
Norman Jacknis, " Theory and Methods for Analyzing Processes of Political Influence and
Policy Making," unpublished doctoral dissertation, Princeton University, 1971, chap. 8.

States should be read not literally as if it were a legal code, but with the flexibility necessary to afford the national government the power it required if the Constitution were to endure through the ages.[47] A generation later, Justice Samuel Miller contended that the Court should strive to maintain the balance between state and federal power that had existed before the Civil War, rather than yield to public opinion as reflected in acts of a radical Congress and the Civil War amendments to the Constitution. Miller's contemporary Stephen J. Field insisted that laissez-faire economic theory was so fundamental as to be implicitly included in the Constitution as well as in the natural order of the universe. In this century Louis D. Brandeis viewed the states as the laboratories of the federal system and generally opposed constitutional restrictions on the states' freedom to conduct economic and social experiments. Harlan Fiske Stone considered freedom of speech and press and political participation to be vehicles for peaceful change and, hence, so basic that the usual presumption of the constitutionality of legislation should be relaxed when they were threatened.

Political scientists have dutifully sought to identify and analyze judicial commitments to the "should" questions, and in the process of doing so, have striven valiantly, if vainly, to prevent their own ethical commitments from infecting their work. But their greatest failing, we think, has resulted less from their lack of success in exorcising evidence of their own value underpinnings (which may in any case be impossible) than from an unwillingness to tackle the "should" questions head-on.* Still, fundamental ethical questions, like Francis Thompson's Hound of Heaven, relentlessly hunt serious scholars down the labyrinthine ways of academe—and, following a ruthless policy of equal protection of the law, bay at judges and lawyers as well.

NOTES

1. For one effort to wrestle with this problem, see Foster H. Sherwood, "The Role of Public Law in Political Science," in Roland Young (ed.), *Approaches to the Study of Politics* (Evanston, Ill.: Northwestern University Press, 1958).

2. Jerome Frank, *Courts on Trial* (Princeton, N.J.: Princeton University Press, 1950), especially chaps. 3, 15; see also his *Law and the Modern Mind* (New York: Brentano's, 1930), and Edmond Cahn, "Fact-Skepticism and Fundamental Law," 35 *New York University Law Review* 1 (1958).

* Walter Berns is a striking exception to this rule. Although we would not agree with all of his premises or conclusions, he has had both the courage and the skill to confront fundamental questions like the relationship between freedom and the good life. See especially his *Freedom, Virtue and the First Amendment* (Baton Rouge: Louisiana State University Press, 1957) and "*Buck v. Bell:* Due Process of Law?" 6 *Western Political Quarterly* 764 (1953). See also David J. Danelski, "A Behavioral Conception of Human Rights," 3 *Law in Transition Quarterly* 63 (1966).

3. See Benjamin Twiss, *Lawyers and the Constitution* (Princeton, N.J.: Princeton University Press, 1942); Clyde E. Jacobs, *Law Writers and the Courts* (Berkeley: University of California Press, 1954); Arnold M. Paul, *Conservative Crisis and the Rule of Law: Attitudes of Bar and Bench, 1887–1895* (Ithaca, N.Y.: Cornell University Press, 1960); and Stuart S. Nagel and Felix V. Gagliano, "Attorney Characteristics and Courtroom Results," 44 *Nebraska Law Review* 599 (1965).

4. Aristotle, *Politics*, Bk. III, chap. 11.

5. For a broader analysis of the political role of lawyers, see Heinz Eulau and John D. Sprague, *Lawyers in Politics: A Study in Professional Convergence* (Indianapolis: Bobbs-Merrill, 1964); Joseph A. Schlesinger, "Lawyers and American Politics: A Clarified View," 1 *Midwest Journal of Political Science* 28 (1957); and Mogens N. Pedersen, "Lawyers in Politics: The Deviant Case of the Danish Folketing," a paper presented at the Shambaugh Conference on Comparative Legislative Behavior Research, the University of Iowa, May 26–30, 1969.

6. Osborn v. Bank of the United States, 9 Wheaton 738, 866 (1824).

7. Quoted in L. F. Crisp, *Australian National Government* (Croydon, Victoria: Longmans, Green, 1965), p. 58.

8. These clauses have given judges ample room to exercise their policy preferences. Compare W. & A. McArthur, Ltd. v. Queensland, (1920) 28 Commonwealth Law Reports 530, with James v. Commonwealth, decided first by the Australian High Court at (1935) 52 Commonwealth Law Reports 570, and then by the British Privy Council at [1936] Appeals Cases 578.

9. Felix Frankfurter, "The Supreme Court of the United States," reprinted in E. F. Pritchard, Jr., and Archibald MacLeish (eds.), *Law and Politics: Occasional Papers of Felix Frankfurter 1913–1938* (New York: Harcourt, Brace & Company, 1939), p. 30.

10. See, for example, the studies by Frederick J. Gaudet *et al.* cited in note 32; the sentencing data cited in Charles Grove Haines, "General Observations on the Effects of Personal, Political, and Economic Influences in the Decisions of Judges," 17 *Illinois Law Review* 96 (1922), reprinted in Glendon A. Schubert (ed.), *Judicial Behavior: A Reader in Theory and Research* (Chicago: Rand McNally, 1964); Albert Somit, Joseph Tanenhaus, and Walter Wilke, "Aspects of Judicial Sentencing Behavior," 21 *University of Pittsburgh Law Review* 613 (1960); Stuart S. Nagel, "Disparities in Criminal Procedure," 14 *U.C.L.A. Law Review* 1272 (1967); and Dean Jaros and Robert I. Mendelsohn, "The Judicial Role and Sentencing Behavior," 11 *Midwest Journal of Political Science* 471 (1967). See also Thomas R. Hensley, "National Bias and the International Court of Justice," 12 *Midwest Journal of Political Science* 568 (1968), for a study linking voting behavior of judges on the World Court to national origins.

11. "Law and the Future," reprinted in Henry M. Christman (ed.), *The Public Papers of Earl Warren* (New York: Simon and Schuster, 1959), p. 226.

12. Albert Somit and Joseph Tanenhaus, *The Development of American Political Science* (Boston: Allyn and Bacon, 1967), especially chap. 6.

13. For a recent account of the Realists, see Wilfred E. Rumble, Jr., *American Legal Realism: Skepticism, Reform and the Judicial Process* (Ithaca, N.Y.: Cornell University Press, 1968). Some of Karl Llewellyn's early writings are collected in his *Jurisprudence: Realism in Theory and Practice* (Chicago: University of Chicago Press, 1962), especially Part I. Jerome Frank's *Law and the Modern Mind* is still a classic work of this genre.

14. Haines, supra note 10. The article was recently reprinted in Schubert (ed.), *Judicial Behavior*; the long quotation is found in Schubert, p. 49.

15. Charles Grove Haines, *The American Doctrine of Judicial Supremacy* (New York: Macmillan, 1914).

16. Charles Grove Haines, *The Role of the Supreme Court in American Government and Politics, 1789–1835* (Berkeley: University of California Press, 1944), p. 48. Haines made much the same point in his "Judicial Review of Legislation in the United States and the Doctrine of Vested Rights and of Implied Limitations on Legislatures," 3 *Texas Law Review* 1 (1924), and in the revised edition of *The American Doctrine of Judicial Supremacy* (Berkeley: University of California Press, 1932).

17. Edward S. Corwin, *The Twilight of the Supreme Court: A History of Our Constitutional Theory* (New Haven, Conn.: Yale University Press, 1934); the quotations are from pp. 184 and 101.

18. Edward S. Corwin, *John Marshall and the Constitution: A Chronicle of the Supreme Court* (New Haven, Conn.: Yale University Press, 1934); the quotations are from pp. 20, 230, 55, and 122.

19. Robert E. Cushman: "National Police Power Under the Commerce Clause of the Constitution," 3 *Minnesota Law Review* 289, 381, 452 (1919); "National Police Power Under the Postal Clause of the Constitution," 4 *Minnesota Law Review* 402 (1920); "National Police Power Under the Taxing Clause of the Constitution," 4 *Minnesota Law Review* 247 (1920).

20. Robert E. Cushman, *Leading Constitutional Decisions* (New York: F. S. Crofts, 1925).

21. Dartmouth College v. Woodward, 4 Wheaton 518 (1819).

22. Slaughterhouse Cases, 16 Wallace 36 (1873).

23. Cushman, supra note 20, p. 34.

24. Gibbons v. Ogden, 9 Wheaton 1 (1824).

25. Cushman, supra note 20, p. 204.

26. Thomas Reed Powell, "The Logic and Rhetoric of Constitutional Law," 15 *Journal of Philosophy, Psychology, and Scientific Method* 654 (1918), reprinted in Robert G. McCloskey (ed.), *Essays in American Constitutional Law* (New York: Knopf, 1957); the quotation is from pp. 88–89 of McCloskey. Typical of Powell's pungent, realistic critiques of the work of the U.S. Supreme Court under Chief Justices Taft and Hughes was "The Judiciality of Minimum Wage Legislation," 37 *Harvard Law Review* 545 (1924). See also one of his last works, *Vagaries and Varieties in Constitutional Interpretation* (New York: Columbia University Press, 1956).

27. The Conferences' results were reported by Arnold Bennett Hall, "Roundtable on Public Law," 20 *American Political Science Review* 127 (1926). For a general discussion of the importance of these Conferences, see Albert Somit and Joseph Tanenhaus, supra note 12, chap. 9.

28. Rodney L. Mott, "Judicial Influence," 30 *American Political Science Review* 295 (1936).

29. Charles G. Haines, "Judicial Review of the Findings and Awards of Industrial Accident Commissions," in Haines and Marshall E. Dimock (eds.), *Essays in the Law and Practice of Governmental Administration: A Volume in Honor of Frank Johnson Goodnow* (Baltimore: The Johns Hopkins Press, 1935).

30. Cortez A. M. Ewing, *The Judges of the Supreme Court, 1789–1937: A Study of Their Qualifications* (Minneapolis: University of Minnesota Press, 1938).

31. Harold D. Lasswell, "Propaganda Detection in the Courts," in Lasswell *et al.*, *The Language of Politics* (New York: George W. Steward, 1949).

32. Frederick J. Gaudet, *Individual Differences in the Sentencing Tendencies of Judges* (New York: Archives of Psychology, Monograph No. 230, 1938); Gaudet, George S. Harris, and Charles W. St. John, "Individual Differences in the Sentencing Tendencies of

Judges," 23 *Journal of Criminal Law, Criminology, and Police Science* 811 (1933); Gaudet, Harris, and St. John, "Individual Differences in Penitentiary Sentences Given by Different Judges," 18 *Journal of Applied Psychology* 675 (1934); Gaudet, "Differences Between Judges in the Granting of Sentences of Probation," 19 *Temple Law Quarterly* 471 (1946).

33. C. Herman Pritchett: "Divisions of Opinion Among Justices of the U.S. Supreme Court, 1939–1941," 35 *American Political Science Review* 890 (1941); "Coming of the New Dissent: The Supreme Court, 1942–1943," 11 *University of Chicago Law Review* 49 (1943); "Dissent on the Supreme Court, 1943–1944," 39 *American Political Science Review* 42 (1945); "The Roosevelt Court: Votes and Values," 42 *ibid.* 53 (1948).

34. C. Herman Pritchett, *The Roosevelt Court: A Study of Judicial Votes and Values, 1937–1947* (New York: Macmillan, 1948; Chicago: Quadrangle Books, 1969, paperback reprint).

35. C. Herman Pritchett, *Civil Liberties and the Vinson Court* (Chicago: University of Chicago Press, 1954), especially chaps. 10 and 11.

36. See Somit and Tanenhaus, supra note 12.

37. Pritchett, supra note 35.

38. See, for instance, John P. Frank's annual articles in the *University of Chicago Law Review* from 1947 to 1952 (vols. 15–20).

39. Glendon A. Schubert (ed.), *Judicial Decision-Making* (New York: Free Press, 1963).

40. Jack W. Peltason, *Federal Courts in the Political Process* (New York: Random House, 1955). Some of these case studies are considered in later chapters.

41. See Kenneth M. Dolbeare, *Trial Courts in Urban Politics: State Court Policy Impact and Functions in a Local Political System* (New York: Wiley, 1967); Dolbeare, "The Federal District Courts and Urban Public Policy: An Exploratory Analysis," in Joel Grossman and Joseph Tanenhaus (eds.), *Frontiers of Judicial Research* (New York: Wiley 1969); Kenneth N. Vines, "The Role of Circuit Courts of Appeals in the Federal Judicial Process," 7 *Midwest Journal of Political Science* 305 (1963); Vines, "Federal District Judges and Race Relations Cases in the South," 26 *Journal of Politics* 337 (1964); and Walter F. Murphy, "Lower Court Checks on Supreme Court Power," 53 *American Political Science Review* 1017 (1959).

42. See Hugh D. Graham and Ted R. Gurr (eds.), *Violence in America: Historical and Comparative Perspectives*, 2 vols. (Washington, D.C.: Government Printing Office, 1969).

43. See Joseph Borkin, *The Corrupt Judge: An Inquiry into Bribery and Other High Crimes and Misdemeanors in the Federal Courts* (New York: C. N. Potter, 1962).

44. Justice Samuel Miller made the classic statement of the relationship between judicial power and public opinion in United States v. Lee, 106 U.S. 196, 223 (1882). Justice Felix Frankfurter eloquently echoed Miller in his own dissent in Baker v. Carr, 369 U.S. 186, 267 (1962): "The Court's authority—possessed of neither the purse nor the sword—ultimately rests on sustained public confidence in its moral sanction." For less prescriptive pronouncements but more empirical findings, see John R. Kessel, "Public Perceptions of the Supreme Court," 10 *Midwest Journal of Political Science* 167 (1966); Kenneth M. Dolbeare, "The Public Views the Supreme Court," in Herbert Jacob (ed.), *Law, Politics, and the Federal Courts* (Boston: Little, Brown, 1967); Jacob, *Debtors in Court: The Consumption of Government Services* (Chicago: Rand McNally, 1969); three articles by Walter F. Murphy and Joseph Tanenhaus: "Public Opinion and the Supreme Court: The Goldwater Campaign," 32 *Public Opinion Quarterly* 31 (1968); "Public Opinion and the Supreme Court: A Preliminary Mapping of Some Prerequisites for Court Legitimation of Regime Changes," in Grossman and Tanenhaus (eds.), supra note 41; "Constitutional Courts and Political Representation," in Michael N. Danielson and Murphy (eds.), *Modern American*

Democracy: Readings (New York: Holt, Rinehart and Winston, 1969); and an unpublished paper by Murphy and Tanenhaus, "The Supreme Court and Its Elite Publics," a paper presented at the Meetings of the International Political Science Association (1970).

45. Peltason, supra note 40.

46. Walter F. Murphy, *Elements of Judicial Strategy* (Chicago: University of Chicago Press, 1964).

47. For an insightful analysis of Marshall's political thought, see Robert K. Faulkner, *The Jurisprudence of John Marshall* (Princeton, N.J.: Princeton University Press, 1968).

2
The Question of Relevance:
The Political Consequences
of Judicial Decisions

We have now said enough to give some idea of the way the study of public law has been developing as well as some notion of the kinds of questions for which political scientists are trying to find answers. We have not, however, justified the interest of political scientists in what courts and judges do; that interest can be justified only to the extent that judicial actions have important political consequences.

The political effects of judicial decisions are intuitively clear to anyone familiar with government systems. In deciding cases between individual citizens, judges typically decide who gets what. "The Judicial Department," Chief Justice Marshall noted, "comes home in its effects to every man's fireside: it passes on his property, his reputation, his life, his all."[1] But the impact of a court decision need not be limited to the actual litigants in the dispute. In settling one controversy, judges may be laying down general principles to govern relations among whole groups of people, such as the liability of employers to employees for accidental injury suffered at work, the obligation of manufacturers to those who buy their products, or the reciprocal rights and duties of landlords and tenants or of unions and management.   Further, in many democracies a public official may be either a defendant or a plaintiff in a lawsuit, and a court's decision may affect the authority of his office—even his right to hold that office—and, consequently, the rights of private citizens to obtain government assistance or to be free from governmental interference.   It is even possible for two government officials or agencies to be the adversary parties,* either directly, as when one sues the other, or indirectly, as in a case in which questions are raised about which official or agency has jurisdiction over a particular kind of problem.

The potential effect of many judicial decisions on the political order is enormous.   Decisions on disputed elections, reapportionment, and voting rights are among the most obvious examples of judicial rulings that have political implications.   Striking down white primaries, poll taxes, "grandfather clauses," and similar gimmicks designed to keep blacks from voting has taken up a large share of the time of U.S. Supreme Court justices.[2] And lower court judges have frequently handled disputes over which candidate has won an election.   For instance, only after three sets of federal judges had heard arguments about fraudulent voting in the Democratic primary was Lyndon B. Johnson's name allowed to stay on the Texas senatorial ballot in 1948.[3]   State judges settle disputes over elections even more often than do federal judges.   Wallace Sayre and Herbert Kaufman point out in their study of New York City politics that

> The courts have sweeping powers in election matters.   The Election Law [of New York State] authorizes voters, candidates, or specified party officers to institute suit against designated election officials. . . .   There is no corner of the electoral process into which the powers of the courts do not reach.[4]

Although judges in other countries apparently receive fewer voting cases, the Canadian, Irish, and Swiss courts have decided controversies involving legislative districting,[5] and the Japanese Supreme Court has been asked to rule both on reapportionment and on the constitutional power of the Prime Minister to dissolve the Diet and call for new elections.[6]   The West German Constitutional Court has twice determined whether a political party could legally nominate candidates for Parliament and in a third case has ruled on

---

* A nondemocratic government may also provide for judicial settlement of disputes between public officials.   The Soviet system, for example, establishes a quasi-administrative, quasi-judicial proceeding that works through agencies known as Arbitrazh.   See Dietrich A. Loeber, "Plan and Contract Performance in Soviet Law," in Wayne R. LaFave (ed.), *Law in the Soviet Society* (Urbana: University of Illinois Press, 1965).   More generally, see Harold J. Berman, *Justice in the U.S.S.R.*, rev. ed. (New York: Random House, 1963).

the fairness of a statute eliminating from a share of parliamentary seats any party that did not receive a minimum percentage of the popular vote.[7]

Electoral cases, however, do not necessarily represent the most important judicial involvement in politics. American decisions regarding free speech, prayers in public schools, school segregation, conscientious objection, wiretapping, and restrictions on police interrogations of suspects may have equal, or even greater, long-range impacts than have electoral cases. Nor are such decisions phenomena unique to America. In Australia[8] and Canada,[9] as well as in Germany, judges have faced questions about federalism, free speech, and political association. Problems of labor relations and criminal justice have plagued Irish judges, as have questions of governmental control of education.[10] The Japanese Supreme Court has had to consider the legal status of foreign and domestic armed forces, freedom of the press, governmental authority to deny passports to citizens, and a cluster of criminal-justice issues that parallel those that swell the dockets of American courts.[11]

With its jurisdiction limited to constitutional interpretation, the West German Constitutional Court has in its short life span confronted a bevy of volatile political issues: rearmament with atomic weapons, national control of television, state authority to conclude treaties without the consent of the federal government, financial subsidies to parties represented in Parliament, and the possibility of the Federal Republic's joining the European Defense Community.[12] Karl Loewenstein's prediction that the West German Basic Law would create "a judicialization of political dynamics"[13] has not materialized, but the Constitutional Court has become a powerful organ of government.

In essaying answers to the broad problems presented to them, judges also help shape national goals. Judicial opinions may become integral parts of a nation's dominant system of beliefs, as have those of John Marshall, Oliver Wendell Holmes, and Louis D. Brandeis. More specifically, a long line of decisions of the U.S. Supreme Court from 1890 to 1936 helped enshrine economic freedom for big business as a dominant national goal. The Great Depression and the New Deal ended that era, but a fresh line of Supreme Court decisions since 1937 has been compatible with—in fact, has sometimes pushed hard toward—tighter government control of the economy and the establishment of equality of opportunity as the overriding objectives of domestic public policy.[14] It would not be wild to predict that the future of democratic government in Japan and, to a far greater extent, in West Germany will be heavily influenced by the ability of judges to formulate prescriptions that will appeal to both public officials and politically attentive private citizens.*

---

* For a fascinating essay instructing officials of the delicate nature of the threads holding a democratic polity together in Japan, see the ironic opinion of Justice Tsuyoshi Mano in the Dissolution case, reprinted in John Maki (ed.), *Court and Constitution in Japan: Selected Supreme Court Decisions, 1948–60* (Seattle: University of Washington Press, 1964), pp. 366ff.

It is necessary to recognize, however, that even highly respected constitutional courts cannot alone stem tides of public sentiment as reflected in the policies of popular chief executives and legislatures.[15]   The U.S. Supreme Court's battle against the New Deal was no less futile for being dogged. Nor in times of crisis can one count on judges always to perform the task of preventing overly zealous officials from transgressing their constitutional bounds.   Judges, too, may be caught up in moods of popular hysteria. More than 100,000 Americans of Japanese ancestry learned to their dismay in World War II that the most solidly entrenched of constitutional courts would not protect their supposedly fundamental right not to be imprisoned without a full and fair trial.   Justice Hugo Black pronounced the Court's constitutional nihil obstat on the government's policy of herding the Nisei into detention camps.   As an outspoken civil libertarian, however, Black could not forbear offering one of his frequent panegyrics to the importance of freedom as well as soothing comfort to those who were being deprived of their rights: "Hardships are a part of war, and war is an aggregation of hardships."[16]

Even when judges are capable of detaching themselves from momentary emotional convulsions, they may be physically unable to intervene effectively in the political processes.   As the once prestigious Argentine Supreme Court plaintively observed after finding itself politically incapable of utilizing its former constitutional authority to review the actions of high officials:

> The exercise of judicial review possessed by courts cannot be a primary and substantial preoccupation: rather, it is the preservation of an efficient judicial order, which offers a way of safeguarding fundamental rights and guarantees without questioning the validity—which would be absurd—of this revolution and of the government which guides it, a government recognized by everyone at home and abroad.[17]

The Political Roles of Constitutional Courts

The question, Can judges save a democracy whose people do not care about their system or are bent on destroying it? is often asked.[18]   The answer has to be that it is unlikely that judges could save their country under such circumstances.   But then, probably no other group of officials could either, unless they could first persuade the people to reorder their values; and as we shall discuss shortly, judges can play a part in this kind of educational process.   A more subtle—and realistic—question is, How and to what extent can judges contribute to the day-to-day operations of a polity as well as to its reform and to its overall stability?

In these respects judges can play politically significant roles, and they

can do so before a number of different audiences.   Among the most important of these audiences are the legal profession and other interest groups,
public officials outside the judiciary, judges of different courts, judges within
the same court, and various segments of the attentive and mass publics.   In
addition, for judges no less than for many presidents, prime ministers,
cabinet officials, and legislators, history is a live audience.   Only a "naif,
simple minded" judge could be unaware that his decisions may affect the
long-run, as well as the immediate, future.

Vis-à-vis audiences outside their own court, judges on most constitutional
courts can play at least seven different but related role* sets: interpreting and
applying legal rules, defining boundaries of authority, supervising, legislating,
representing, stabilizing, and educating.

Rule Interpreting and Applying

The interpretation and application of rules is the traditional adjudicative
role.   Litigants bring specific cases and controversies before courts; and
judges, interpreting and applying more or less general rules, decide those
cases.   The jurisdictions of particular courts differ, as do the complexity and
importance of the issues at stake; but the function is essentially the same:
settling disputes that can be phrased as "legal issues."   In systemic terms
one can characterize this role as that of receiving demands, processing them,
and converting them into decisional outputs.

Defining Boundaries of Political
Authority

The party bringing a case before a court may be a private citizen, a representative of an interest group, or a government official.   The defendant may also
be a private citizen, a representative of an interest group, or a government

---

* In this context we are using the term "role" to refer to the actual behavior, or more accurately
the effect of actual behavior, of judges rather than to normative expectations about how judges
should behave.   We are using "role" here in a way quite similar to Newcomb's concept of "role
behavior."   See T. M. Newcomb, *Social Psychology* (New York: Dryden Press, 1951), p. 330.
Still, we would add, none of these roles is logically incompatible with what large segments of a
national sample of American adults described as the U.S. Supreme Court's role in American
government.   Furthermore, only the legislative role raises questions of compatibility with
normative legal doctrines that are widely shared among writers on law and jurisprudence.   We
would also argue that to deny that a legislative function is proper for judges requires an argument
divorced from reality.   Whether or not in the best of all worlds judges should make rules, in this
world they often must if they are to decide cases.
In the last section of chapter 5, we return to the concept of "role," but there we shall use
the term to refer to normative expectations about judicial behavior.   For a discussion of the many
meanings of the concept of "role," see Neal Gross, Ward S. Mason, and A. W. McEachern,
Explorations in Role Analysis (New York: Wiley, 1958), esp. chap. 2.

official. In addition, public officials who disagree with one another often take to law to settle their differences. Even when a dispute is already in progress, a court may also allow any or all of these three classes of persons to intervene as an amicus curiae, a friend of the court, and to outline their interests and present their arguments about the proper ruling.

As we have already noted, the political significance of judicial decisions can thus escalate from merely determining "mine" and "thine" between private citizens to settling relative priorities among more widely shared social interests and then to influencing the scope of authority of government officials as well as the manner in which that authority can be exercised. Constitutional interpretation is important in this process, but so is interpretation of statutes and executive orders. Questions such as, Did the legislature forbid misleading television advertisements? and If the legislature did forbid such activity, on which government agency did it confer enforcement authority? may generate as much short-run policy as a constitutional dispute.

By declaring certain acts permissible or impermissible under the constitution, statutes, or executive orders, judicial decisions put forth guidelines prescribing limits to the authority of particular public officials. In the complex institutional matrices of modern democracies, judges may offer definitions of authority among officials of the national government, between national and local government officers, and between what is within the control of any political official and what is a right of a private citizen or interest group. The effects of a judicial definition of boundaries may be trivial or important, and this significance has to be weighed in terms of tangible results and psychological satisfactions and in long-run as well as short-run terms.

Even more acutely than when only rights of private citizens or groups are at issue, boundary definitions are likely to engender resistance. When the losing litigant is a private citizen, retiring to the nearest tavern to damn the court may be his only recourse beyond appeal to a higher tribunal. If a losing litigant is an interest group or one of its representatives or is supported by such an organization, a larger fund of resources may be available to permit use of the legislative or administrative processes or both to seek redress. Public officials, of course, usually have the means immediately at hand to turn their disappointment at a defeat into resistance, which may take even the form of striking back at the court.

A role corollary to that of defining boundaries of authority is one to which we have already alluded: determining the eligibility of certain political parties to place candidates' names on the ballot or deciding, when elections are disputed, which claimant is entitled to public office. This function also overlaps considerably with what in a few pages we shall describe as the representational role of courts.

Supervising

The role of a superior court as supervisor of lower court judges is easy to conceptualize, since it is implicit in the notion of a judicial hierarchy. Historically, the British King's Bench and even Parliament—which was known as the High Court of Parliament—performed a supervisory function vis-à-vis the Court of Common Pleas; and the framers of the American Constitution—as have the authors of many other constitutions, such as those of Australia, Canada, India, Ireland, and Japan—opted for the continuation of this system in providing that the supreme court should have appellate jurisdiction in a wide range of cases.

However easy it is to understand in the abstract, the supervisory role is difficult to execute. As we shall explain later in this chapter, the occasions for disagreement among judges are frequent, and opportunities for lower court judges to escape close surveillance abound. Thus successfully playing a supervisory role requires considerable tact, skill, energy, patience, and luck.

Legislating

In performing these various kinds of roles judges cannot always rely on existing rules, as Corwin, Cushman, Haines, Powell, and their contemporaries amply demonstrated for the U.S. Supreme Court. On occasion judges must create new rules to apply and interpret; and this is true whether the case involves private rights, legislative acts, executive orders, or constitutional provisions. Typically, this creativity occurs within narrow bounds. But every now and then, the range of creativity may be quite broad. Examples of this in the United States include the inauguration of judicial review itself and the establishment and later the disestablishment of the "original package" rule, Social Darwinism, and the "separate but equal" doctrine. In Australia examples include the flowering and deflowering of reciprocal tax immunity and the dogma that the Commonwealth Constitution contains a mutual set of implied restrictions on both state and national—though usually national—power. A scholar interested in American politics needs only to sample *The Congressional Record* to see how frequently charges are made about judicial legislation, the Supreme Court Reports to see how often such charges are justified, or the vague clauses of the American Constitution to see how inevitable such a practice is.

In playing this legislative role, judges act both as policy makers in their own right and as umpires of the policy-making prerogatives of other public officials—as both players and referees in a political contest. It is not surprising, then, that they are often thrown into conflict with members of other branches of government, for professional politicians are typically jealous of invasion, even by judges, of what they think is their preserve of power. Sometimes, however, the conflict is more apparent than real; an elected politician may not actually be unhappy to have someone else handle a complex problem about which public opinion is bitterly divided, especially when the time to run for reelection is approaching.   Still, real conflicts occur often enough for prudent judges who are truly committed to the attainment of their jurisprudential—or policy—goals to be sensitive to potential sources of support who can counter opposition from those who will be disappointed by particular decisions.

Representing

By defining boundaries of authority, applying old rules or creating new rules for new problems, and supervising similar work of lower courts, the political involvement of judges is frequently highly visible.   Knowledgeable leaders of groups—whether defined in terms of specific economic or professional interests, regionalism, or ethnic and religious affiliations—may see constitutional court judgeships as prestigious awards to which their members are entitled as a recognition of their accepted status in the polity.   Moreover, such leaders are apt to think it important that judges at least sympathetically understand their policy preferences.

These desires may be manifested by direct pressure on appointing officials or anticipated by those officials, and they can lead to representation[19] in the sense of "standing for."[20]   That is, court appointees may reflect, as they do in federal polities like Canada, Switzerland, the United States, and West Germany, the various regions into which the country is divided.   Or perhaps there will be a representation of religious and ethnic groups.*   In the United States there is now a tradition of usually having a Catholic and a Jew on the Supreme Court, and the appointment of Thurgood Marshall probably began a new tradition of having a black man on the Court as well. In Ireland one of the five Supreme Court justices is usually a Protestant, offering a kind of representation not only for a religious minority but also for an ethnic and economic minority, since Protestant barristers are apt to be of English background, descendants of the old Dublin ascendancy, and members of the upper economic stratum of society.   In Canada, as in Switzerland, regional representation largely includes ethnic and religious representation.   By law, three of the nine Canadian justices of the Supreme

---

* The concept of constitutional courts as representative institutions was caricatured during the Senate debates in March 1970 on the confirmation of G. Harrold Carswell for the U.S. Supreme Court.   Responding to widespread evaluations of Carswell that ranked him in the lower ranges of mediocrity, Senator Roman L. Hruska of Nebraska rose to defend his President's nominee: "Even if he were mediocre, there are a lot of mediocre judges and people and lawyers, and they are entitled to a little representation, aren't they?"

Court are from Quebec and are usually French Catholics; the other justices are from the English-speaking provinces and are usually Protestants, although one of the Quebecois may be Protestant and one of the English-speaking justices, Catholic. Swiss judges are elected by Parliament on an informal basis of proportional representation that gives the major parties—and the major ethnic and religious groups—a share of seats on the bench similar to the proportion of seats each has in Parliament.

Judges can play a more direct representational role by providing not only a forum but also political clout for groups who lack sufficient power to have a meaningful voice in the legislative and executive processes. This was the kind of role Harlan Fiske Stone was referring to in the third paragraph of his famous *Carolene Products* footnote.[21] Certainly, constitutional court judges in a number of other countries have actively performed this sort of representational function. Usually, however, judges necessarily act negatively in this respect. That is, they can more effectively protect groups like Jehovah's Witnesses against discrimination, as the Canadian and U.S. Supreme Courts have done, than they can change the entire political system to conform to the Witnesses' desires. Yet the struggle for black civil rights in the United States indicates that judicial action can also have a positive effect. By declaring discrimination invalid, judges can arouse the consciences of other officials and of important groups within the electorate. Judges can also stir the offended group to achieve its full potential. Perhaps in the long run the most significant effect of *Brown v. Board of Education*[22] will be that it awakened a new consciousness of group identity among blacks and a fresh awareness of the possibilities of removing the discrepancy between their supposed and actual rights. As Eldridge Cleaver, sometime Minister of Information of the Black Panthers, put it:

> Prior to 1954, we lived in an atmosphere of novocain. Negroes found it necessary, in order to maintain whatever sanity they could, to remain somewhat aloof and detached from "the problem." We accepted indignities and the mechanics of the apparatus of oppression without reacting by sitting-in or holding mass demonstrations. Nurtured by the fires of the controversy over segregation, I was soon aflame with indignation over my newly discovered social status, and inwardly I turned away from America with horror, disgust and outrage.[23]

Judges may perform an ancillary representational role in protecting the integrity of the processes through which issues are discussed and officials are chosen. Again, Stone spelled out this function in his *Carolene Products* footnote. In free speech and voting-rights cases the American Supreme Court, like constitutional courts in Canada, Ireland, and West Germany, has put Stone's prescription into practice.

Stabilizing

Important public policies are apt to be controversial, and disagreement often involves the legitimacy as well as the wisdom of governmental action. Sometimes denials of governmental authority are only shallow propaganda charges, but not infrequently doubts are seriously, sincerely, and widely held. Given the inability of those who draft constitutions to provide for, or even to foresee, all possible crises, occasions for real doubts to arise are likely to be quite numerous.

In playing its other roles, a constitutional court may also perform a stabilizing role in three different ways. First, it can provide an additional forum to which persons and groups whose interests have been defeated in the other policy-making processes may take their causes and continue their struggles. These contestants can argue either that the relevant constitutional or statutory clauses do not grant government officials the authority they are exercising or, alternatively, that one or both of these legal documents command government officials to respect certain claims on which they are in fact trespassing. In this sense, one can speak of the judicial process as a surrogate for violence, substituting, just as in private litigation, trial by lawsuit for trial by combat; operating, in Thomas Jefferson's terms, " to render unnecessary an appeal to the people, or in other words a rebellion, on every infraction of their rights. . . ."[24]

Second, judges can legitimate controversial public policies, and in fact judges normally sustain the validity of national statutes when they are challenged. For example, despite its actions in 1935 and 1936, the U.S. Supreme Court in its first 180 years declared only about eighty-five acts of Congress unconstitutional, and far more rarely has it held invalid a recent congressional statute. The Japanese Supreme Court in its first twenty years did not invalidate a single important act of the Diet,* and from 1938 to 1969 the Irish Supreme Court and High Court upheld the constitutionality of about two out of every three of the more than seventy statutes challenged before them. In the one hundred years from 1867 to 1966 the Privy Council and the Canadian Supreme Court declared unconstitutional fifteen of the thirty-eight Dominion statutes. That represents a high percentage when compared to American standards; still more than three out of five challenged statutes passed muster. Even the Italian Constitutional Court, which has had to determine the validity of a number of criminal statutes adopted by

---

* On several occasions the Japanese Court did declare minor acts invalid and on a number of occasions individual justices have asserted in separate opinions the unconstitutionality of statutes and cabinet orders. See the discussion of these actions by Dan Fenno Henderson, " The Scope of Justiciability in Constitutional Law," in Henderson (ed.), *The Constitution of Japan: Its First Twenty Years, 1947–67* (Seattle: University of Washington Press, 1968).

the old Fascist regime, upheld during its first fourteen years more than sixty percent of the contested acts.[25]

Judicial affirmations that political choices of elected officials are permitted by the constitution may help quiet doubts and so serve a legitimizing function for public officials, for particular elite groups, or for a broad spectrum of the general public.[26] Insofar as a court decision legitimizes controversial policies in the minds of politically relevant people, then, just as in providing a forum for peaceful, nonelectoral overthrow of legislative and executive policy choices, judges will be helping to stabilize the polity.

Here, as in other aspects of their work, judges may act dysfunctionally as well as functionally. A judicial decision may, as the Dred Scott case[27] did in pre-Civil War America, contribute to a polarization of opinion within the society. Whether a particular decision will settle doubts and have a legitimizing effect, harden opposing views, or make no impact on opinion at all is a matter for empirical research,* just as are questions about the material and psychological effects of holding a statute unconstitutional.

The third sense in which a constitutional court can play a stabilizing role is one that did not seem plausible to us until we had begun analysis of answers to questions about the U.S. Supreme Court that were asked of a national sample of adults. If a constitutional court is respected, the very fact that it exists may increase popular support of the regime. Many people do not make the fine and largely artificial distinction among legislating, adjudicating, and administering—or if one prefers more current jargon, rule making, rule applying, and rule adjudicating. For many people government is all cut from the same cloth. If they know about and respect a constitutional court, they are quite likely to support the entire regime.

Educating

As Chief Justice Marshall saw so clearly, public awareness and support are essential if a constitutional court is to establish itself as a major political institution. Other perceptive chiefs, like Kotaro Tanaka in Japan and Cearbhall O'Dalaigh in Ireland, have shared Marshall's appreciation of the need for a constitutional court to gain, in Corwin's phrase, a firm "hold on the imagination of the country." When judges appeal to the broader public with reasoned argument, they are playing the role of educator, and how well the judges on a court perform the educator's role will affect their

---

* We have been trying to determine the extent to which reasonable conditions exist in the United States for the Supreme Court to perform this legitimating function. Some of the data discussed later in this chapter and in chapter 7 are from this investigation. See also our "Public Opinion and the United States Supreme Court: A Preliminary Mapping of Some Prerequisites for Court Legitimation of Regime Changes," in Joel Grossman and Joseph Tanenhaus (eds.), *Frontiers of Judicial Research* (New York: Wiley, 1969).

success in playing some of their other roles, such as representing, stabilizing, and legislating.

Constitutional court judges typically file written opinions along with their decisions. In common law countries these opinions are generally heavily documented and carefully, indeed elaborately, reasoned. They tend to be more succinct in civil law countries, although occasionally civil law judges find it expedient to produce opinions that run to more than a hundred pages. The object of these documents is less to explain the processes of decision making than to persuade readers of the reasonableness of the conclusion and also to identify the basic principles on which this and related public policy choices should rest.

Although few Americans are apt to make a steady diet of Supreme Court reports, a fair share of the college-educated population has at some time been exposed to at least a handful of leading opinions by some of the Court's most eloquent teachers. Moreover, the mass media periodically carry stories about judicial pronouncements that impress editors as worthy of wide dissemination. Hardly a term of Court fails to generate a handful of causes célèbres. In a desire to reach a broader public, the Supreme Court has even modified some of its historic procedures to facilitate news reporters and analysts. Traditionally, the Court met at noon and handed down opinions only on Mondays—often a wad of judgments that could be but slowly digested. In part to enable reporters for afternoon newspapers to meet their deadlines, the justices have changed the opening of their sessions to 10 A.M. And to allow editors more time to read and explain the Court's opinions, the justices no longer restrict announcement of decisions to one day of the week.[28]

The justices, of course, do not have to depend directly and solely on their own resources to generate knowledge about their work. The importance of what they do ensures that many public officials and interest-group leaders will become aware of a substantial portion of the Court's rulings; and the long-range significance of the Court in the political system has made its existence and some notion about its general operations a part of the information conveyed by the processes of political socialization. Children, even youngsters in early school grades, are conscious of the Court's existence and tend to express great respect for it as an institution.[29]

In surveying random samples of American adults in 1964 and 1966, we found that the Court is rather visible. Sixty-five percent of our respondents could respond appropriately to a query about the nature of the Court's job; 49 percent could name at least one justice; and about 45 percent could recall something the Court had done recently that they had liked or disliked. All these responses were to open-ended questions, which tend to elicit less information than people possess because an individual may not be able to recall during the stress of an interview all that he actually knows.

TABLE 2.1

Specific likes and dislikes about U.S. Supreme
Court decisions

Subject	1964 (N = 915)	1966 (N = 1,063)
Civil rights of Negroes	38%	25%
School prayers	30	24
Criminal justice cases	6	16
Reapportionment	5	1
Other	20	34
	99%	100%

Questions: "Is there anything in particular that the
Supreme Court in Washington has done that
you have disliked (liked)?" (Up to 4 mentions
on each question were counted.)

For the attentive public (as we arbitrarily labeled the one-sixth of the respondents who were best informed about politics), the percentage able to articulate likes or dislikes or both climbs from 45 to 77.   As education increases, so does familiarity with what the justices have been doing.   Seventy percent of those who had some college background mentioned likes and dislikes, and among college graduates the percentage was 78.   A subsequent sampling of the Princeton class of 1968 revealed that a whopping 86 percent could make informed responses to a similar inquiry.

What people know about the decisions of the U.S. Supreme Court may not be precise or detailed, but as Table 2.1 shows, it is generally relevant. An occasional response, to be sure, may be far-fetched.   One person spoke disapprovingly of the Court for "getting mixed up in this war."   Another praised the justices because "they gave us Medicare."   But on the whole the answers were meaningful, if somewhat lacking in legal sophistication.

Judges, like other educators, are not always successful in merchandising the truth as they see it—especially in the very short run.   Table 2.2 indicates

TABLE 2.2

Total number of comments about U.S. Supreme
Court, 1964 and 1966

	1964 (N = 915)	1966 (N = 1,063)
Favorable	29%	29%
Unfavorable	71	71
	100%	100%

TABLE 2.3

Specific versus diffuse evaluations of the
U.S. Supreme Court, 1966

Specific comments	How well the Supreme Court does its job				
	Very well	Well in some ways, not so well in others	Not very well	No answer	Total
Likes only	75	4	2	18	99
Likes and dislikes	75	13	29	11	128
Dislikes only	112	46	145	67	370
No answer	187	20	22	459	688
Total	449	83	198	555	1,285

that unfavorable references to recent Court activity outnumbered favorable comments by a wide margin. This is not so damaging to the Court as it might at first appear. As the data in Table 2.3 show, fewer than half of those who criticized the Court on particular issues were prepared to say that on the whole it was not doing a very good job. Altogether, those unhappy about the Court's overall performance constituted only slightly more than one-third of those who assessed the kind of job the Court was doing.* Even among white Southerners, the single group most hostile to the Court, people who felt that the Court was not doing its job very well comprised no more than 40 percent of those who responded to the job-assessment question.

The U.S. Supreme Court, it seems, has a reservoir of good will that is so deep that it has not been dangerously drained by controversial decisions in the areas of civil rights, schoolhouse religion, and criminal justice—any more than it was during the tangles over economic policy in the 1930s and subversive activities in the 1950s. This is not to say, of course, that the well is bottomless.

In dealing with the educational role of courts, we have drawn our illustrations from studies of the U.S. Supreme Court. In a preliminary report on a companion investigation in West Germany, Rudolph Wilden-mann found that about 42 percent of adults claimed awareness of the functions of their Constitutional Court, and most of these people could supply a reasonably informed response to a follow-up question asking for a definition of those functions. Research now under way in Canada,

---

* Since only people who could respond to a prior open-ended question about the nature of the Court's work were asked how well it was doing its job, those who believed that the Court was not doing a very good job make up less than one-sixth of all people interviewed, and those who thought the Court was performing very well constitute only 35 percent of the sample.

Ireland, and Norway, as well as further study in West Germany, should soon yield information for the constitutional courts in those countries comparable to that available for the U.S. Supreme Court.

Judges may, as Learned Hand protested, be ill equipped by training to play their educational role, and in fact, they may often play it badly.[30] Still, to paraphrase Justice Robert H. Jackson, judges play that role by force of their commissions, rather than by reason of their competence.[31] And no one who remembers how suddenly after May 17, 1954, ministers of all faiths in the United States experienced the revelation that God Almighty had always forbidden school segregation can doubt that the potential to affect at least those whom we call "opinion leaders" may be considerable. The Supreme Court, Frank Murphy commented when nominated to be an associate justice, is "the Great Pulpit" in American politics.[32] Other constitutional courts may provide smaller pulpits, but any pulpit presents an opportunity, as Martin Luther demonstrated.

Measuring Influence

Political scientists have yet to distinguish themselves by their efforts to evaluate the impact of specific judicial decisions. The subject is as treacherous as antiquity's fabled Serbonian bog. First, a decision, especially one interpreting the Constitution, may foreclose whole ranges of choice in the minds of some public officials and private citizens. The effect may be negative, and so practically invisible, in that public officials may simply no longer seriously consider some alternatives. That kind of effect is no less important because it cannot be seen and measured. Second, the principles judges put forth may, by the very fact that they have been propounded by a respected government institution, become imbedded—or, which is more likely, more firmly imbedded—in the political culture of a nation. Certainly, one could argue that John Marshall's nationalism became part of the dominant American heritage, just as one could argue that whatever was the immediate impact of *Brown v. Board of Education* on the racial composition of public schools, Chief Justice Earl Warren's opinion cut the moral as well as the legal ground from under white racism.

Third, in modern democracies public policy is rarely, if ever, made by a single person or by a single institution. As our previous discussion tried to emphasize, legislators and administrators—not to mention members of the general public—may be involved in policy formation both before and after a judicial decision. In this process judges may succeed in excluding some alternatives, and they may encourage use of others; but in the end too many actors have played parts, too many factors have been at work for an analyst to reweave in exact order the parti-colored threads of public policy.

The development of Canadian federalism provides a succinct illustration. Instructed by the American example about the difficulties of leaving to local authorities all residual power, the framers of the British North America Act of 1867—the Canadian Constitution—provided in Section 91 that the Dominion Parliament should "make laws for the peace, order, and good government of Canada in relation to all matters not coming within the classes of subjects by this Act assigned exclusively to the legislatures of the provinces. . . ." Section 91 of the British North America Act goes on to list "for greater certainty, but not so as to restrict the generality of the foregoing terms of this section," a number of topics over which the Dominion has exclusive authority.

These provisions stated about as clearly as the stilted jargon of legal draftsmanship permits that the overriding principle of Canadian federalism was to be national supremacy. Yet decades of judicial interpretation—both by the Privy Council in Westminster and the Supreme Court in Ottawa—have endorsed a different concept. Time and again, British and Canadian judges have struck down Dominion legislation as if the British North America Act read like the Tenth Amendment to the American Constitution. As the Privy Council, displaying some of its usual pithy prose, noted in 1925:

> It appears to their Lordships that it is not now open to them to treat *Russell v. The Queen* as having established the general principle that the mere fact that Dominion legislation is for the general advantage of Canada, or is such that it will meet a mere want which is felt throughout the Dominion, renders it competent if it cannot be brought within the heads enumerated specifically in s. 91.[33]

Even when construing powers explicitly enumerated as among those of the Dominion, such as "regulation of trade and commerce," British, and to a lesser extent Canadian, judges conceded only a very narrow meaning to the words.[34] Thus the Canadian provinces have accrued a degree of states' rights on the American model, and Dominion officials have found themselves having to justify their activity by specific grants in the British North America Act, as if the provision relating to "the peace, order, and good government" had never been written.

It might be tempting to credit—or saddle—judges with sole responsibility for establishing a theory of federalism in Canada under which the provinces operate "not as fractions in a unit but as units in a multiple";[35] but the physiology of Canadian as well as American politics is too complex to be explained in such simplistic terms.[36] The French-speaking minority, proud of its heritage and conscious of social and cultural differences from English-speaking Canadians, has been the dominant group in a single province, rather than being scattered more or less randomly about the country. Concentration of more than 80 percent of French Canadians in the province of Quebec has worked to intensify the political influence of separatists and has hitched to a powerful cultural force the interests of local officials in provincial autonomy. The Maritime Provinces, too, have been less than eager to be dominated by outlanders. In addition, like their friends to the South, many Canadians from Ontario and even the newer Western provinces have feared big government.[37]

The Dominion Parliament had an easy legal path open to free itself of unwanted judicial rulings. The jurisdiction—in fact, the very existence— of the Canadian Supreme Court and, after 1931, appeals to the Privy Council depended entirely on statutes; neither jurisdiction nor appeals rested on a constitutional provision. But to have taken the straight road of repeal would have required a far greater degree of consensus than existed in Canada. By 1949 that consensus had been reached on ending appeals to Westminster but not on curbing judicial review from Ottawa as well. Nor, given the swelling resentment among Quebecois against Anglo-Saxon rule, could the national government have dared attempt a direct and sharp switch away from a wide scope for provincial autonomy.

The nub of the matter is that judicial decisions tended to help one side in a series of struggles about the nature of the union, but these struggles occurred in a complex political situation in which many other forces were at work. Legitimation of provincial authority was in part a judicial effort to cope with the reality of two nations under one government, more an effect than a cause of decentralizing forces. Moreover, the matter has not yet ended. Federalism in Canada, like federalism in the United States, is a constantly changing bundle of political relationships. Judicial decisions are likely to continue to play a part in that development, but, again, as only one among many parts in a larger drama.

These difficulties of measurement are formidable, but the tendency of public law scholars to shy away from close analyses of the impacts of judicial decisions cannot be attributed solely to such problems. The teaching and research methods political scientists have favored are to some extent responsible. Traditionally, political scientists have relied heavily on the techniques made familiar through courses in constitutional law. Such courses, as they are taught in American colleges and universities, have attempted to lay what is in fact an indispensable basis for understanding what judges have held in specific cases, what reasons they have given to justify their choices, and what principles they have endorsed as guidelines for their own and others' conduct. Those courses typically require students to read, summarize, and with the help of gentle prodding from the instructor, analyze decisions and opinions—almost always of the U.S. Supreme Court —arranged topically under such headings as "civil rights," "control over commerce," and "President and Congress." From examination of these primary source materials, students are expected to gain knowledge of legal procedures as well as of the nation's fundamental constitutional problems and the solutions that judges have offered to those problems.

Case analysis is basically both textual analysis—scrutiny of the internal structure and implications of judicial reasoning—and contextual analysis —examination of the setting in which the problem arose and, to a much lesser extent, the effect a decision may have had. Political scientists have usually agreed with Lord Coke that understanding the law—at least what judges have said is the law—requires more than common sense or poetic imagination. These are helpful and the latter perhaps essential, but even together they are not sufficient. The logic of judicial reasoning is not always the logic of Aristotle, Euclid, Hume, or Mill; it may be a peculiar intellectual process that marches off from conclusions in search of major and minor premises.[38] Judges frequently busy themselves with weaving fictions to allow irreconcilable propositions at least to appear reconciled. This shuffling of premises, spinning of myths, and chopping of logic is not merely a game of charades—though occasionally it has that quality. The purpose of the process is to help solve society's problems or, failing that, to help society live with its problems, perhaps by calling those problems by different names or smothering them in soothing adjectives and adverbs.

An important concern in both political science departments and law schools has been the stitching together into doctrinal wholes of the reasons judges offer in specific cases, so that students, scholars, lawyers, public officials, and even judges themselves might better understand the development of law and policy in particular areas. The earlier scholars mentioned in chapter 1—Corwin,[39] Cushman,[40] Haines,[41] and Powell[42]—were adept at this kind of analysis, often adding to imaginative textual exegesis erudite explanations of the historical background of controversies. Their work has been carried on by men like William M. Beaney,[43] David Fellman,[44] Robert J. Harris,[45] and Robert G. McCloskey.[46] Even political scientists primarily associated with different approaches—Alpheus T. Mason,[47] C. Herman Pritchett,[48] and Glendon A. Schubert,[49] for instance—have recognized the importance of case analysis by writing and editing works in this sub-field and, perhaps more importantly, by teaching historically and doctrinally oriented constitutional law courses at both the graduate and undergraduate levels.

As fundamental, however, as the case approach is to a general understanding of the work of judges, it does have significant limitations for impact analysis. It has not, for example, been much concerned with what actually happened—as opposed to what a court said or implied should happen—after a judicial decision. Yet even though the usual casebook has not, except in a sentence or two appended as an editorial note, gone deeply into the aftermath of a decision,* this fault is not totally irreparable. Several casebooks have included remarks about later lower court decisions or political reactions,[50] and one, edited by Pritchett and Alan F. Westin,[51] has stressed the result of Supreme Court decisions.

The central problem here is that the case approach has given judges center stage in the drama of politics. Judges are important political actors, but they play as members of a very large cast. However necessary it is to begin an analysis with judges' decisions and opinions, we have to look further to learn what the consequences of a decision were, and usually further than the judicial subsystem itself. One has to see what happened to the litigants, how public officials—police, school administrators, presidents, prime ministers, governors, legislators—lawyers, and even segments of the public reacted both immediately and in the long run. Moreover, one has to find out how future judges chose among alternatives when similar issues, perhaps generated out of the controversy surrounding the first decision, arose. Most difficult of all is determining what difference a decision or set of decisions made in public policy.

We need to know, first, what happens if the case, as it usually is in the American system, is retried by a lower court after a Supreme Court ruling. The broad principles of law that appellate court judges have announced may or may not affect the final results as far as the litigants themselves are concerned. In *Miranda v. Arizona* Ernesto Miranda was apparently the victor in the famous criminal appeal that held that police must immediately inform an arrested person of his constitutional rights to silence and counsel, provide him with a lawyer—free of charge if need be—and allow that lawyer to be present and to give advice during any interrogation.[52] This was a landmark case in American constitutional law, and because of its doctrine the justices ruled that a "confession" Miranda had given to police was inadmissible in evidence against him. But neither the general doctrine nor the specific decision freed Miranda. Even without the confession he was convicted again when he was retried in Arizona.

In an Irish case of similar notoriety, Philip Quinn was vindicated by two Supreme Court rulings, one holding that he had been illegally arrested and another convicting two Irish and two British policemen of contempt of court for their abuse of his constitutional rights.[53] Quinn, nevertheless, served his term in an English jail, since the police had succeeded in getting him across the border into Ulster before Irish judges could intervene.

These are notable, but not necessarily rare, instances. A study done by the editors of the *Harvard Law Review* showed that only about half the

---

* One of the features, as we noted in chapter 1, that made Robert E. Cushman's *Leading Constitutional Decisions* so popular was that he, unlike many other editors of constitutional law casebooks, was interested in the impact of Supreme Court rulings and included a number of notes about the reactions that decisions begat.

litigants from state courts who won in the U.S. Supreme Court were actually victorious when their cases were heard again on retrial.[54]

Lower Court Reactions

What effect a decision has on the litigants is one important datum, but only one, in what may be a general pattern of response by lower court judges when they apply the principles approved by higher courts. Where, as in Canada and Ireland, advisory opinions are permitted,[55] a constitutional court can sometimes completely by-pass lower court judges. But, by and large, constitutional courts hear a variety of kinds of litigation and are to a great extent dependent on a lower court bureaucracy to carry out their decisions as well as to apply their general principles to future controversies.

The vague and amorphous nature of many of these general principles can permit or sometimes even force lower court judges to exercise a considerable degree of freedom. In fact, they may apply principles other than those intended by high court judges or apply the "correct" principles in different ways. Because constitutional courts are collegial bodies, agreement on an institutional opinion often involves compromise: insertions of qualifying words, phrases, and even paragraphs to general principles. These compromises further complicate already difficult problems of communication. Even the most intelligent and diligent trial judge can be left in doubt about the precise nature of the doctrine his superiors have recently endorsed. Where, as in Australia, there is a tradition of seriatim rather than institutional opinions, a lower court judge may be presented with three or more different sets of principles, many of them mutually incompatible, supposedly controlling the issue at bar. In either situation he must exercise some range of choice, even when he is sincerely and humbly trying to do no more than carry out his senior colleagues' wishes.

If a lower court judge has different goals from those of the constitutional court judges—and except in a few countries like Japan and to some extent India, constitutional court judges do not have responsibility for the training, selection, or promotion of lower court judges—he can take advantage not only of this leeway but also of that created by the sheer volume and costs of litigation. In the United States, for example, federal district courts hold more than 14,000 trials each year and settle in less formal ways another 14,000 cases.[56] No one really knows the precise extent of state court business, but the annual number of non-traffic cases probably exceeds 10 million and perhaps even 20 million. Only a minuscule percentage of state cases raise questions of federal law, but even if 1 percent did, that figure would represent from 500 to 1,000 times the number of cases the U.S. Supreme Court justices could intelligently discuss, decide, and write opinions on in a single term. A number of factors, including satisfaction with trial decisions and the costs of further action, help reduce the number of appeals. Less than half of the trial decisions of federal district courts and almost none of the informal dispositions are appealed. Estimates of similar state statistics are of doubtful accuracy; but given the huge number of petty criminal prosecutions and small civil suits, the proportion is probably far smaller.[57]

What this all means is that Supreme Court justices cannot supervise closely the work of all lower court judges. Even supervision of federal courts presents serious difficulties, and the justices have to depend heavily on the courts of appeals to oversee district judges. This problem, of course, varies in gravity from country to country, depending on density of population and propensity to litigate. In Ireland, where there are only about 200 practicing barristers, all of whom have offices in the same building that houses the Supreme Court, knowledge about lower court actions is likely to be quickly and widely disseminated.

At first glance it might seem that West German Constitutional Court judges would not have to face bureaucratic resistance. They do not hear appeals, and theirs is the only tribunal authorized to decide questions of federal constitutional law. In fact, however, an important part of their jurisdiction covers cases that other judges, in the course of regular litigation, perceive as raising constitutional issues and send on for review. Thus judges in other courts can drag their heels and so restrict the Constitutional Court's opportunities to exercise its full authority, since these cases can be transferred to the Constitutional Court only on a motion initiated by a lower court judge. Kommers has written about West Germany:

> It is quite clear from the record that the high federal courts have been anything but eager to invoke the Constitutional Court's jurisdiction. Only on rare occasions have they done so. . . . These courts have actually evidenced some resentment of the [Constitutional] Court's prerogatives. In one instance, the Federal High Court frontally challenged an earlier decision of the Constitutional Court upholding the Federal Government's 1951 reorganization of the German civil service.[58]

Italian experience has been similar to that of West Germany. Older judges, brought up in a civil law system to which judicial review was an alien concept, have frequently ignored the requirement of sending to the Constitutional Court cases involving interpretation of the basic law. Younger Italian judges, on the other hand, have apparently been quite ready to accept the Court's authority.[59] In both Germany and Italy the outlook is for more rather than less judicial cooperation with the Constitutional Court, but the potential for resistance remains.

Reactions of Other Public Officials

Since many apparently important judicial decisions require action by other public officials to translate them into actual policy, the reactions of these officials can often be a critical factor in determining what real effect a decision will have. Officials may greet a court ruling with joy or anger, interest or ennui. They may praise it, condemn it, or ignore it. They may earnestly and avidly attempt to carry out its principles into public policy, or they may try to subvert it, to pass a new statute, to obtain a fresh administrative ruling, or to amend the constitution to obviate its impact.[60] Not infrequently in American politics some officials react in each of these ways to the same decision and, in what has become a hackneyed phrase, an output from the judicial branch of government becomes an input for the legislative and executive processes.

Federalism can immensely complicate the problems here. Local officials in various parts of a country may react differently from each other just as national officials may differ among themselves. It is not improbable that one group of national officials will ally with a group of state or provincial officials to support a court decision while a second group of national and local officials will join in trying to obstruct implementation. Indeed, this is a fairly accurate description of what has happened after the School Segregation cases. Such a chaotic condition is far more probable in a country like America where political parties are loose alliances of feudal baronies, where the executive branch is chosen separately from the legislative, and where a tradition of civil-service subservience to elected leaders is only weakly grounded, than it is in countries where parties are tightly disciplined, the executive chosen by the legislature, and the civil service wedded to a tradition of obedience to elected rulers.

In the past decade some public law scholars have de-emphasized the kind of legal case analysis we have just discussed in favor of studying judicial votes. Some of the methods devised for analyzing judicial voting behavior are scrutinized in chapters 5 through 7 and need not now detain us. We might point out here, however, what may in any case be almost self-evident: The votes judges cast cannot tell us any more about impact than judicial opinions can—if votes can tell us as much. Like opinions, votes help us most when we wish to understand what judges do and why they do it, rather than the political consequences flowing from judicial behavior.

Studies of Impact

Although students of public law, whether traditionalists or behavioralists, have generally avoided systematic efforts to assess the impact of judicial decisions, there have always been some exceptions.   And in recent years there has been a growing body of empirical studies exploring the effects of specific rulings.[61]   As with much of the literature produced by American scholars, most of this writing has dealt with controversies decided by the U.S. Supreme Court.   A number of articles and books, both old and new, focus on efforts by senators and congressmen to modify doctrines of constitutional or statutory law or to attack judicial power itself,[62] and there are several analyses of administrative responses to court decisions.[63]   The issues political scientists and lawyers have examined range from school segregation, released time for religious instruction, prayers and Bible reading in public schools, admission of illegally seized evidence in judicial proceedings, police interrogation of suspects, loyalty-security programs, censorship, freedom of association, portal to portal pay, offshore oil leases, and reapportionment.

These researchers have demonstrated that the effect of Supreme Court decisions varies from issue to issue, from time to time, from institution to institution, and even from community to community at the same time. *Brown v. Board of Education* brought about some fairly quick integration among the border states but for almost ten years made almost no changes in the patterns of school attendance in the Deep South.   It provoked a number of lengthy lawsuits, provided golden opportunities for racists to win public office, and caused anxiety among both blacks and whites; but until the passage of the Civil Rights Act of 1964 with its provisions for cutting off federal funds from programs operated in violation of the Constitution, most black children in states like Mississippi and Alabama remained in all-black schools.   Even the 1964 act did not bring about instant integration, but it did trigger a number of changes.[64]   By 1970 about 40 percent of black children in the South were attending racially mixed schools. Fulfillment of the Nixon administration's earlier campaign decision to buy white Southern votes at the expense of black civil rights slowed down the process again.   Moreover, it is quite possible that fear of school integration has spurred the white exodus from urban centers to suburbia, thus increasing rather than decreasing de facto segregation all around the nation.

The story of religious rites and instruction in public schools is also mixed.   Some districts fully and immediately complied with decisions outlawing released time programs, prayers, and Bible reading.   Others only partially complied.   Still other school officials have consistently ignored, and others have defiantly flouted, Court pronouncements.   They have done so because they believe that local communities want religion in the public schools and because they know that the only practical way of reversing their policy decisions is for some parent to file a lawsuit—an action that, because it would be punished by social sanctions, is improbable.

At another level of analysis, studies of the impact of Supreme Court decisions like *Miranda v. Arizona* and its insistence on an accused's rights to silence and counsel during interrogation after arrest or detention have shown equally widespread variations. Even when police have sincerely attempted—and the attempt has not been universal—to carry out what the Court has said was a set of constitutional commands, the effect on behavior of accused persons has not been uniform. A study by the editors of the *Yale Law Journal*, based on around-the-clock observations of all interrogations in the New Haven police headquarters during eleven weeks of the summer after the *Miranda* decision, reported that in only 25 of 118 instances did police give suspects all the advice required by *Miranda*, although most suspects received some advice about their rights.[65] In part, this low percentage of police compliance may have been due to an initial lack of understanding of *Miranda*, for both the amount and quality of advice improved as police became more accustomed to the new rules. Significantly for the impact of *Miranda* on law and order, the Yale study concluded that "the police were no less successful in the interrogations where they had given relatively adequate advice than in the others." Furthermore, while finding no evidence of physical coercion, the editors believed that there was a high correlation between confessions and aggressive interrogation and that the *Miranda* rules were not particularly effective in reducing that kind of psychological coercion.

Along similar lines, scholars from Georgetown University's Institute of Criminal Law and Procedure investigated the effects of *Miranda* on defendants' behavior in the District of Columbia. They reported:

> Two central findings stand out in our study. First, approximately 40 percent of the defendants who were arrested in the post-*Miranda* period stated that they had given statements to the police. Second, an astonishingly small number of defendants—1,262—requested counsel from the Precinct Representation Project, even though volunteer attorneys were readily available around the clock, seven days a week. This number represented only 7 percent of the 15,430 persons arrested for felonies and serious misdemeanors in the District of Columbia during fiscal 1967.[66]

The authors found several keys to understanding why so many people had not availed themselves of the *Miranda* rules. First was ignorance. Thirteen out of eighty-five defendants whom the researchers interviewed did not understand what the right to silence meant; twenty did not comprehend their right to counsel. Some were not very intelligent people; others simply could not think clearly under stress. Second, the accused included a number of cynics. Some of the defendants said they feared police brutality if they did not cooperate; others believed that they would have to answer questions if an attorney were present or that the lawyer assigned to them would be working for the police.*   Third, some of the defendants were sure they would be convicted and thought that it would go easier on them if they cooperated.

A survey conducted by the office of the district attorney of Philadelphia asserted that as a result of *Miranda* and the rulings that had immediately preceded it, *voluntary statements* from arrested persons dropped from an estimated 90 percent in 1964 to 41 percent in the seven-month period ending on February 25, 1967.[67]   In apparent contrast, a similar study by the district attorney of Los Angeles county showed no substantial decrease in the number of *confessions* obtained by police before and after *Miranda*.[68]   As had Nathan Sobel,[69] a New York state judge, the Los Angeles district attorney concluded that confessions were not really vital to successful prosecutions.

In another kind of reaction to *Miranda*, Congress passed the Crime Control Act of 1968.   This statute openly contradicts the principles behind the *Miranda* ruling by stipulating that federal judges may admit in evidence confessions obtained from suspects who were not informed of their rights to silence and counsel, as long as the confession was "voluntary."   The Senate Committee on the Judiciary acknowledged the constitutional problem that this law raises but added:

> After all, the *Miranda* decision itself was by a bare majority of one, and with increasing frequency the Supreme Court has reversed itself.   The committee feels that by the time the issue of constitutionality would reach the Supreme Court, the probability rather is that this legislation would be upheld.[70]

As with the School Segregation, school prayer, and *Miranda* decisions, the reapportionment rulings have been bitterly attacked on the floor of Congress; and a number of senators and representatives have proposed legislation and constitutional amendments to authorize a certain amount of gerrymandering.   Like congressional efforts directed at the school prayer[71] and Segregation cases, but unlike those aimed at *Miranda*, these attacks on the reapportionment decisions have failed.   On the surface, the reactions of state legislatures to *Baker v. Carr*,[72] *Reynolds v. Sims*,[73] and their progeny have been rather uniform.   Every state legislature has redistricted itself at least once, and Florida and New Mexico each did so five times between 1962 and 1968.   In addition, there have been smaller but still considerable

---

* We found in a survey of a national probability sample of adults that it was not uncommon for people of low education and little political knowledge to conceive of government as a monolithic "they," or even a "he," and to make no meaningful distinctions among public officials such as the President, congressmen, and Supreme Court justices.   Although our survey did not include direct questions on the right to counsel, from reading responses to other inquiries, we would find it quite consistent for less-informed people to imagine police, lawyers, and judges as one group with the same interest.

numbers of changes in electoral districts for the U.S. House of Representatives. There, however, the uniformity ends. Actual reapportionment plans vary from complete redistricting to meet standards of fairness to the use of new tricks to preserve the old order. Time and again, state and federal courts have struck down the more crude of these efforts; but even in 1968 thirteen states still had legislative districts that varied as much as 30 percent in size from each other.

Two years later the struggle showed few signs of ending. Politicians are aware that where one draws electoral lines is as important as how many people live within those lines. Even where redistricting had been prompt and honest, there have been few dramatic changes in legislative behavior or public policies. Some blacks and many Republicans have been elected in the South; all around the country fewer legislators are coming from rural areas and more from the suburbs. Still, one looks in vain for radical changes in the substantive content of legislative decisions. There have been some shifts, but few if any sweeping reforms. Indeed, in some areas—Ohio, for instance—there have been signs of a rural-suburban coalition joining together to preserve the status quo against the demands from the central city for social reforms. Anyone familiar with the complicated nature of the legislative process would not have expected the shifting of boundaries of constituencies to have brought about a revolutionary change in that process—especially since the interests of suburbanites, who suffered most under the old malapportionment, are not identical nor even necessarily congruent with those of the inner-city inhabitants. Changes are being made, however, although slowly, as suburban and urban areas elect a new generation of politicians.[74]

In each of the four instances mentioned, Presidents have also been involved, although except on the race question they have been able to dodge much of the controversy flowing from these particular decisions. Both President Eisenhower and President Kennedy used troops to carry out court orders requiring desegregation, Eisenhower with misgivings about the basic racial policy he was supporting. President Johnson reluctantly signed the Crime Control Act. He apparently seriously considered vetoing it, but he wanted some of the bill's provisions and also needed the support of conservatives for his policies in Vietnam. In his 1968 campaign Richard Nixon repeatedly attacked the Court for being soft on criminals; and once in the White House, he used his influence to secure enactment in 1970 of a tough crime control act for the District of Columbia and of antinarcotics legislation that was more stringent than the 1968 bill Lyndon Johnson had thought unconstitutional.

The studies we have been discussing have been mostly aimed at determining the short-range impact of judicial decisions and setting up as yardsticks behavior by public officials or, less commonly, of affected private citizens in a time span closely limited to the date of the decision. But a judicial ruling may have a long-range effect on public policy, and it may have an indirect, but still critical, effect on private and public behavior. Furthermore, there is no reason to expect that a decision will have the same kind of impact over different time periods. Had a political scientist in 1835 looked at the effect of John Marshall's decision in *McCulloch v. Maryland* (1819),[75] he would have concluded that his case was more interesting as a monument to judicial impotence than as an example of judicial power. Marshall's ruling that states could not tax or regulate the Bank of the United States did not end the dispute, but marked one battle in a war the Bank eventually lost. State officials continued to harass the Bank, and Andrew Jackson, refusing to be bound by the Supreme Court's decision that Congress had authority to establish a national bank, withdrew federal deposits from the institution.

Yet today most lawyers, political scientists, and historians who study American constitutional development would assert that *McCulloch* was a most influential decision. As in *Gibbons v. Ogden* (1824),[76] Marshall laid down fundamental principles of national supremacy. Neither case settled either the specific controversy before the Court or the larger problem of federal-state relations. The basic issue of national versus state power was not settled until 1865, when General Ulysses S. Grant, sitting at Appomattox Court House, accepted General Lee's surrender. Even now, the precise line of authority between Washington, D.C., and the states is both fuzzy and shifting.

Neither does the importance of these cases lie in the fact that Marshall's opinions described a legal relationship, for most assuredly his description was a prescription. Rather, the importance is twofold: First, Marshall was not merely trying to settle specific policy disputes; he was proclaiming national goals and doing so in eloquent terms from a pulpit that would command wide attention. His vision of a "vast Republic, from the St. Croix to the Gulf of Mexico, from the Atlantic to the Pacific,"[77] was then a dream, but it was a dream that other men of his own and later generations shared and cherished. Second and concomitantly, the Supreme Court's decisions in these cases and Marshall's forceful rhetoric became a set of instruments in a long political struggle—one element, but an important element, in a protracted political contest.

Thus the impact of any decision also must be gauged in intangible terms. "We live by symbols," Justice Oliver Wendell Holmes noted, and a judicial ruling, a statute, or an executive order may be more important for its symbolic value than because of its actual effect on material welfare. The antitrust laws, as both lawyers and political scientists have pointed out, have done little to curb monopoly in the United States; still, their existence on the statute books apparently provides a great deal of comfort for some people.[78]

Similarly, it can be argued that the real importance of the West German Constitutional Court's ruling banning the neo-Nazi Socialist Reich party[79] lies in the fact that a powerful government institution publicly reaffirmed rejection of a totalitarian past.

Elucidating the Obscure

Oliver Wendell Holmes once said that demonstrating the obvious can be more important than elucidating the obscure. But the obvious and the obscure frequently shade into each other; equally frequently what is obvious to one man is obscure to another. It may be obvious that judicial decisions can have major political effects, but political scientists have not offered broadly applicable explanations of why decisions have produced such substantially different results. This failure is due in part to the causes we have already discussed—the inherent difficulties of measurement and the inherent shortcomings of the case approach. But failure has also been due in part to a dearth of conscious efforts to identify the psychological, political, economic, and social factors likely to shape the influence a decision will have. What political scientists have tended to produce are richly detailed and interesting descriptions of insular events, rather than close analyses and efforts to move beyond the instance at hand by developing testable generalizations.

In his study of the reaction of school principals to the U.S. Supreme Court's prayer decision, William K. Muir, Jr., has suggested a number of factors that predispose individuals to comply with judicial decisions that contradict their own value preferences.[80] On a larger scale, Stephen Wasby has extracted from a mass of literature on impact an inventory of more than 130 "hypotheses" about the elements that condition the effect of judicial rulings.[81] Most of these propositions are implicit rather than explicit; many are overlapping; many more are mutually contradictory; and none has been rigorously tested. Thus the analyst has to face the fact that there is no body of theory with which he can work, nor even proved narrow-gauged propositions from which he can begin—only a knot of problems and a mass of data.

Perhaps the first step toward creating at least the basis for general explanations would be for future studies to identify more clearly than have most previous efforts the exact problem sought to be clarified. If the object is to provide a detailed portrait of one aspect of the judicial process, the work may serve a useful set of teaching purposes but should not be expected to contribute directly to theoretical understanding. If the object is to advance knowledge in a more general fashion, then the target has to be carefully ringed. What kind of impact is being investigated? On whom is the impact being made?   It is possible but hardly probable that the responses of all private citizens, interest-group leaders, judges, legislators, lower bureaucrats, and higher executives will be influenced in the same way by the same factors.

Next, from his understanding of the problem and his examination of the morass of available literature, the analyst will have to specify the elements that he thinks most significantly affect differences in compliance among the people he is studying.   This step is much easier to prescribe than to perform.*   We have no magic list, but we suggest as a starting point a variation on the items that Richard Neustadt[82] offered to explain responses to presidential decisions.

Identifying such elements, of course, begins rather than ends analysis. Earlier discussion stressed that the tasks of measuring the extent of their presence, the degree of their interaction, and the contribution they make to the final outcome (assuming an outcome can ever be classified as "final") constitute formidable undertakings; but the difficulties are directly proportional to the importance of the attempt and the rewards that success would yield.   It would seem that the first and the greatest contribution of political scientists to the study of public law would be a set of explanations of what—and how—forces shape the impact of judicial decisions on the governmental system.   That contribution has yet to be made.

NOTES

1. Remarks at the Virginia Constitutional Convention of 1829–1830, quoted in Robert K. Faulkner, *The Jurisprudence of John Marshall* (Princeton, N.J.: Princeton University Press, 1968), p. 70.

2. White primaries: Smith v. Allwright, 321 U.S. 649 (1944); Terry v. Adams, 345 U.S. 461 (1953).
Poll taxes: Harper v. Virginia, 383 U.S. 663 (1966).
Grandfather Clauses: Guinn v. United States, 238 U.S. 347 (1915); Lane v. Wilson, 307 U.S. 268 (1939).
See generally South Carolina v. Katzenbach, 383 U.S. 301 (1966), sustaining the constitutionality of the Voting Rights Act of 1965.

3. Johnson v. Stevenson, 170 F. 2d 108 (1948); 335 U.S. 801 (1948); 336 U.S. 904 (1949).   The district court decision is unreported.   These citations are to rulings by the U.S. Court of Appeals for the Fifth Circuit and memorandum orders by the U.S. Supreme Court.

4. Wallace S. Sayre and Herbert Kaufman, *Governing New York City* (New York: The Russell Sage Foundation, 1960), pp. 204–205.   See also Kenneth M. Dolbeare, *Trial Courts in Urban Politics: State Court Policy Impact and Functions in a Local Political System* (New York: Wiley, 1967).

* See, for example, the imaginative but frustrated attempt of Robert H. Birkby, "The Supreme Court and the Bible Belt," 10 *Midwest Journal of Political Science* 304 (1966).

5. Canada: Attorney General for Prince Edward Island v. Attorney General for Canada, [1905] Appeals Cases 37.

Ireland: O'Donovan v. The Attorney General, 1961 Irish Reports 114; *In re Art. 26 and the Electoral Bill, 1961*, 1961 Irish Reports 169.

Switzerland: See F. W. O'Brien, "*Baker v. Carr* Abroad," 72 *Yale Law Journal* 46 (1962).

6. Dissolution Case, reported in John Maki (ed.), *Court and Constitution in Japan: Selected Supreme Court Decisions, 1948–1960* (Seattle: University of Washington Press, 1964), p. 366. As far as we can determine, the reapportionment case has not been translated into English. It was decided by the Grand Bench of the Supreme Court in 1964 and is officially reported at Hanreishu, XVIII, No. 2,270 (civil). In both instances the Japanese Supreme Court ducked the substantive issue by invoking an analogue of the political question doctrine, a favorite tactic of the justices. For a discussion of the Japanese use of this means of avoiding politically loaded decisions, see the articles by John Maki, Isao Sato, and Kisaburo Yokota in Dan Fenno Henderson (ed.), *The Constitution of Japan: Its First Twenty Years, 1947–67* (Seattle: University of Washington Press, 1968).

7. The West German cases are discussed by Donald P. Kommers, "The Federal Constitutional Court in the West German Political System," in Joel B. Grossman and Joseph Tanenhaus (eds.), *Frontiers of Judicial Research* (New York: Wiley, 1969); several of these opinions are excerpted in John C. Lane and James K. Pollock (eds.), *Source Materials on the Government and Politics of Germany* (Ann Arbor, Mich.: Wahrs, 1964). The decision outlawing the Communist party has been translated and edited by Wolfgang P. von Schmertzing, *Outlawing the Communist Party: A Case History* (New York: The Bookmailer, 1957).

8. For a discussion of the Australian cases, see L. F. Crisp, *Australian National Government* (Croyden, Victoria: Longmans, Green, 1965), especially chap. 3, and Geoffrey Sawer, *Australian Federal Politics and Law, 1929–1949*, 2 vols. (Melbourne: Melbourne University Press, 1963).

9. For the opinions of the Canadian court, see Bora Laskin (ed.), *Canadian Constitutional Law: Cases, Text and Notes on Distribution of Legislative Power* 2d ed. (Toronto: The Carswell Company, 1960), and Peter H. Russell (ed.), *Leading Constitutional Decisions: Cases on the British North America Act* (Toronto: McClelland and Stewart, 1965); for analyses see W. R. Lederman (ed.), *The Courts and the Canadian Constitution* (Toronto: McClelland and Stewart, 1964), and B. L. Strayer, *Judicial Review of Legislation in Canada* (Toronto: University of Toronto Press, 1968).

10. See the Irish cases discussed in John M. Kelly, *Fundamental Rights in the Irish Law and Constitution* 2d ed. (Dublin: Allen Figgis, 1967), pp. 162–170, 263–311, and 233–239.

11. See Maki, supra note 6, for the opinions in these Japanese cases.

12. See the article by Kommers and the source book edited by Lane and Pollock, supra note 7.

13. Karl Loewenstein, "Justice," in E. H. Litchfield (ed.), *Governing Postwar Germany* (Ithaca, N.Y.: Cornell University Press, 1953), p. 262.

14. See the interesting discussion by Arthur S. Miller, "An Affirmative Thrust to Due Process of Law," 30 *George Washington University Law Review* 399 (1962).

15. For a general discussion, see Robert A. Dahl, "Decision-Making in a Democracy: The Supreme Court as a National Policy-Maker," 6 *Journal of Public Law* 279 (1957).

16. Korematsu v. United States, 323 U.S. 214, 219 (1944). See also Hirabayashi v. United States, 320 U.S. 81 (1943), and Ex parte Endo, 323 U.S. 283 (1944). The best analysis of the policy of putting the Nisei in detention camps is Morton Grodzins, *Americans Betrayed: Politics and the Japanese Evacuation* (Chicago: University of Chicago Press, 1949). During World War II Canada followed a somewhat similar policy to that of the

United States in regard to citizens of Japanese ancestry.   See Forrest E. La Violette, *The Canadian Japanese and World War II* (Toronto: University of Toronto Press, 1948), and also the decision of the British Privy Council sustaining the legality of part of the Canadian program: Cooperative Committee on Japanese Canadians v. Attorney General for Canada, [1947] Appeals Cases 87.

17. Quoted by Tilman Tonnies Evers, "Die 'Gesetzesdekrete' Argentinischer Revolutionsregierungen," *Verfassung und Recht in Übersee* (1968), p. 350.

18. Judge Learned Hand probably asked this question more often than anyone outside of a political science classroom.   See especially his *The Bill of Rights* (Cambridge, Mass.: Harvard University Press, 1958), and Irving Dilliard (ed.), *The Spirit of Liberty: The Papers and Addresses of Learned Hand* (New York: Knopf, 1954).

19. See Walter F. Murphy and Joseph Tanenhaus, "Constitutional Courts and Political Representation," in Michael N. Danielson and Murphy (eds.), *Modern American Democracy* (New York: Holt, Rinehart and Winston, 1969).

20. Hannah F. Pitkin, *The Concept of Representation* (Berkeley: University of California Press, 1967), chaps. 4–5.

21. United States v. Carolene Products Co., 304 U.S. 144 (1938).

22. Brown v. Board of Education, 347 U.S. 483 (1954).

23. Eldridge Cleaver, *Soul on Ice* (New York: Dell, 1968), pp. 3–4.

24. Thomas Jefferson, "Notes on Virginia," in Philip S. Foner (ed.), *Basic Writings of Thomas Jefferson* (New York: Willey Book Company, 1944), p. 139.

25. Alberto Marradi, "Report on the Progress of a Multi-Nation Research on Supreme Courts," a paper presented at the Meetings of the International Political Science Association (1970).   For a fascinating analysis of the workings of the Italian court system, see Giorgio Freddi, "Legitimacy and Opposition in the Italian Judiciary: A Study of Organizational Conflict," unpublished doctoral dissertation, University of California at Berkeley, 1970.

26. The idea of a legitimizing role for constitutional courts has been around for some time.   As far as we are aware, a Canadian Member of Parliament, Edward Blake, was the first to articulate the notion with any precision and clarity.   His remarks are quoted at length in Gerald Rubin, "The Nature, Use and Effect of Reference Cases in Canadian Constitutional Law," 6 *McGill Law Journal* 168 (1959), reprinted in Lederman, supra note 9, pp. 227–228.   More recently Robert Dahl, a political scientist, and Charles L. Black, Jr., a lawyer, have further developed the concept.   See Dahl, supra note 15, and Black, *The People and the Court: Judicial Review in a Democracy* (New York: Macmillan, 1960), especially chap. 3.

27. Dred Scott v. Sandford, 19 Howard 393 (1857).

28. David C. Grey, *The Supreme Court and the News Media* (Evanston, Ill.: Northwestern University Press, 1968); Grey, "The Supreme Court as a Communicator," 5 *Houston Law Review* 405 (1968); Chester Newland, "Press Coverage of the U.S. Supreme Court," 17 *Western Political Quarterly* 16 (1964).

29. See David Easton and Jack Dennis, *Children in the Political System: Origins of Political Legitimacy* (New York: McGraw-Hill, 1969), and Robert D. Hess and Judith V. Torney, *The Development of Political Attitudes in Children* (Chicago: Aldine, 1967).

30. Learned Hand, "The Contribution of an Independent Judiciary to Civilization," in Irving Dilliard (ed.), *The Spirit of Liberty: Papers and Addresses of Learned Hand* 2d ed. (New York: Knopf, 1954); Hand's *The Bill of Rights* (Cambridge, Mass.: Harvard University Press, 1958).

31. West Virginia v. Barnette, 319 U.S. 624, 640 (1943).

32. Quoted in J. Woodford Howard, *Mr. Justice Murphy: A Political Biography* (Princeton, N.J.: Princeton University Press, 1968), p. 228.

33. Toronto Electric Commissioners v. Snider, [1925] Appeals Cases 396, 412–413.

34. See the cases discussed in G. P. Browne, *The Judicial Committee and the British North America Act* (Toronto: University of Toronto Press, 1967), chap. 7.

35. Argument of counsel in: St. Catherine's Milling and Lumber Co. v. The Queen, [1889] Appeals Cases 46.

36. For more sophisticated analyses see Edward M. Corbett, *Quebec Confronts Canada* (Baltimore: The Johns Hopkins Press, 1967), and Pierre Elliott Trudeau, *Federalism and the French Canadians* (New York: St. Martin's Press, 1968).

37. Mildred A. Schwartz, *Public Opinion and Canadian Identity* (Berkeley: University of California Press, 1967), p. 93.

38. For a discussion of this problem, see Charles A. Miller, *The Supreme Court and the Uses of History* (Cambridge, Mass.: The Belknap Press of Harvard University Press, 1969), chap. 1, and Julius Stone, *Legal System and Lawyers' Reasonings* (Stanford: Stanford University Press, 1964).

39. For Edward S. Corwin's writings see chapter 1, notes 17–18. See also the bibliography in Alpheus T. Mason and Gerald Garvey (eds.), *American Constitutional History: Essays by Edward S. Corwin* (New York: Harper & Row, 1964), pp. 216–229. David J. Danelski notes [" Public Law: The Field," in David L. Sills (ed.), *International Encyclopedia of the Social Sciences* (New York: Macmillan, 1968), XIII, 177] that fourteen of Corwin's articles were chosen by a committee of the American Association of Law Schools for inclusion in the four-volume work *Selected Essays on Constitutional Law* (Chicago: The Foundation Press, 1938). Two of Corwin's case analyses were still being used as textbooks in 1970: *The Constitution and What It Means Today* 12th ed. (Princeton, N.J.: Princeton University Press, 1958); Corwin and Jack W. Peltason, *Understanding the Constitution* 4th ed. (New York: Holt, Rinehart and Winston, 1967). The 3rd and 4th editions of the latter book were revised solely by Peltason, since Corwin had died some time earlier. Corwin's magnum opus in the area of case analysis was the huge volume he edited for Congress, *The Constitution of the United States of America: Analysis and Interpretation* (Washington, D.C.: Government Printing Office, 1953).

40. For a sample of Robert E. Cushman's writings, see chapter 1, notes 19–20. For a number of years (1925–1948) Cushman also published an annual article in the *American Political Science Review* on the work of the Supreme Court during its previous term.

41. For the more important of Charles Grove Haines' writings, see chapter 1, notes 15–16.

42. Several of Thomas Reed Powell's writings are cited in chapter 1, note 26. Twenty-three of his articles were included in *Selected Essays on Constitutional Law*, Danelski, supra note 39.

43. See, for instance, William M. Beaney, *The Right to Counsel in American Courts* (Ann Arbor: University of Michigan Press, 1955); Beaney, "The Constitutional Right to Privacy in the Supreme Court," in Philip B. Kurland (ed.), *1962 Supreme Court Review* (Chicago: University of Chicago Press, 1962); Beaney, "The Right to Privacy and American Law," 31 *Law and Contemporary Problems* 253 (1966); Beaney, "The Griswold Case and the Expanding Right to Privacy," 1966 *Wisconsin Law Review* 979; Alpheus T. Mason and Beaney, *The Supreme Court in a Free Society* (Englewood Cliffs, N.J.: Prentice-Hall, 1959); Mason and Beaney (eds.), *American Constitutional Law* 4th ed. (Englewood Cliffs, N.J.: Prentice-Hall, 1968); and Max Freedman, William M. Beaney, and Eugene V. Rostow, *Perspectives on the Court* (Evanston, Ill.: Northwestern University Press, 1967).

44. Alternating with Robert J. Harris, David Fellman took over from Robert E. Cushman the task of preparing the annual article on the Supreme Court for the *American*

Political Science Review for several years, then Fellman continued the project alone from 1952 until 1961. Among his other writings are "The Right to Counsel under State Law," 1955 *Wisconsin Law Review* 281; *The Defendant's Rights* (New York: Holt, Rinehart and Winston, 1958); and "The Constitutional Rights of Association," in Philip B. Kurland (ed.), *1961 Supreme Court Review* (Chicago: University of Chicago Press, 1961).

45. For several years after 1948 Robert J. Harris alternated with David Fellman in writing the annual article on the work of the U.S. Supreme Court for the *American Political Science Review*. See also Harris, "The Decline of Judicial Review," 10 *Journal of Politics* 1 (1948); "Due Process of Law," 42 *American Political Science Review* 32 (1948); *The Judicial Power of the United States* (Baton Rouge: Louisiana State University Press, 1940); and a somewhat more broadly oriented work, *The Quest for Equality: The Constitution, Congress, and the Supreme Court* (Baton Rouge: Louisiana State University Press, 1960).

46. See especially, Robert G. McCloskey, *The American Supreme Court* (Chicago: University of Chicago Press, 1960), one of the most useful introductions to the Court in American politics. See also his edited work *Essays in Constitutional Law* (New York: Knopf, 1957), and his trilogy on the Warren Court: "The Supreme Court Finds a Role: Civil Liberties in the 1955 Term," 42 *Virginia Law Review* 735 (1956); "Useful Toil or Paths of Glory: Civil Liberties in the 1956 Term of the Supreme Court," 43 *ibid*. 803 (1957); and "Tools, Stumbling Blocks, and Stepping Stones: Civil Liberties in the 1957 Term of the Court," 44 *ibid*. 1029 (1958). One of his last writings was "Reflections on the Warren Court," 51 *ibid*. 1229 (1965).

47. See Mason and Beaney, supra note 43.

48. C. Herman Pritchett, *The American Constitution* 2d ed. (New York: McGraw-Hill, 1968); Pritchett (ed.), *American Constitutional Issues* (New York: McGraw-Hill, 1962).

49. Glendon A. Schubert (ed.), *Constitutional Politics* (New York: Holt, Rinehart and Winston, 1960).

50. For example, Walter F. Murphy and C. Herman Pritchett (eds.), *Courts, Judges, and Politics* (New York: Random House, 1961), especially chap. 16; Pritchett and Alan F. Westin (eds.), *The Third Branch of Government* (New York: Harcourt, Brace & World, 1963). See also the essays in Theodore L. Becker (ed.), *The Impact of Supreme Court Decisions* (New York: Oxford University Press, 1969).

51. Supra note 50.

52. Miranda v. Arizona, 384 U.S. 436 (1966).

53. State (Quinn) v. Ryan. 1965 Irish Reports 70.

54. Note, "Evasion of Supreme Court Mandates in Cases Remanded to State Courts Since 1941," 67 *Harvard Law Review* 1251 (1954). See also Note, "Supreme Court Disposition of State Decisions Involving Non-Federal Questions," 49 *Yale Law Journal* 1463 (1940), and Walter F. Murphy, "Lower Court Checks on Supreme Court Power," 53 *American Political Science Review* 1017 (1959).

55. For Canadian practice see Gerald Rubin, supra note 26. For Irish practice see Loren P. Beth, *The Development of Judicial Review in Ireland, 1937–1966* (Dublin: Institute for Public Administration, 1967), pp. 14–16.

56. The Director of the Administrative Office of United States Courts publishes an *Annual Report* (Washington, D.C.: Government Printing Office) on the business of federal courts. These statistics, like so many published by the federal government, are arranged so as to obfuscate as much as to clarify. It is, for instance, almost impossible to discern how many cases district judges actually decide and how many are settled by negotiation or by death of one or both parties.

57. James Willard Hurst, *The Growth of American Law: The Law Makers* (Boston: Little, Brown, 1950), p. 178, reports some statistics on federal and state appeals for the late

1920s.   Kenneth M. Dolbeare, *Trial Courts in Urban Politics* (New York: Wiley, 1967), p. 3, found that in his sample of 388 trial court decisions about 25 percent were appealed.

58. Kommers, supra note 7, p. 114.

59. Mauro Cappelletti, J. H. Merryman, and J. M. Perillo, *The Italian Legal System* (Stanford: Stanford University Press, 1967), pp. 75–79, generally agree with us here, although, based on interviews with Italian judges and lawyers, we go somewhat further than they do.   See also Freddi, *op. cit.*, supra note 25, for a more general account of the Italian judiciary.

60. For a more detailed discussion see Walter F. Murphy, *Elements of Judicial Strategy* (Chicago: University of Chicago Press, 1964), chap. 2.

61. See especially Pritchett and Westin, supra note 50, and Becker, supra note 50, for collections of case studies.   See also David R. Manwaring, *Render unto Caesar: The Flag-Salute Controversy* (Chicago: University of Chicago Press, 1962); Samuel Mermin, *Jurisprudence and Statecraft* (Madison: University of Wisconsin Press, 1963); Jack W. Peltason, *58 Lonely Men: Southern Federal Judges and School Desegregation* (New York: Harcourt, Brace & World, 1961); Harrell R. Rodgers, *Community Conflict, Public Opinion and the Law* (Columbus, Ohio: Charles E. Merrill, 1969); Richard M. Johnson, *The Dynamics of Compliance: Supreme Court Decision-Making from a New Perspective* (Evanston, Ill.: Northwestern University Press, 1967); David H. Everson (ed.), *The Supreme Court as Policy-Maker: Three Studies on the Impact of Judicial Decisions* (Carbondale: Public Affairs Research Bureau, Southern Illinois University, 1968); and Stephen L. Wasby, *The Impact of the United States Supreme Court: Some Perspectives* (Homewood, Ill.: Dorsey, 1970); Kenneth M. Dolbeare and Phillip E. Hammond, *The School Prayer Decisions: From Court Policy to Local Practice* (Chicago: University of Chicago Press, 1971).   For two studies of a German case, see Ronald F. Bunn, *German Politics and the Spiegel Affair* (Baton Rouge: Louisiana State University Press, 1968), and David Schoenbaum, *The Spiegel Affair* (Garden City, N.Y.: Doubleday, 1968).   More generally, see Ronald F. Bunn and William G. Andrews (eds.), *Politics and Civil Liberties in Europe: Four Case Studies* (Princeton, N.J.: D. Van Nostrand, 1967).

62. Charles Warren, "Legislative and Judicial Attacks on the Supreme Court of the United States," 47 *American Law Review* 1 and 161 (1913), and his *Congress, the Constitution, and the Supreme Court* rev. ed. (Boston: Little, Brown, 1935); Alan H. Monroe, "The Supreme Court and the Constitution," 18 *American Political Science Review* 737 (1924); C. Herman Pritchett, *Congress versus the Supreme Court, 1957–1960* (Minneapolis: University of Minnesota Press, 1961); Walter F. Murphy, *Congress and the Court* (Chicago: University of Chicago Press, 1962); William M. Beaney and Edward N. Beiser, "Prayer and Politics," 13 *Journal of Public Law* 475 (1964).

63. In addition to the literature cited, especially notes 61–62, see, for example, Robert H. Birkby, "The Supreme Court and the Bible Belt," 10 *Midwest Journal of Political Science* 304 (1966); William K. Muir, Jr., *Prayer in the Public Schools: Law and Attitude Change* (Chicago: University of Chicago Press, 1967); Gordon Patric, "Impact of a Court Decision: Aftermath of the McCollum Case," 6 *Journal of Public Law* 455 (1957); Frank J. Sorauf, "*Zorach v. Clauson*: The Impact of a Supreme Court Decision," 53 *American Political Science Review* 777 (1959); Richard M. Johnson, "Compliance and Supreme Court Decision-Making," 1967 *Wisconsin Law Review* 170; and H. Frank Way, Jr., "Survey Research on Judicial Decisions: The Prayer and Bible Reading Cases," 21 *Western Political Quarterly* 189 (1968).   Although parallel studies of other countries are rare, see generally for judicial control of administrative action: M. A. Fazal, *Judicial Control of Administrative Action in India and Pakistan* (London: Oxford University Press, 1969), and Kiminobu Hashimoto, "The Rule of Law: Some Aspects of Judicial Review of Administrative Action," in Arthur T. von Mehren (ed.), *Law in Japan: The Legal Order in a Changing Society* (Cambridge, Mass.: Harvard University Press, 1963).

64. For an analysis of the background and effect of the 1964 act, see Gary Orfield,

The Reconstruction of Southern Education: The Schools and the 1964 Civil Rights Act (New York: Wiley, 1969).

65. Project, "Interrogation in New Haven: The Impact of *Miranda*," 76 *Yale Law Journal* 1519 (1967).   This article is excerpted in part in Becker, supra note 50.

66. Richard J. Medalie, Leonard Zeitz, and Paul Alexander, "Custodial Police Interrogation in Our Nation's Capital: The Attempt to Implement *Miranda*," 66 *Michigan Law Review* 1347, 1351–1352 (1968).   This article is also excerpted in Becker, supra note 50.

67. U.S. Senate, Committee on the Judiciary, *Hearings: Controlling Crime Through More Effective Law Enforcement*, 90th Cong., 1st sess., 1967, pp. 200–201.

68. *Ibid.*, p. 341.

69. Nathan Sobel, "The Exclusionary Rules in the Law of Confessions," *New York Law Journal* (November, 1965), p. 1.

70. U.S. Senate, Committee on the Judiciary, Report No. 1097, *Omnibus Crime Control and Safe Streets Act*, 90th Cong., 2d sess., 1968, p. 51.

71. See especially the article by Beaney and Beiser, supra note 62.

72. Baker v. Carr, 369 U.S. 186 (1962).

73. Reynolds v. Sims, 377 U.S. 533 (1964).

74. The most thorough analysis of the impact of the reapportionment decisions is Robert G. Dixon, *Democratic Representation: Reapportionment in Law and Politics* (New York: Oxford University Press, 1968).

75. McCulloch v. Maryland, 4 Wheaton 316 (1819).

76. Gibbons v. Ogden, 9 Wheaton 1 (1824).

77. McCulloch v. Maryland, supra note 75 at p. 408.

78. For discussions see Thurman Arnold, *The Symbols of Government* (New Haven, Conn.: Yale University Press, 1935), and Murray Edelman, *The Symbolic Uses of Politics* (Urbana: University of Illinois Press, 1967).

79. The Socialist Reich Party Case, 2 BverfGE 1 (1952).   The opinion is reprinted in Lane and Pollock, supra note 7, p. 229.

80. Muir, supra note 63, pp. 132–134.

81. Wasby, supra note 61, chap. 8.

82. Richard E. Neustadt, *Presidential Power: The Politics of Leadership* (New York: Wiley, 1960), p. 19.

3
Access and Influence

Because the decisions of judges can have the kinds of effects we discussed in the last chapter, political scientists have been interested in questions relating to access to judicial power and influences on its exercise. Who can energize judicial machinery? How can that be done? How can one influence judges to select one policy alternative over another? and How may one go about "correcting" judicial "errors"? are all crucial intellectual concerns of political scientists as well as practical concerns of litigants, lawyers, and public officials.

Access by Government Officials

Courts, constitutional or otherwise, are in one important sense usually passive instruments of government. They lack, as the late Justice Robert

H. Jackson once said, a self-starter.[1]   Normally, someone outside of the judicial system has to bring a suit or invoke a set of special circumstances to transform judicial power from a potential to a kinetic state.   In most polities with constitutional courts, individual citizens and government officials have opportunities—though not necessarily equal opportunities—to exploit the access that is legally available.

Public officials might want to use the courts to carry out their own policies, legitimize a current or projected policy, or block the policies of other officials.   Practice in federal courts in the United States provides national officials with several special means of formal access to courts. Federal officers, like state officials, can institute criminal proceedings and intervene directly in certain kinds of civil suits between private parties.   If one state government sues another or sues the government of the United States, or if the federal government sues a state, the case may be heard in the U.S. Supreme Court under its original—that is, trial—jurisdiction.   In fact, although it is not required by any written rule, the Supreme Court is quite likely to agree to review lower court decisions if asked to do so by the Department of Justice.[2]   In the bulk of civil litigation, however, American public officials usually have to walk much the same long, dusty road as private citizens.

The desirability of quickly settling constitutional doubts and the tortoise-like speed of many legal proceedings have led some countries—and a number of American states—to provide for a kind of judicial preview before legislation goes into actual force.   In Norway the Parliament may ask the Constitutional Court for advice before a bill is enacted.   In France several agencies of government may request an opinion from the Constitutional Council, and the Irish Constitution permits the President to ask for an opinion on a bill's constitutionality before he signs it into law.

The Indian President may go even further and ask the Supreme Court for advice on almost any question of law, but even this potential for the injection of judicial advice does not equal the potential that exists in Canada, where there is a series of opportunities for constitutional preview and for review at any early stage in a law's life.   First, the Governor General in Council—an ancient legalism for the cabinet—may ask the Supreme Court for an advisory opinion on almost any issue,* including the constitutionality

---

* The Canadian statute is wonderfully broad:
  Important questions of law or fact touching (a) the interpretation of the *British North America Acts*; (b) the constitutionality or interpretation of any Dominion or provincial legislation; (c) the appellate jurisdiction as to educational matters, by the *British North America Act, 1867*, or by any other Act or law vested in the Governor in Council; (d) the powers of the Parliament of Canada, or of the legislatures of the provinces, or of the respective governments thereof, whether or not the particular power in question has been or is proposed to be exercised; or (e) any other matter, whether or not in the opinion of the Court *ejusdem generis* [of the same nature] with the foregoing enumerations, with reference to which the Governor in Council sees fit to submit any such question; may be referred by

of bills pending in or enacted by provincial legislatures or the Dominion Parliament. Second, either house of the Dominion Parliament may ask the Court for an opinion on any private bill. Third, each province has authorized its cabinet to seek advice from its highest provincial court and to do so on a scale comparable to that open to the Dominion government. Fourth, the British North America Act itself also establishes a kind of nonjudicial preview in allowing the Dominion cabinet to "disallow" any act of a provincial legislature that the cabinet deems either to exceed provincial power or to conflict with Dominion authority or policy. Even at this stage the Supreme Court can become involved, since the cabinet may well ask the Court's advice.

The binding power of preview differs from country to country. In France and India[3] the opinion given by the judges is purely advisory. In contrast, the Irish Constitution provides that the Supreme Court's "advisory" opinion practically closes the constitutional issue forever. It can be reopened only by an amendment approved by both the national legislature and a popular referendum. This is the only instance in which the Irish Supreme Court is bound by the rule of stare decisis. The Canadian practice seems to fall between that of France and India on the one hand and Ireland on the other. There is no doubt that in terms of strict law the answers given by the Canadian Supreme Court, as the first Justice Taschereau noted in 1894, "will bind no one, not even those who put them, not even those who give them. . . ."[4] Practice, however, has brought about a series of changes. Stare decisis tugs at the sleeves of all common law judges, especially where, as in Canada, judges tend to be legal positivists. In fact, at one time the Canadian justices were referring to their advisory opinions as having the same authority as decisions in actual cases. The trend seems to have changed again, and the Court is now treating advisory opinions as carrying great weight as precedents though not as being absolutely binding.[5] For their part, elected officials could find it embarrassing to ignore or contravene advice publicly given by respected judges, especially where that advice tends to be tantamount to a decision on a particular issue.

At one time the West German Constitutional Court had authority to give advisory opinions; but after the emotionally heated controversy over the legality of Germany's joining the European Defense Community proved deeply embarrassing to the Government, the Court, and the President, Parliament repealed the statute. A modified form of constitutional preview is still available, however, in West Germany. The government of a *Land*

the Governor in Council to the Supreme Court for hearing and consideration; and any question touching any of the matters aforesaid, so referred by the Governor in Council, shall be conclusively deemed to be an important question.

Revised Statutes of Canada, 1952, chap. 259, as amended by Stats. Can., 1956, chap. 48. B. L. Strayer, *Judicial Review of Legislation in Canada* (Toronto: University of Toronto Press, 1958), pp. 259–260, reprints the entire statute dealing with advisory opinions.

(state), one-third of the members of the Bundestag, or the federal Government itself may petition the Constitutional Court for "abstract review" of the "formal and material compatibility of Federal law or *Land* law with this Basic Law, or on the compatibility of *Land* law with Federal law"[6] after such a statute has been enacted, even if it has not yet been enforced.

Although American, Australian, and Japanese officials cannot utilize their respective judicial systems quite so readily as can Canadian, German, or Irish officials, governments in these first three countries can bring test cases in an effort to legitimize, execute, or block controversial policies. Alternatively, public officials can proceed to carry out a policy through administrative processes in reasonably sure knowledge that some individual, organization, or other set of government officers will quickly challenge its legality or constitutionality. Each of these procedures usually takes longer than constitutional preview, and much can happen in the time between administrative and judicial decisions; but in the end judges are likely to be drawn into the web of policy making.

Access by Private Citizens

In each instance of preview just discussed, the initiating party has to be a government official. Private citizens do not have this option open to them. Moreover, a few countries limit all access to the constitutional court to government officials. In most countries, however, private citizens have a number of ways to utilize judicial power. First of all, individuals or leaders of interest groups can pressure public officials to protect or attack certain policies by using any of the special routes of access open to government. For instance, in the United States a local medical association might ask a district attorney to prosecute a man practicing medicine without a license, or the National Association for the Advancement of Colored People might try to persuade officials of the Department of Justice to bring more prosecutions under civil rights statutes. In Germany members of a labor union might ask a *Land* officer to challenge the constitutionality of a federal law that affected their bargaining position vis-à-vis management. Even in Italy, where private citizens cannot bring a suit directly to the Constitutional Court, this kind of indirect approach through pressure on regional or national officials is possible. How effective such requests would be in any democratic nation would depend on a number of factors, not least of which would be the votes officials would estimate they would gain or lose by complying and their general sympathy with the policy goals they would be asked to promote.

A second alternative, available to private citizens only if the government itself is pursuing an objectionable policy, is to violate the statute or executive order in question and, when prosecuted, set up as a defense a claim that the regulation is unconstitutional. In Connecticut, for example, Dr. C. Lee Buxton and the Planned Parenthood League flagrantly flouted that state's legislation against advising use of contraceptives. They eventually succeeded in bludgeoning state officials into prosecuting them and, after losing in Connecticut courts, won on the constitutional issue in the U.S. Supreme Court.[7] A third procedure, one usually chosen after the fact, is for a citizen who suddenly finds himself in the clutches of the police to set up a constitutional or statutory right as a defense.

Both the second and third procedures entail serious risks.* If the court upholds the validity of the applicable statute under the constitution or the legitimacy of the police action under a statute, the tester faces a fine or imprisonment or both. In Japan, for instance, Article 9 of the Constitution declares that the " people forever renounce war " and avow never to maintain armed forces; but demonstrators who in 1957 trespassed on a U.S. Air Force installation in protest against American military bases as a violation of that Article lost their case. The Japanese Supreme Court, to the annoyance of some of the justices and many scholars, implied that the constitutionality of the treaty was not a question that judges could decide and, besides, that the treaty was constitutional.[8] Despite the Court's problems with logic, the demonstrators received minor punishment.

Most countries provide a fourth set of ways to challenge governmental action—ways that do not involve risks of criminal penalties. These means are less dangerous than direct confrontation, but they are usually not without their own technical and substantive difficulties. It may be possible for one private citizen to sue another or to sue a corporation to prevent the defendant from taking advantage of or obeying certain legislation. More directly, a citizen can often go to court and claim that, although at this instant he is not being injured by private or governmental action, he stands in grave and immediate danger of injury. In this situation the citizen asks the court for a definition of his rights and usually for an order restraining private citizens or government officials from taking the threatened action if it would interfere with those rights. He may name as those whose rights are to be defined and possibly to be protected not only himself but perhaps all other persons similarly situated. In common law countries the definition of rights is known as a declaratory judgment, the restraining order as an injunction, and the suit that includes in its sought-after protection the rights of a large group of other persons as a class action.

Some countries have been very generous in allowing private citizens to request declaratory judgments or their analogues. None has been more so

---

* The risks of invoking a constitutional defense under these conditions are even greater in countries like Italy, where the trial judge cannot himself decide a constitutional claim but can only send it to the Constitutional Court if he thinks the issue is substantively important to a decision in the case. Furthermore, if he refuses to send the case to the Constitutional Court, a private citizen cannot go to the Constitutional Court and appeal the trial judge's decision.

than Colombia, which permits any citizen to contest any statute he believes invalid, whether or not the statute affects him personally. Normally, however, courts require an individual to show real or threatened injury before permitting him to challenge the constitutionality of a statute or the legality of administrative action. Even the Swiss, who allow citizens a broad right to attack the validity of a cantonal (but not a federal) statute within thirty days of its promulgation, still demand that the litigant show how the act would harm his rights if it were enforced.[9]

Lest they be inundated with litigation, judges in the United States have set rather tight rules to control access to judicial power. Federal and, typically, state judges require not only that potential litigants meet the formal requirements of jurisdictional statutes but also that they have "standing to sue."[10] Essentially, the latter phrase means, first, that the individual bringing a case has to show that he is suffering or is immediately threatened with injury; mere possibility of injury is not sufficient. Second, the right must be a legally protected one, not merely a "moral" or "natural" right. Third, the right must be a personal one of the plaintiff, not the right of another person; a general claim that a law is unjust, unfair, or unconstitutional does not fulfill the standing requirements. Fourth, the two parties to the suit must be truly adversaries. Their interests have to be in conflict; they cannot be friends who merely want the court to settle a difference of opinion. Fifth, if the contested action is that of a government agency, that action must be final to be "ripe" for review. Unless there are exceptional circumstances, a potential litigant has to demonstrate that he has used all available administrative procedures to secure redress. Sixth, the decision sought must be one that is within the province of the judiciary to give, not a dispute on which a judge may merely tender advice or one whose solution the Constitution entrusts to other organs of government.

The sheer volume of litigation is forcing judges of the West German Constitutional Court to develop their own criteria for deciding when a litigant who meets jurisdictional standards can invoke judicial power.[11] The Basic Law provides that a citizen whose constitutional rights are threatened by any governmental action—national or *Land*, administrative, judicial, or legislative—can bring suit directly in the Constitutional Court by filing what is technically called a constitutional complaint. As one might have expected, many people looked on these provisions as an open invitation to litigate, and the Court is currently receiving about 1,400 constitutional complaints a year. The West German judges have established committees to screen out the more frivolous of these cases so that the Court can hear and decide the more serious ones. The judges sit in committees of three and by unanimous consent can dismiss a petition. If, however, one judge on a committee thinks a complaint presents a sufficiently important issue or indicates a real danger to a citizen's rights, the appropriate senate of the Constitutional Court must hear the case.

Australian, Canadian, and Irish judges have at times implicitly or explicitly endorsed standing rules that are fairly similar to those of American judges, but they usually apply them much more liberally.* Even in the United States there have been some relaxations of standing rules in the past, and more appear likely in the future. In litigation involving religious schools[12] and the rights of blacks to buy housing on an equal basis with whites,[13] the Supreme Court treated the standing requirements rather generously, in the first instance allowing teachers to assert the rights of parents, and in the second, allowing whites to assert the rights of blacks. One of the old standing rules has been that a taxpayer could not challenge the constitutionality of a federal program, since his monetary interest in any expenditure was too small to give him a real interest.[14] Since rigid application of this rule would make it difficult to contest any act of Congress that subsidized either one religion or a group of religions, the Supreme Court has modified the standing rule to permit taxpayers to challenge federal grants as violating the First Amendment ban against establishment of a religion.[15]

Protecting courts from being swamped is one of the prime functions of rules on standing, but one cannot understand such rules in the United States or elsewhere if one looks at them only as a set of strict, legal criteria or even as a set of jurisdictional sieves. The protean nature of these rules also permits judges to use them as instruments of diplomacy to avoid problems that they believe would be better handled by other agencies of government or, at least, better postponed. The U.S. Supreme Court, for instance, twice used the standing rules to duck the Connecticut birth control issue. When the Court finally did confront the problem, it did so at a time when birth control had become an accepted part of American culture, rather than a dirty word.

A pair of Japanese cases provide illustrations of judicial ability to use standing rules so as to avoid being sucked into the vortex of a dangerous political struggle and yet maintain the appearance of being legalistically rather than politically oriented. In 1950, when the Korean War forced the United States to pull the bulk of its troops out of Japan, General Douglas MacArthur authorized the Japanese government to establish a "national police reserve." This quaint euphemism for a small army was designed to mask an evasion of Article 9 of the Constitution.† Two years later, when

---

* Speaking through Mr. Justice Brian Walsh, the Irish Supreme Court has rejected the view that anyone can challenge the constitutionality of a statute, but the Court has also refused to endorse standing rules as strict as those sometimes applied by the U.S. Supreme Court. *East Donegal Cooperative Livestock Mart et al. v. Attorney General*, unreported as of early 1971 but decided in 1970. For Canadian practices, see B. L. Strayer, *Judicial Review of Legislation in Canada* (Toronto: University of Toronto Press, 1968), pp. 96–125.

† Article 9 reads:
   Aspiring sincerely to an international peace based on justice and order, the Japanese people forever renounce war as a sovereign right of the nation. . . . In order to accomplish the aim of the preceding paragraph, land, sea, and air forces, as well as other war potential, will never be maintained. The right of belligerence of the state will not be recognized.

the American military occupation officially ended, Mosaburo Suzuki, Secretary General of the Social Democratic party, petitioned the Supreme Court for a declaration that the police reserve was unconstitutional. The justices, however, said they could find no "concrete legal dispute."[16] Suzuki had failed to show how any specific, individual right of his was being violated or threatened with injury, and so the Court dismissed the case. A year later, when the Conservative Prime Minister dissolved the Diet and called a national election, a Social Democrat again brought suit, alleging that the Constitution provided for dissolution and new elections only on a vote of no confidence, not at the pleasure of the Government. But the Court relied on the doctrine of the Suzuki case to avoid a decision on the merits.[17]

Lawyers have generally done most of the research on formal rules of access to courts. Their basic technique is first to identify jurisdictional statutes and (especially in common law countries) appropriate court opinions and then to collect, classify, and perhaps rank the relevant regulations. In studying foreign systems, political scientists may often have to do this kind of work themselves, although lawyers have on occasion compiled superb treatises and casebooks that provide full and accurate explanations.

Ferreting out informal rules that judges apply is somewhat more difficult. It may necessitate scrutinizing private papers, briefs of counsel, and transcripts of written records and oral argument, as well as quantitative analysis to determine to what extent judicial behavior squares with announced rules and to test hunches that might account for patterns of actual behavior. Once again the interests of lawyers and political scientists overlap, but political scientists will need to do more of the spade work here than in discovering formal rules. One of these common concerns involves the criteria that U.S. Supreme Court justices apply in deciding whether or not to grant certiorari, that is, to review a case. The formal rules are quite simple.[18] They are also quite general, quite vague, and, as lawyers have delighted in showing, quite haphazardly applied.[19] Joseph Tanenhaus and three colleagues used multivariate analysis—techniques we discuss in chapter 7—to test several hypotheses relating to the "cues" that justices apparently pick up as they read the several thousand annual requests for review.[20] These scholars found that a request by the United States government for review or the presence of a civil liberties issue (other than criminal justice) greatly increased the chances of the justices' agreeing to hear the case, as, to a lesser extent, did dissent within the lower court.

Strategies to Obtain Access

With the stakes of judicial decisions high, litigants, whether private citizens or government officials, are apt to devise strategies in initiating and carrying on lawsuits. Since legal procedures typically are complicated, expensive, and time consuming, money, organization, and technical skills—which can often be hired—may be critical factors in winning a case. Thus government agencies and organized groups frequently have real advantages over private citizens acting alone. Not the least of these advantages is the accumulated experience of a relatively permanent professional staff who specialize in particular kinds of work and who have the time not only to plan litigation on their own but also to search out lawsuits already in progress that they can join as amicus curiae. The size of an organization's membership also provides opportunities to find cooperative litigants who meet the standing requirements or who are even willing to risk martyrdom by violating objectionable regulations. Government agencies usually need only to enforce or ignore regulations to provoke a lawsuit.

In a series of case studies, Professor Clement E. Vose has demonstrated the careful way in which lawyers for several American organizations have gone about exploiting judicial power.[21] Vose's most detailed account, that of the NAACP's strategy in bringing suits to declare racially restrictive real-estate covenants unenforceable, showed how the association's legal staff picked its litigants, timed its suits, and coordinated its operations with those of other friendly organizations.[22] Vose's main materials were the actual trial and appellate records; the briefs of counsel on both sides as well as of amici curiae; and, most revealing, interviews with those who participated in the cases. The result was a dramatic narrative showing NAACP leaders acting much like the general staff of an army, commanding here—and not always being obeyed—pleading there, and constantly coordinating with each other and possible allies to attain the goal of victory in the U.S. Supreme Court.

The factors that make for success in one governmental process may have very different weights in another, as the many successes of the NAACP and, in both Canada and the United States, of an even smaller and less powerful group, the Jehovah's Witnesses, illustrate. The liberal justices of the U.S. Supreme Court might have decided racial issues the same way no matter how skillfully the NAACP and its allies had played their parts. But the facts remain that the cases were brought to the Court and were conducted with devotion, skill, and meticulous attention to detail—for instance, by having counsel rehearse oral argument before a group of Howard Law School professors each of whom played the part of an individual Supreme Court justice.

The judicial process in other countries offers similar opportunities for private citizens and organizations to take their causes to the judges. One of the most notable Irish cases involved reapportionment. In 1959, with its own rigid discipline and against only spasmodic and ineffective opposition from Fine Gael, the larger of the two opposition parties, the government party, Fianna Fail, pushed through the Parliament a districting plan that overrepresented the rural Western areas, where Fianna Fail was stronger, at the expense of urban areas, especially Dublin, where Fianna Fail was

weaker.   Angered at the apparent acquiescence of their party leadership in
what they viewed as a government power play, a group of Fine Gael back-
benchers rallied behind Senator John O'Donovan, who brought suit in the
High Court, asking for a declaration that the 1959 electoral act was unconstitutional.   Counsel for O'Donovan included Sean MacBride, the former
leader of one of the small independent parties that had once joined in a
coalition government with Fine Gael; two Fine Gael members of the Dail,
the lower house of Parliament; and one Fine Gael senator.   Since the Constitution of the Republic of Ireland stipulates that "so far as it is practicable,"
members of the Dail should represent the same number of constituents, and
since the census figures demonstrated that the 1959 act established some rural
areas with populations 20 to 40 percent smaller than those in the Dublin
region, the High Court declared the statute unconstitutional.[23]   The Government did not appeal but, instead, obtained a new act in 1960 creating districts
of approximately equal size.*

   The "constitutional complaint" in West Germany provides a ready
route for private action, as does the possibility of raising a constitutional
right as a defense in a regular lawsuit.   Political parties have two additional
means of utilizing judicial power.   First, the West German Basic Law allows
an independent agency of government to seek what is in effect a declaratory
judgment that its authority has been violated by another agency of government.   This kind of proceeding—technically called an *organstreit* and sometimes translated as a "separation of powers" complaint—opens the possibility of continuing partisan conflict in the Constitutional Court, not only
because different parties may control governmental institutions at the *Land*
and federal levels, but also because the Court has ruled that, at least where
elections or electoral laws are involved, a political party is an organ of
government for the purpose of this aspect of the Court's jurisdiction.[24]

   Second and less directly, if a political party controls a *Land* government
or a sizable minority of seats in the federal Parliament or can ally itself with
other parties, party leaders can use that power to invoke what is called
"abstract judicial review."   This procedure eases the usual burden on a
petitioner of demonstrating a real or immediately threatened injury to a
legally protected right.   All that is required is a showing that a difference of
opinion exists on a constitutional issue.   Only three groups, however, can
ask for abstract judicial review: the federal Government; one-third of the
members of the Bundestag, the lower house of the national legislature; or a

---

* The President referred the new bill to the Supreme Court and obtained an opinion that it was
constitutional: See *In re Art. 26 and the Electoral Amendment Bill, 1961*, 1961 Irish Reports 169.
Redistricting, it should be noted, did not prevent the Government from winning a majority of
legislative seats in the national elections of 1961, 1965, and 1969.   Shortly after O'Donovan's
court victory, he left the Fine Gael party and was defeated when he ran as a Labour candidate
in 1965; but he was elected in 1969.   Richie Ryan, O'Donovan's solicitor, remained in the party
and became a member of its shadow cabinet.   The Government later showed its magnanimity
by promoting to the Supreme Court the High Court judge who had decided the case.

Land government. It is unlikely, of course, that the federal Government would want to challenge the legality of its own actions, though it might want to have questions of legitimacy immediately settled. On the other hand, a minority group in the legislature might well wish to challenge the action of the majority. Since in German politics *Laender* have often been controlled by the Social Democratic party, and since until 1969 the Christian Democratic party was dominant in the Bundestag, occasions for conflict have been frequent, and abstract review has provided a ready judicial forum for such conflicts.

In 1958 the Social Democratic government of Hesse, for instance, successfully brought suit to declare unconstitutional the federal statute allowing corporations to claim political contributions as tax deductions. This statute had encouraged German businessmen to help finance the more conservative Christian Democrats. Despite the fact that up to that time the Christian Democrats had outpolled the Socialists in national elections, the Social Democrats had a much greater number of dues-paying members than the Christian Democrats, and thus the Christian Democrats had greater financial problems. To allay those problems, the Christian Democrats, with an absolute majority in Parliament, next enacted a plan by which the federal government provided subsidies for all parties who had representatives in the Bundestag. The government of Hesse, against the wishes of the national leadership of the Social Democrats, pressed its advantage and challenged this new statute. Once more the Constitutional Court decided against the federal government.[25]

The even more controversial national television case revolved around the efforts of Konrad Adenauer to establish a video network to be financed by the federal government.[26] Adenauer's tactics were both high-handed and heavy-handed, disturbing many members of his own party. In the middle of negotiations with *Laender* governments to establish some kind of joint direction over a television corporation, *Der Alte* formally established a private television company solely under national control. The Social Democrats were quite cognizant of the political potential involved in a nation-wide television system under the financial thumb of a rival political party, and the Social Democratic governments of four *Laender*, including Hesse, immediately took the case to the Constitutional Court. The judges ruled that Article 30 of the Basic Law gives the *Laender* exclusive authority in the field of cultural affairs and that the Bund government's control of a television network would violate the guarantee of freedom of opinion and information in Article 5.

Influencing Judicial Output

In this chapter we have been concentrating on the problem of energizing judicial power via lawsuits. This is a necessary but not a sufficient condition for obtaining a favorable judicial decision. Access in itself provides only an avenue for influencing judicial output. Let us turn, then, to methods of influencing what judges do. Bribing, of course, is an obvious means of impelling a judge to make a " correct " ruling. Occasionally, as in Oklahoma and Illinois in the 1960s, there is a scandal involving judges;[27] but by and large in developed countries the standards of judicial honesty are quite high. Another means of influence is force, which is usually applied by government agencies or revolutionary organizations. Judges in Nigeria, Greece, and Argentina have in recent years been among those who have been removed from office or have had their authority curbed by military juntas or civilian dictatorships. The fist of military power has also occasionally touched American judges. In the Civil War, for instance, Lincoln kept a federal judge in the District of Columbia under virtual house arrest when it seemed likely that the judge would order the release of some Southern sympathizers.[28] And in Hawaii during World War II the military commander threatened a federal district judge with arrest. Undeterred, the judge held the general in contempt; and after a peace maker from the Department of Justice arranged a compromise procedure that permitted a test case, the Supreme Court—after, not during, the war—sustained the authority of the judge.[29]

Fortunately for constitutional government, political officials in democratic nations almost always restrict themselves to other means of influence, such as bringing cases and relying on evidence and argument to convince judges. In a general sense, speeches by a president or a prime minister or by leading members of the legislature may persuade judges of the correctness —or merely the necessity—of a certain political course. Politicians are aware that judges often read their speeches—not always by choice, but because counsel are likely to quote extensively from such material in their arguments of a case*—and often direct their speeches to that select judicial audience. Even when judges are not fully convinced of the correctness of specific policies, they may treat such policies with deference and resolve doubts in favor of the government. This is little more than a restatement of the so-called presumption rule, followed in most constitutional courts: Judges presume a legislative act to be constitutional; the burden of proof that a statute is invalid falls upon the challenging party.

---

* Historically, common law judges would not allow counsel to cite speeches of legislators or reports of committees on the grounds that the judicial task was to decide what the statute as worded meant, not what legislators had intended it to say. Judges of the Privy Council applied this ban to constitutional interpretation—which they saw as basically no different from statutory interpretation anyway. Justices of the U.S. Supreme Court were less strict about this problem and by the second decade of this century had abandoned the restriction. One of the results has been that speeches on the floor of Congress are often aimed more at judges than at legislators and may form a network of mutually contradictory interpretations as each senator or congressman tries to make sure that there will be some record of his particular interpretation that a court might construe as authoritative. On the other hand, Australian and Canadian constitutional court judges have tended to follow the Privy Council's practice.

The ability of counsel, whether working for a private or a government client, to influence a court through the normal channels of argument is shaped to some extent by the procedures of the court and the kinds of evidence judges will admit. In appearing before a tribunal that allows only oral advocacy, a lawyer is apt to use strategies and perhaps substantive arguments very different from those he would employ were the court to restrict him to submission of written briefs.

Procedures vary widely among courts. In Ireland argument before the Supreme Court is almost completely oral; briefs as they are known in the United States are simply not used. The Australian and Canadian courts also depend more heavily on oral advocacy than does the American Court. The Swiss, on the other hand, permit only written briefs. A lawyer may sit and watch the judges discuss the case among themselves, but he cannot take part in that debate. Like the U.S. Supreme Court, the West German Constitutional Court permits both written and oral argument, though the West German lawyers apparently rely more on briefs than do their American colleagues. Argentine constitutional court judges also depend primarily on written argument, but it is considered proper for counsel to talk privately with one or more members of the court to explain his case.

Closely related to the procedures of advocacy is the question of what kinds of evidence a court will admit. Justices of the U.S. Supreme Court seem hungry for "societal facts," information that will put the case into a concrete situation, and will receive and search out on their own all sorts of writings by statisticians, government officials, lawyers, social workers, economists, and even political scientists. Judges of the West German Constitutional Court have, if anything, displayed more systematic enthusiasm in their search for hard social, economic, and historical data on which to ground their decisions. Not only are they likely to be informed through their private reading but they also sometimes invite, on their own motion, experts to testify before them.[30]

Not all judges are receptive to factual considerations in cases involving constitutional or statutory interpretation, nor have they always been so in America.* As late as the 1920s some of the more conservative members of

* Edward S. Corwin tells the story that during the oral argument of Adams v. Tanner, 244 U.S. 590 (1917), a case contesting the constitutionality of a Washington statute ending private employment agencies, Chief Justice Edward Douglas White picked up the state's brief, which had amassed voluminous evidence about the abuses of such agencies, and remarked that he could have compiled a brief twice that thick to support an argument for outlawing the legal profession. Four of the other justices were also unimpressed with the evidence, and the Court, by a 5 to 4 vote, held the statute unconstitutional. See Corwin's *Liberty Against Government* (Baton Rouge: Louisiana State University Press, 1948), pp. 151–152. As late as 1923 a majority of the U.S. Supreme Court characterized the social science data presented in a Brandeis-type brief as "interesting, but only mildly persuasive." Adkins v. Children's Hospital, 261 U.S. 525, 560 (1923).

the U.S. Supreme Court looked askance at their colleagues when they cited law review literature, and many judges and commentators in the United States remain skeptical of the value of social science evidence as well as of the propriety of a judge's relying on "extralegal" writings.[31]   Judges in Australia and Canada are far more reluctant than their American cousins to acknowledge that the broader social, economic, and political contexts of cases interest them.[32]   In large part this suspicious attitude is probably due to an insistence that judges find law, not make it.   They apply principles; legislators consider facts.   The flaws in this reasoning are so obvious that few judges would frankly endorse it, and there are some signs that Commonwealth countries are coming closer to the approach used by the American and German courts.   Whatever the problems of evaluating social science evidence, the alternative of relying on judicial notice—facts that a judge will accept as common knowledge—has even more dangerous implications in a complex world in which few people have much deep knowledge outside their narrow specialties.

Irish judges have never made much of the problem, in part because in the past the conservative British legal orientation presented Irish lawyers with a model of a judicial system that generally eschews such evidence, in part because the education of Irish barristers puts few of them in touch with modern social science, and in part because a tradition of oral advocacy is not conducive to the use of social statistics.   Especially in recent years, however, Irish judges have shown no ideological bias against social science evidence.   The reapportionment cases revolved around a pair of factual questions: Were there significant discrepancies in the numbers of voters needed to elect members of the Dail?   If there were, could these discrepancies be justified because of difficulties of travel and communication?   Similarly, in the suit challenging the constitutionality of the country's program to put fluoride in drinking water, the courts received all sorts of evidence on the physical effects, positive and negative, of fluoridation.[33]

One can find a great deal of literature describing, praising, and criticizing judicial use of societal facts, but for political scientists, here, just as in other aspects of advocacy, the central question—What difference does it make in the substance of a decision and on the effect of that decision?—remains largely unexplored.   The question, of course, is a tricky one, especially since an outside observer cannot be sure that in citing or not citing certain kinds of evidence—articles in social science or law journals, for example—a judge has or has not been influenced by them.   Indeed, one cannot even be sure he has read them if he cites them or that he has not read them if he omits reference to them.   The difficulty of the question, however, is proportional to its importance.   A judge who is content to consider only abstract principles and to ignore social, economic, and political reality is likely to come to very different conclusions from a judge who has an appreciation of the complexity of the problems before him and the likely consequences of alternative decisions.*

Public pronouncements of government officials and arguments of lawyers are not the only sources of judicial knowledge. Judges may discuss broad problems, and sometimes specific cases, with friends who may supply an added degree of learning or practical experience.[34] Since the literacy rate among judges is high, they may also gather wisdom, not necessarily cited in their opinions, from newspapers, books, and professional journals. In chapter 2 we noted that judges may help shape a nation's political culture, but judges are also products of a political culture and may in turn be molded in their thinking by the climate of opinion in which they live. "The great tides and currents which engulf the rest of men," Justice Cardozo once wrote, "do not turn aside in their course and pass the judges by."[35]

Thus another way to influence judges is to influence community values. On the broadest plane, authors of treatises on politics, economics, history, jurisprudence, and philosophy—and even novelists—may orient the thinking of large numbers of the population. As John Maynard Keynes observed, "The ideas of economists and political philosophers, both when they are right and when they are wrong, are more powerful than is commonly understood. Indeed, the world is ruled by little else."[36] And jurists are not immune to the contagion of ideas. The effect of writers like Gunnar Myrdal on the thinking of educated Americans, including judges, about race relations is a striking example of the potential here.[37] At a more practical level, authors of law reviews may alert a judge to a specific problem.[38] Even if judges do not have the time or inclination to do much reading, by living in a community they can become sensitized to certain kinds of problems—an economic depression; race riots; a crisis in education; or a war, major or minor, hot or cold. How a judge ranks these problems in importance and the degree of sympathy with which he views different kinds of solutions depend in part on his personality and life history. For instance, five of the U.S. Supreme Court justices who sat in judgment on the constitutionality of early New Deal legislation had been born during or before the Civil War, the other four during Reconstruction. Even the most liberal of them—

---

* On the other hand, there is the case of Oliver Wendell Holmes and Louis D. Brandeis, who were not only close friends but also tended to vote together. Brandeis was an empiricist who reveled in statistical analysis. His idea of relaxation was to read a report of the Coal Commission. He was also a believer in judicial activism and openly and ardently sympathized with a number of social causes. Holmes, in contrast, claimed to hate facts and preferred to argue from abstract principles. Moreover, he was an apostle (prophet might be more apt) of judicial self-restraint and professed toward reform the cynical distrust of a true Social Darwinist. Nevertheless, these two judges generally arrived at the same result by their very different approaches, an agreement made easier by their colleagues' devotion to judicial activism and to the opposite social causes from those endorsed by Brandeis. For a discussion of Holmes and Brandeis, see Alexander Bickel, *The Unpublished Opinions of Mr. Justice Brandeis* (Cambridge, Mass.: Harvard University Press, 1957), esp. chap. 10; Samuel J. Konefsky, *The Legacy of Holmes and Brandeis* (New York: Crowell Collier and Macmillan, 1956); and Walter F. Murphy, *Wiretapping on Trial* (New York: Random House, 1965), chap. 6.

Brandeis, Stone, and Cardozo—were far more suspicious of both the legitimacy and the wisdom of federal regulation of the economy than have been Supreme Court justices who lived through the Great Depression as relatively young men and matured in an era whose economic thinking was dominated by Keynes and his disciples.

Similarly, the increasing importance of the Supreme Court in the Irish political system follows hard upon the coming of age of a new generation of judges and lawyers. In the early years of Irish independence, the bench and bar were largely staffed by men trained in the English judicial tradition, in which there was no written constitution and no judicial review. Many younger barristers and judges have rejected the British model and have been influenced by American writings and court decisions. As lawyers, these younger men have been willing to ask for exercises of judicial power on a scale closer to American than to British practice; as judges, these younger men have been more willing to exert that power.

In contrast, Australian High Court judges are now less apt to cite U.S. Supreme Court decisions than they were at the turn of the century. The course of American constitutional law has changed—it changed in Australia, too, but then to some extent swung back toward its earlier track—and at least at the Supreme Court level American judges have become much more candid about their policy-making roles. Australian judges, on the other hand, still prefer to speak of their function as limited to discovering "the law," and thus are not likely to find much nourishment in Legal Realism.

It will be fascinating to see how, if at all, a future generation of German judges too young to have had any direct contact with Nazism other than the horrors of the last stages of World War II differs from their older brethren. It may well be that the intensive professional training all West German judges go through will be dominant over the more diffuse political culture in shaping outlooks.* Japan will also present an interesting case study. As David Danelski has pointed out, most of the men who served on the Japanese Supreme Court through 1967 had matured in a relatively liberal period of Japanese history.[39] The next generation of judges will have been brought up during the more authoritarian regimes from the 1930s until 1945.

Influencing the general political culture is a long-range way of shaping judicial decisions. A much more immediate means of maximizing chances of winning a lawsuit is forum shopping, looking around and choosing a court where the judge or judges are most likely to decide favorably. For

---

* Professor Rudolph Wildenmann, of the State University of New York at Stony Brook and the University of Mannheim, and his associates in Germany have under way in 1971 a study of German political culture that should shed considerable light on this general question. Included in the interview schedules are not only several national samples but also groups of such elites as lawyers, judges, and other government officials.

often a lawyer does have a choice of where to begin.   In the United States, for example, a black litigant pressing a civil rights claim would probably do better by starting in a federal district court rather than in a state court, especially if he were living in the South.   Even in federal systems like Australia and Canada where there is a single judicial hierarchy, a litigant might fare better in the courts of one region rather than another.   If a constitutional issue is involved, it may, of course, happen that the supreme court will eventually decide, or at least be asked to decide, the case; but that court would usually do so on the basis of records and rulings built up in lower courts.   It is also probable that one's chances of winning in a court of last resort are increased if one has won below, especially if one is allowed to build up a favorable factual record.   In any event, a case may terminate in a lower court.

If a court uses panels of judges, as in Australia, Canada, and occasionally in Japan and Ireland, and in ten of the eleven U.S. Courts of Appeals, an element of chance is injected into the whole process.[40]   In West Germany the Constitutional Court is divided into two senates with such strict separation of membership as to constitute for all practical purposes two different and rather permanent courts.   Jurisdiction, too, is divided, though questions inevitably arise on the borders of power.

The controversy in 1952 over Germany's joining the proposed European Defense Community provides a marvelous—or horrible—example of the wild forum shopping that such a multiple court arrangement permits.[41]   The story is a jumble of maneuvers and countermaneuvers.   Initially, one-third of the members of the Bundestag, all Social Democrats, petitioned the first senate of the Constitutional Court—popularly known as the "red," or anti-Government, senate—for abstract judicial review and an injunction against German participation in the EDC.   Later, the Social Democrats amended their petition to include a request for an injunction against the Bundestag's consenting to ratification of the defense agreements.   Before the first senate could decide the case, the German President, Dr. Theodor Heuss, petitioned the Constitutional Court to give an advisory opinion on the constitutionality of the treaty.   The jurisdictional statute in force at that time permitted the Court to offer advisory opinions, but only as a full Court, with both senates sitting together.   Further complicating the picture was the peculiar political position of the President.   Under the German Constitution he is not a member of the Government and is supposed to be politically neutral; thus some members of the parties that had formed a coalition Government viewed his invocation of judicial power as officious interference and publicly attacked both him and the Court.   Nevertheless, since the President had authority to request the Court's advice, the Government decided to present its side to the judges.

After the President's request for an advisory opinion, but before the full Court could offer its views, the first senate ruled that the petition of the Social

Democrats had been premature; abstract judicial review was available only after an act was passed, not while it was merely under consideration. A short time later, but still before the full Court had offered an advisory opinion, a majority of members of the Bundestag, most of them from the parties that formed the coalition Government, invoked the jurisdiction of the second senate of the Constitutional Court, the allegedly pro-Government senate, to hear disputes between organs of the federal government. The coalition members of the Bundestag asked for a declaration that the suit of the Social Democrats was an interference with the right of the majority to enact legislation and also that, in any event, a majority of the Bundestag was competent to approve a treaty.

Angered by these blatant maneuvers, the full Court immediately ruled that its advisory opinion, whatever it would be, would bind both senates. The President was then subjected to heavy pressure. The Government feared the judges would rule that the treaties were invalid and apparently asked the President to withdraw his request. In addition, some members of the Bundestag were sharply criticizing the Constitutional Court for acting like a politically partisan body biased toward the Social Democrats. In the face of the Government's request and in order to get the Court out of the box in which he had put it, the President rescinded his request.

A few months later the second senate dismissed the majority's suit on procedural grounds, hewing so close to the letter of the law as almost to disappear in its ink. The senate ruled that although the Bundestag as an institution could bring suit, a majority of its members had no standing. The judges pretended to be oblivious to the fact that a resolution of a majority of the Bundestag commits that institution on such matters. After this rebuff, a majority of Parliament proceeded to consent to ratification of the treaties. Once again, one-third of the members of the Bundestag, mostly members of the Social Democratic party, renewed their action in the first senate, pointing out now that a formal piece of legislation had been passed. The judges prudently procrastinated. General elections were called during this period of deliberation, and the Adenauer coalition increased its representation to the point where they achieved the necessary two-thirds majority to amend the Basic Law in such a way as to eliminate constitutional doubts about specific parts of the treaties. The amendment also added a declaration that the EDC agreements were in conformity with the Basic Law[42]—an interesting and definitive "advisory opinion" by the legislative branch of government. The President then signed the treaties. Anticlimactically, the French National Assembly thereupon rejected the agreement, and the EDC died. Shortly thereafter, the German Parliament repealed the statutory provisions permitting the Constitutional Court to give advisory opinions, thus limiting, though by no means eliminating, forum shopping as a possibility on constitutional issues.

" Correcting " Judicial Decisions

Political actors may find it expedient to "correct" as well as to provoke judicial decisions. Possible channels for remedial action include changing judges' minds by means of additional lawsuits and fresh arguments, selecting new judges who may also wish to rectify past "mistakes," and promoting a climate of opinion that is supportive of the kind of change the actors desire. On the last point, political campaigns may be pitched in such a way, as was Franklin D. Roosevelt's in 1936, as to bring about what is, in effect, a popular referendum on the legitimacy of a particular policy course. If successful, this approach can persuade judges that their earlier views were either wrong or too doubtful to prevail against strongly and widely held public opinion. This is certainly a plausible, if only a partial, interpretation of the turnabout that Chief Justice Charles Evans Hughes and Justice Owen Roberts executed in 1937 in regard to the constitutionality of New Deal legislation.

Most democracies have other means of overcoming judicial obstacles. If a problem has been caused by judicial interpretation of a statute, the Government can try to persuade the legislature to pass a more clearly worded piece of legislation. This alternative is likely to be more fruitful in countries like Canada or Ireland where parties are disciplined and one party controls the legislature than in countries like West Germany where two or more parties govern in a coalition. It is likely to be least effective in countries like the United States, where parties are undisciplined.

If a court has interpreted the constitution as forbidding or commanding a given policy, a formal amendment is usually possible,* though serious practical difficulties are always involved. An amendment, as in Germany during the EDC controversy, may anticipate an adverse judicial decision and clear the constitutional ground for a new policy. Alternatively, an amendment can be directed at a particular decision—in the United States, for example, the Sixteenth Amendment legitimated a federal income tax, overturning a doctrine that the Supreme Court had laid down in 1895—or it may strike directly at judicial power itself, as the Eleventh Amendment did in removing from federal courts jurisdiction to hear cases in which a private citizen sues a state government for money.

---

* India—at least until the decision in Golak Nath v. Punjab, (1967) Supreme Court Reports 1643, is overturned—is an exception in that fundamental rights as listed in the Constitution may not be abridged even by regular constitutional amendments. This decision is obviously an extraordinarily important one in Indian constitutional development. For discussions, see H. C. L. Merillat, *Land and the Constitution in India* (New York: Columbia University Press, 1970), especially pp. 242–252; H. M. Seervai, *Constitutional Law of India* (Bombay: N. M. Tripathi, 1968), chap. 30; and Jagat Narain, "Constitutional Changes in India—An Inquiry into the Workings of the Constitution," 17 *International and Comparative Law Quarterly* 878 (1968).

The jurisdiction of the German, Indian, and Irish constitutional courts, at least to hear cases interpreting their constitutions, is explicitly and firmly grounded in fundamental law; but in Argentina, Australia, Canada, Japan, and the United States, the legislature can alter or even revoke jurisdiction by statute.   In 1867, for example, the Radical Republicans took away the jurisdiction of the U.S. Supreme Court to hear a class of cases that threatened to evoke decisions denying the constitutionality of much of Reconstruction.[43] The Canadian Supreme Court is particularly vulnerable to retaliation, since it has historically been viewed as a creature of the legislature.   Although bills occasionally have been introduced to abolish the Court, the Dominion Parliament has so far tended to use its power to extend rather than restrict the authority of the Court.   The Judicial Committee of the Privy Council, on the other hand, has not fared so well.   India abolished appeals to it in 1949, and during that same year Canada, after three-quarters of a century of heavily province-oriented decisions from Westminster, finally cut off appeals from its Supreme Court to the Council.

In all countries with which we are familiar, the number of constitutional court judges is fixed only by statute, and "court packing" is among the more drastic weapons in the government's arsenal.   Removal of wrong-headed judges remains the ultimate political weapon against recalcitrant members of constitutional courts.   In most countries removal procedures are simpler than the American impeachment proceedings, requiring only a joint resolution of both houses of the legislature, for example, in Australia, Canada, India,* and Ireland.   The Japanese provide for impeachment trials by a special tribunal composed of members of both houses of the legislature.   But most countries rarely resort to this kind of radical surgery.   Argentina is an exception.   After its takeover, the Perón regime forced all the members of the Supreme Court off the bench and replaced them with more trusted lawyers. When Perón was deposed, the new Government removed Perón's judges. Two decades later, the Ongania regime, after its coup, forced all the sitting Supreme Court judges to resign, reappointing several of them along with some of its own men.

On the other hand, no constitutional court judge has yet been dismissed in Australia, Canada, India, Ireland, Japan, Norway, Switzerland, West Germany,† or the United States.   In 1804 the Jeffersonian forces in the American House of Representatives did impeach Justice Samuel Chase, but they could not muster the required two-thirds majority in the Senate to secure a conviction.   As Jefferson remarked, impeachment is largely a

---

* In India, those voting for removal must constitute a majority of the living, elected membership of each house and two-thirds of the members present.

† During the years before 1971, when West German Constitutional Court judges were eligible for reelection, Parliament on three occasions declined to reelect a member of the Court.

"scarecrow" in the American political system. The unhappy experience of Abe Fortas illustrates, however, that there are informal ways of securing a judge's resignation or retirement. Several times in American history the members of the Supreme Court have persuaded one of their colleagues to retire—Robert Grier and Stephen Field in the nineteenth century, for example, and Joseph McKenna and Oliver Wendell Holmes in the twentieth. Although the Fortas case had policy overtones, the publicly related issue was the propriety of the justice's financial dealings. In each instance in which the Court has asked a judge to leave, it was because health or old age was preventing the man from doing his job.

As with many of the other kinds of research discussed in this chapter, detailed studies of political activity to "correct" judicial decisions have been confined mostly to American politics and more especially to the American Supreme Court. Charles Warren's two-volume *The Supreme Court in United States History* is studded with case studies of eighteenth- and nineteenth-century presidential and legislative attacks on Court decisions as well as on the Court itself. Warren extracted some of his material and published several articles and monographs dealing specifically with this topic.[44] He was a lawyer turned historian, and a staunch defender of, and frequently a polemicist for, judicial power. Charles G. Haines, a political scientist whose work we briefly described in chapter 1, also wrote two volumes which dealt extensively with the Supreme Court's relations with other branches of government, covering the period from 1789 to 1864.[45] In contrast to Warren and partially to rebut him, Haines was critical of the way in which the justices had used their power. In 1961 C. Herman Pritchett published an account of the Warren Court's early problems with Congress.[46] Like Warren and Haines, Pritchett relied mainly on published material.

Judicial biographies, like Albert J. Beveridge's of John Marshall[47] and Alpheus T. Mason's of Harlan Fiske Stone,[48] also often contain historical studies of legislative or presidential efforts to overturn Supreme Court decisions. Biographers, by utilizing not only published sources such as newspaper stories, congressional hearings, committee reports, and floor debates but also interviews and letters from judges, have sometimes been able to supply a view of the struggle from inside the Court. In 1938 two newspapermen, Joseph Alsop and Turner Catledge, published an "inside" account of the struggle in the Senate over President Roosevelt's Court-Packing plan.[49] And in 1962 one of the authors of this text published *Congress and the Court*,[50] a case study dealing with the attempts of public officials and interest-group leaders from 1957 to 1959 to strike back at the Warren Court for its decisions regarding race relations in particular and civil liberties in general. Both these books relied heavily on material obtained from confidential interviews with executive officials, lobbyists, senators, congressmen, and their staffs.

One of the more obvious lessons that emerges from these researches is that it is no easy matter to overturn constitutional doctrines embodied in Supreme Court decisions, a conclusion supported by evidence from Ireland and, to a lesser extent, from India. The Irish government has for years been chafing under the effects of a decision that held unconstitutional an effort, along American lines, to provide that workers in an industry should choose a single union to represent them.[51] Apparently officials have never felt sufficiently strong to try to amend the Constitution. In 1968 when the Fianna Fail party tried to have an amendment adopted that, contrary to the holding in the reapportionment case,[52] would have allowed legislative districts to vary up to 16.6 percent in size, the measure was resoundingly defeated in the required popular referendum. In its first sixteen years the Indian Parliament amended its Constitution five times to overturn specific Supreme Court decisions, generally rulings on property rights.[53] In 1967, however, the Court struck back in a dramatic, albeit somewhat confusing, judgment and invalidated one of these constitutional amendments expanding governmental power over private property. By a shaky and hotly disputed 6 to 5 vote, the Court ruled that: (1) A constitutional amendment is a law; (2) the Constitution* specifically prohibits laws abridging fundamental rights; (3) property rights are among those fundamental rights listed in the Constitution; and (4) therefore, a constitutional amendment restricting property rights is itself unconstitutional.[54] The majority hinted, but did not decide, that it might be possible to modify constitutional provisions regarding fundamental rights either through a specially called constituent assembly or through the somewhat more elaborate amending procedure the Constitution provides for changing the basic structure of the government.

Experience in other countries has been much like that in the United States: Whereas many private citizens, journalists, leaders of organized groups, and government officials at all levels may be angered at a particular judicial decision and work passionately for change, other citizens, opinion leaders, and public officials are likely to be delighted at what the judges have done and will oppose change.

Successful legislative counteraction is more likely to be achieved if the opponents of a judicial decision restrict themselves to trying to enact a new and apparently innocuous statute and if they go about their work quietly, abstaining from open attacks on the court itself that would alert potential defenders.[55] That certainly has been true in the United States. And it is interesting that, in early 1970 when the Indian Supreme Court declared unconstitutional the government's nationalization of the country's fourteen largest banks, the reaction of the Prime Minister was not to issue an

---

* Article 13 (2): "The State shall not make any law which takes away or abridges the rights conferred by this Part [of the Constitution regarding fundamental rights] and any law made in contravention of this clause shall, to the extent of the contravention, be void."

angry call for a constitutional amendment, but to assure her supporters that what they wanted could be lawfully attained by a more carefully drawn statute.

Also it is interesting to see how often people switch sides in these institutional struggles. In the United States during the 1930s, for instance, liberals led the attack on the Supreme Court. But in the 1950s and 1960s they were the arch defenders of judicial power, while conservatives became the great foes of the judiciary. These shifts do not deny that support for the judiciary runs deep in American political culture, but they do indicate that in politics idealism and self-interest are often closely and subconsciously linked. Even sophisticated and intelligent men of good will sometimes assume that what is good for themselves is good for their country.

Judges and Policy Choices

We began this chapter by noting that, in the sense that someone has to trigger courts, they are passive instruments of government.* It should be evident, however, that once a suit is brought, judges can be very active policy makers. They can manipulate technical and procedural rules to avoid or delay a decision on the merits. And they can tailor their decisions and opinions not only to meet what the litigants ask but to do so in a way that will receive sufficient support in the political system to promote goals the judges want and still survive efforts at "correction."[56]

A judge may be more limited in the courses of action from which he can choose than are legislative and administrative officials, but a judge usually has wide room for choice of both ends and means; and he can employ strategic planning much like any other public official. His basic instruments are the legal weapons of his court—authority to decide cases, to issue orders, and to publish opinions justifying his selection among alternatives. The effectiveness of his deployment of those instruments depends on his sense

---

* We would not, however, exaggerate the passivity of judges. Constitutional adjudication may raise as many new ghosts as it lays old ones to rest. When this occurs, as it frequently does, judges are willy-nilly, if indirectly, setting the stage for subsequent litigation. Hence, when in 1866 the U.S. Supreme Court held the military commission that sentenced Lambdin P. Milligan to be hanged unconstitutional [Ex parte Milligan, 4 Wallace 2 (1866)], litigation attacking the constitutionality of the military governments set up by the Reconstruction Acts inevitably—and quickly—followed. A judge, however, may do much more. He may, for example, invite new litigation, as Black, Douglas, and Murphy once did by indicating that if another compulsory flag salute statute were brought to the Supreme Court, they would reverse their earlier position and vote against its validity [Jones v. Opelika, 316 U.S. 584 (1942)]. Or a judge may yield to chivalry, as did Justice Stone to the Secretary of Labor at a cocktail party, when he suggested the line of argument the Court would find constitutionally congenial when reviewing the Social Security Act [Alpheus T. Mason, *Harlan Fiske Stone: Pillar of the Law* (New York: Viking, 1956), p. 408]. Or a judge may encourage new legislation by dropping hints about the kinds of statutes likely to surmount constitutional obstacles, as Justice Brennan did for controlling obscenity [Fanny Hill v. Massachusetts, 383 U.S. 413 (1966)] and Chief Justice Fuller [Leisy v. Hardin, 135 U.S. 100 (1890)] for divesting liquor of its protection under the commerce clause.

of timing, his capacity to perceive and counter or utilize the ideas and forces that are politically dominant or are about to become dominant. His effectiveness also depends on his ability to persuade others not only of the correctness of his choices but also of the strength of his character and the firmness of his determination. In part his effectiveness may depend on his ability directly or indirectly to muster support among other political actors. He may, as did Holmes and Brandeis, write opinions that serve as intellectual beacons; or he may, as was the case with William Howard Taft, do his major work outside the courtroom, rallying actual and potential allies around his policies. He may attempt both.

In effectively planning to achieve his goals, a judge would have to take into consideration the views of colleagues on the bench, whether of a higher or a lower or the same court; legislators; administrators; future litigants; leaders of organized interest groups and their relative skills in mustering support in other branches of government; journalists; news commentators; professional scholars; and, not least, the general climate of public opinion. This is not to caricature judges as conniving Machiavellians conspiring to govern a country by clever subterfuge and intrigue. The point is rather that judges, no less than other political actors, may recognize that judicial decisions can have important effects on the larger political system and are under no obligation to function as pawns. They can, within limits, act to achieve their policy goals, which may or may not coincide with the goals litigants are pursuing. Judges can, moreover, often reenter the political thicket to stave off efforts to " correct " earlier decisions.

NOTES

1. Robert H. Jackson, *The Supreme Court in the American System of Government* (Cambridge, Mass.: Harvard University Press, 1955), p. 24.

2. See Joseph Tanenhaus *et al.*, "The Supreme Court's Certiorari Jurisdiction: Cue Theory," in Glendon A. Schubert (ed.), *Judicial Decision-Making* (New York: Free Press, 1963).

3. For France see Brian Chapman, "The French Conseil d'Etat," 12 *Parliamentary Affairs* 164 (1959); Henry Parris, "The Conseil d'Etat in the Fifth Republic," 2 *Government and Opposition* 89 (1967); and Francine Batailler, *Le Conseil d'Etat: Juge Constitutionnel* (Paris: R. Pichon et R. Durand-Auzias, 1966). For Indian practice see the *Constitution*, Art. 143; the discussion by H. M. Seervai, *Constitutional Law of India* (Bombay: N. M. Tripathi Private, 1967), pp. 855–857, 1026–1027; and the Court's own handling of the problem in *In re Kerala Education Bill*, (1958) Supreme Court Reports 995.

4. *Manitoba Education Reference*, (1894) Supreme Court Reports 577, 678.

5. See Gerald Rubin, "The Nature, Use and Effect of Reference Cases in Canadian Constitutional Law," 6 *McGill Law Journal* 168 (1959), reprinted in W. R. Lederman (ed.), *The Courts and the Canadian Constitution* (Toronto: McClelland and Stewart, 1964); and B. L. Strayer, *Judicial Review of Legislation in Canada* (Toronto: University of Toronto Press, 1968), chap. 7.

6. West Germany, *Basic Law*, Art. 93(2).

7. Poe v. Ullman, 367 U.S. 497 (1961); Griswold v. Connecticut, 381 U.S. 479 (1965). Compare an earlier case in which the Court also dodged the issue: Tileston v. Ullman, 318 U.S. 44 (1943).

8. The Sunakawa Case, reprinted in John M. Maki (ed.), *Court and Constitution in Japan: Selected Supreme Court Decisions, 1948–1960* (Seattle: University of Washington Press, 1964), p. 298.

9. Fred L. Morrison, "The Judicial Process in Switzerland: A Study of the Swiss Federal Court" (unpublished Ph.D. dissertation, Princeton University, 1966), chap. 2. See also Morrison's "The Swiss Federal Court: Judicial Decision-Making and Recruitment," in Joel B. Grossman and Joseph Tanenhaus (eds.), *Frontiers of Judicial Research* (New York: Wiley, 1969).

10. See Walter F. Murphy and C. Herman Pritchett (eds.), *Courts, Judges, and Politics* (New York: Random House, 1961), chap. 7.

11. See Donald P. Kommers, "The Federal Constitutional Court in the West German Political System," in Grossman and Tanenhaus, supra note 9.

12. Pierce v. Society of Sisters, 268 U.S. 510 (1925).

13. Barrows v. Jackson, 346 U.S. 249 (1953).

14. Frothingham v. Mellon, 262 U.S. 447 (1923).

15. Flast v. Cohen, 392 U.S. 83 (1968).

16. Suzuki Case, Maki, supra note 8, p. 362.

17. Dissolution Case, Maki, supra note 8, p. 366.

18. See Rule 19, Supreme Court Rules.

19. See Fowler V. Harper and Alan S. Rosenthal, "What the Supreme Court Did Not Do in the 1949 Term—An Appraisal of Certiorari," 99 *University of Pennsylvania Law Review* 293 (1950); Harper and Edwin D. Etherington, "What the Supreme Court Did Not Do During the 1950 Term," 100 *ibid.* 354 (1951); Harper and George C. Pratt, "What the Supreme Court Did Not Do During the 1951 Term," 101 *ibid.* 439 (1953); and Robert W. Gibbs, "Certiorari: Its Diagnosis and Cure," 6 *Hastings Law Journal* 153 (1955).

20. Tanenhaus *et al.*, supra note 2.

21. Clement E. Vose, *Caucasians Only: The Supreme Court, the NAACP, and the Restrictive Covenant Cases* (Berkeley: University of California Press, 1959); "Litigation as a Form of Pressure Group Politics," 319 *The Annals* 20 (1958); "The National Consumers' League and the Brandeis Brief," 1 *Midwest Journal of Political Science* 267 (1957); "Interest Groups, Judicial Review, and Local Government," 19 *Western Political Quarterly* 85 (1966).

22. Shelley v. Kraemer, 334 U.S. 1 (1948); Hurd v. Hodge, 334 U.S. 24 (1948); Barrows v. Jackson, 346 U.S. 249 (1953).

23. O'Donovan v. The Attorney General, 1961 Irish Reports 114.

24. See Kommers, supra note 11, pp. 79–89.

25. The cases are discussed in Kommers, supra note 11. The first decision is excerpted in John C. Lane and James K. Pollock (eds.), *Source Materials on the Government and Politics of Germany* (Ann Arbor, Mich.: Wahrs, 1964), p. 231; Kommers has translated longer selections from the second Party Finance case in Theodore L. Becker (ed.), *Comparative Judicial Politics* (Chicago: Rand McNally, 1970).

26. See Kommers, supra note 11, and also Edward McWhinney, *Constitutionalism in Germany and the Federal Constitutional Court* (Leyden, Netherlands: A. W. Sythoff, 1962), pp. 60–64. The opinion in the Television Case is excerpted in Lane and Pollock, supra note 25, p. 138.

27. See Joseph Borkin, *The Corrupt Judge* (New York: C. N. Potter, 1962).

28. Gerald I. Jordan, "The Impact of Crises upon Judicial Behavior," a paper presented at the 1960 Meetings of the American Political Science Association.

29. Duncan v. Kahanamoku, 327 U.S. 304 (1946). Robert E. Cushman again tells much of the story in his note to the case. See his *Leading Constitutional Decisions* 12th ed. (New York: Appleton-Century-Crofts, 1963), pp. 86–91.

30. Hans W. Baade, "Social Science Evidence and the Federal Constitutional Court of West Germany," 23 *Journal of Politics* 421 (1961).

31. The outcry from segregationists over the famous footnote 11 to the School Segregation cases would alone fill a large volume. For reasoned discussions of the Court's use of the particular evidence introduced in that litigation, see Edmond Cahn, "Jurisprudence," 30 *New York University Law Review* 150 (1955), and "Jurisprudence," 31 *ibid.* 182 (1956); Herbert Garfinkel, "Social Science Evidence and the School Segregation Cases," 21 *Journal of Politics* 37 (1959); and Jack Greenberg, "Social Scientists Take the Stand," 54 *Michigan Law Review* 953 (1956). For more general treatments of the problem in American courts, see Joseph Tanenhaus, "Social Science in Civil Rights Litigation," in Milton Konvitz and Clinton Rossiter (eds.), *Aspects of Liberty* (Ithaca, N.Y.: Cornell University Press, 1958); and Murphy and Pritchett, supra note 10, chap. 9 and literature cited.

32. In awarding costs to the Jehovah's Witnesses in the case of Saumur v. Quebec, (1953) 2 Supreme Court Reports 299, the Canadian Supreme Court specifically excluded payment for costs of preparing the Brandeis Brief the Witnesses had presented. See the discussion in Edward McWhinney, *Judicial Review* 4th ed. (Toronto: University of Toronto Press, 1969), pp. 210n–211n. See also the overt refusal of the Australian High Court to consider social and economic data in its decision invalidating bank nationalization. Bank of New South Wales v. Commonwealth, 76 Commonwealth Law Reports 1 (1948). McWhinney discusses this case on pp. 80–81, 90–91.

33. Ryan v. The Attorney General, 1965 Irish Reports 294.

34. Harlan Fiske Stone, for example, often corresponded with his friends in the law schools—Felix Frankfurter, Karl Llewellyn, and John Basset Moore, among others—about general constitutional problems as well as about the work of the Court in the very recent past. See Alpheus T. Mason, *Harlan Fiske Stone: Pillar of the Law* (New York: Viking, 1956). Frank Murphy went somewhat further and apparently sought the advice of Edward G. Kemp, his roommate, about pending cases. See J. Woodford Howard, Jr., *Mr. Justice Murphy: A Political Biography* (Princeton, N.J.: Princeton University Press, 1968), pp. 242, 244, 254.

35. Benjamin N. Cardozo, *The Nature of the Judicial Process* (New Haven, Conn.: Yale University Press, 1921), p. 168.

36. John Maynard Keynes, *The General Theory of Employment, Interest, and Money* (New York: Harcourt, Brace & World, 1936), p. 383.

37. Gunnar Myrdal, *An American Dilemma* (New York: Harper & Row, 1944).

38. Note, for example, the influence of Charles Warren's article "New Light on the History of the Federal Judiciary Act of 1789," 37 *Harvard Law Review* 49 (1923), which eventually brought about the death of a dual system of common law in the states via Erie Railroad v. Tompkins, 304 U.S. 64 (1938). See Chester A. Newland, "Legal Periodicals and the U.S. Supreme Court," 3 *Midwest Journal of Political Science* 58 (1959), and Clyde E. Jacobs, *Law Writers and the Courts* (Berkeley: University of California Press, 1954).

39. David Danelski, "The Supreme Court of Japan: An Exploratory Study," in

Glendon A. Schubert and David Danelski (eds.), *Comparative Judicial Behavior* (New York: Oxford University Press, 1969), p. 149.

40. Marvin Schick's *Learned Hand's Court* (Baltimore: The Johns Hopkins Press, 1970) contains rich data from Judge Charles Clark's papers on the impact of various panel combinations on work of the U.S. Court of Appeals for the Second Circuit during the years when Learned Hand was chief judge.

41. For detailed accounts, see Edward McWhinney, supra note 26, pp. 34–40; and Karl Loewenstein, "The Bonn Constitution and the European Defense Community Treaties," 64 *Yale Law Journal* 805 (1955).

42. West Germany, *Basic Law*, Art. 142a.

43. Ex parte McCardle, 7 Wallace 506 (1869).

44. Charles Warren, "Legislative and Judicial Attacks on the Supreme Court of the United States," 47 *American Law Review* 1 and 161 (1913); Warren, *Congress, the Constitution, and the Supreme Court* rev. ed. (Boston: Little, Brown, 1935).

45. Charles G. Haines, *The Role of the Supreme Court in American Government and Politics 1789–1835* (Berkeley: University of California Press, 1944); Haines and Foster H. Sherwood, *The Role of the Supreme Court in American Government and Politics 1835–1864* (Berkeley: University of California Press, 1957).

46. C. Herman Pritchett, *Congress versus the Warren Court 1957–1960* (Minneapolis: University of Minnesota Press, 1961).

47. Albert J. Beveridge, *The Life of John Marshall*, 4 vols. (Boston: Houghton Mifflin, 1916–1919).

48. Mason, supra note 34.

49. Joseph Alsop and Turner Catledge, *The 168 Days* (Garden City, N.Y.: Doubleday, Doran, 1938).

50. Walter F. Murphy, *Congress and the Court: A Case Study in the American Political Process* (Chicago: University of Chicago Press, 1962).

51. See, in particular, National Union of Railwaymen v. Sullivan, 1947 Irish Reports 77, and Educational Company of Ireland v. Fitzpatrick, 1961 Irish Reports 345. This problem is discussed in *Report of the Committee on the Constitution* (Dublin: The Stationery Office, 1967). These and similar cases are analyzed in John M. Kelly, *Fundamental Rights in the Irish Law and Constitution*, 2d ed. (Dublin: Allen Figgis, 1967), pp. 162–170.

52. O'Donovan v. Attorney General, 1961 Irish Reports 114, and In re Article 26 and the Electoral Amendment Bill, 1961, 1961 Irish Reports 169.

53. These changes are discussed in Jagat Narain, "Constitutional Changes in India— An Inquiry into the Working of the Constitution," 17 *International and Comparative Law Quarterly* 878 (1968). With some exaggeration Narain writes on p. 882: "The history of Indian Constitutional change can be epitomized as largely a story of successive attempts on the part of Parliament to overrule judicial interpretation of the Constitution—a story in which the constitutional guarantees as to property rights played a dominant role." See also the literature cited in the footnote on p. 83.

54. Golak Nath v. Punjab, (1967) Supreme Court Reports 1643.

55. Note, "Congressional Reversal of Supreme Court Decisions: 1945–1957," 71 *Harvard Law Review* 1324 (1958).

56. For a general discussion of the problems of policies, tactics, and strategies, see Walter F. Murphy, *Elements of Judicial Strategy* (Chicago: University of Chicago Press, 1964).

4
Judicial Recruitment, Training, and Tenure

Judges usually derive considerable political power from their participation in the processes of determining goals and allocating values for society. Judgeships are also tangible values in themselves. Because they carry power, they bestow prestige, as well as a comfortable living, on incumbents; and terms of office are usually long. Men who are ambitious for these good things of life are often attracted to the bench. Furthermore, political actors who identify themselves with particular regions or ethnic groups may covet judgeships for their own people as symbols of their importance in society or as means of achieving policy goals. It is thus hardly surprising that there is frequently intense competition for a judicial post, and party leaders can turn this competition to their own advantage. As Sayre and Kaufman explain in their analysis of politics in New York City:

The court system provides much of the fuel for engines . . . . Predominant among the ranks of those who give unstintingly of their time and energy and money to their party are lawyers striving for positions on the bench, and both lawyers and non-lawyers endeavoring to establish claims on other court posts. On the one hand, this enables the parties to recruit, hold, and motivate a large body of willing, industrious, and often able workers in their cause. On the other hand, it helps the parties maintain a measure of discipline in their ranks and among officeholders who owe their position to their respective parties.[1]

As we shall explain later in this chapter, political leaders in other countries—especially Australia, Canada, West Germany, and Ireland—have reserved at least a portion of the important judgeships to reward those among the party-faithful who are also talented lawyers. In Norway a similar process has been in operation. The Ministry of Justice has been a fertile spawning bed for judicial candidates. The reason is not, as in many Roman law countries, that judges are pretty much civil servants working under the minister of justice, but rather that the ministry uses judgeships as a means of attracting skilled and ambitious young lawyers. Opportunities for administrative advancement are limited, but the chances of a bright young attorney's becoming a judge are quite good if he works for the ministry.[2]

If judges exercise power and if judgeships are desirable objects in themselves, then Who becomes a judge? How are judges recruited and trained? and How long can they serve? are questions that are as central to the interests of political scientists as they are to practicing and academic lawyers, public officials, and perhaps even aspirants to judicial office.

Selection Processes

The selection process for constitutional court judges is usually openly partisan in the sense that recruitment is under the direct control of popularly elected officials. In Australia, Canada, India, and Ireland the cabinet appoints judges, although this fact may be clouded by legal rhetoric about the role of the governor general or the President. The American two-step procedure of presidential nomination plus senatorial confirmation adds additional partisan complexities. Argentina has adopted the same procedure, although the peculiarities and instabilities of both democratic and authoritarian regimes there have brought about a very different kind of process. The Japanese policy of cabinet appointment* followed by popular referendums at the next regular election and at ten-year intervals has so far added no new political dimension, since all Supreme Court justices have been approved by thumping majorities running close to 90 percent.[3]

* The Chief Justice is officially appointed by the Emperor.

The two houses of the Swiss Parliament sit together and elect the judges of the Constitutional Court.[4] This vote is usually little more than a formality. Normally, party leaders of the various parties divide the number of judgeships among each other in the same proportion as each controls seats in Parliament. The real selection process occurs within each major party.

The West German Parliament also elects the Constitutional Court judges. But the process is complicated because Parliament is a bicameral institution and the Constitutional Court is composed of two separate senates, each with jurisdiction over specific kinds of constitutional disputes. Each house of Parliament elects half of the members of each senate of the Court. The lower house, the Bundestag, appoints a committee of twelve, reflecting as closely as possible the strength of each party in the Bundestag itself. The committee then selects the judges by a two-thirds vote. The upper house, the Bundesrat, elects its share of judges directly, but again a two-thirds majority is necessary. The actual choice among candidates, as Kommers points out, is made informally by negotiation, if not outright bargaining, among party leaders, since a single party has seldom had a simple, much less a two-thirds, majority in Parliament.[5] As one would expect, the party backgrounds of West German Constitutional Court judges correspond fairly closely to party strengths in the two houses of Parliament.

As usual, the most detailed analyses of the realities of the appointing process have been done in the American context. David J. Danelski, for instance, used Department of Justice files and the private papers of a number of men prominent in American politics in the 1920s to reconstruct the events surrounding the appointment of Pierce Butler to the Supreme Court.[6] In a broader-gauged study, Harold W. Chase also had access to Justice Department files and interviewed most of the officials involved in federal judicial selection during the Kennedy and early Johnson administrations.[7] Joel B. Grossman utilized archival material, government documents, newspaper sources, and interviews to sketch the activities and influence of one pressure group, the American Bar Association, in the choosing of federal judges.[8]

From these and other investigations it is evident that the American appointing process is a hotbed of political activity. Interest-group leaders, party officers, journalists, government officials, candidates, and even university professors vie with each other to exert influence and counterinfluence. Efforts such as the Missouri plan to depoliticize the selection process by providing a much wider role for the bar at the expense of elected officials seem to have the principal effect of shifting the arena of struggle from the legislative or executive process into the politics of local bar associations.[9]

Although political activity over judicial appointments may be less frenzied in other polities, it is not likely to be less important, judging from the results. In the end public officials may decide to trade an appointment of a preferred candidate for one less preferred in exchange for a promise of support from some groups on other issues.   This is less likely to be true in countries like Canada, Ireland, and Japan, where political parties are disciplined and usually control either a majority or close to a majority in the legislature, than it is in nations like the United States where parties tend to be less disciplined.   As we have already noted, the frequent necessity for coalition Governments and the requirement of a two-thirds majority to elect Constitutional Court judges force interparty negotiations in West Germany, with judgeships only one of many kinds of political prizes.   The same sort of bargaining occurs in Italy and Switzerland.

Judges may also become involved in choosing their colleagues.   In the United States their participation has been sporadic and informal.   Taft, when Chief Justice, assiduously and effectively injected his massive frame into the appointing processes for all federal judgeships.   His activity was unique only in its brazenness and energy.   The Japanese and Indian constitutions explicitly bring Supreme Court judges into the appointing process. In Japan the cabinet chooses lower court judges from a list of nominees drawn up by the Supreme Court,[10] but any part the justices have in picking their own colleagues is purely informal.   In naming judges to the high courts of Indian states, the President—in actual fact, the Prime Minister and his cabinet—is supposed to consult with the Chief Justice of India, the governor of the state, and, except in the case of the appointment of a high court chief justice, with the chief justice of that high court.[11]   In addition, the Constitution commands that, before appointing associate justices of the Supreme Court, the President should consult with the Chief Justice.   The Constitution also allows the President to seek the advice of other Supreme Court and high court judges.[12]   It appears that the Chief Justice has, in fact, played an active part in this process.

In some countries appointing officials are restricted in whom they can choose, not only by other political actors but by specific constitutional or statutory requirements as well.   In West Germany six of the sixteen Constitutional Court members must be chosen from the ranks of career judges. A Japanese statute stipulates that all Supreme Court justices must be forty or more years of age, and at least ten of them must have had either a minimum of ten years' experience as judges of high courts or district courts or twenty years' experience as prosecutors, practicing attorneys, law professors, or judges of minor courts.   The remaining justices need only meet the age minimum of forty and be persons of " broad vision and extensive knowledge of law."   The Indian Constitution contains similar provisions: A Supreme Court appointee must have served five years as a judge on a high court *or* practiced for ten years as an advocate before a high court *or* be "a distinguished jurist."[13]   Article 135 of the Italian Constitution states that a Constitutional Court judge must have been a judge of another court, a law professor, or a lawyer with twenty years' experience.   Three of the nine

Canadian Supreme Court justices must be from Quebec, and all nine must either have been provincial judges or have practiced as barristers or advocates for ten years.   The only formal requirement in Norway is that the candidate shall have earned a law degree with honors.   In Australia any member of the bar who has practiced for five years is eligible for appointment to the High Court.

The Americans and the Irish have not set up formal qualifications for constitutional court judges, but each has important informal requirements. In both countries an appointee must be a lawyer, and in Ireland he must be not only a barrister but also a member of the Inner Bar—a Senior Counsel, an accolade accorded as recognition of professional prestige and success. American justices have also been drawn from the more prestigious ranks of the bar.   No Supreme Court justice has yet been primarily a specialist in divorce or criminal law, and only one was basically a labor lawyer.   When an American justice has spent most of his pre-Court career in private practice —and such judges have been in the minority—he has typically worked in prosperous firms, dealing with wealthy, corporate clients.

Informal requirements have also grown up in those countries that have established statutory or constitutional criteria.   Despite the broad wording of the Australian statute to encompass solicitors, High Court judges have all been barristers.   The Japanese do not have a bifurcated bar in the British tradition, but Supreme Court nominees have been largely graduates of the elite Tokyo or Kyoto law schools; similarly, Norwegian judges have generally been graduates of the University of Oslo.   The factionalism that has so often paralyzed Italian politics kept the Constitutional Court from being formed until 1956 and has pushed the contending parties toward selecting law professors as Constitutional Court judges.   Professors, although not necessarily politically neutral, have generally been less openly partisan than many other candidates; and in Italy, as in most civil law countries, professors have great prestige.

As we noted in chapter 2, appointing officials also have to consider ethnic and geographic factors in selecting judges.   In the United States a tradition has built up of having a Catholic and a Jew on the Supreme Court,* and now probably a black as well.   In addition, the Court at any one time has customarily included men from each region of the country.   By statute three seats on the Canadian Supreme Court are reserved for citizens of Quebec; unwritten rules require that Ontario have three residents on the Court and that the Maritime Provinces and the West have representatives as well.[14]   There is in West Germany an effort to weigh geographical con-

---

* The tradition is not ironclad.   From 1932 to 1938 there were two Jews (Brandeis and Cardozo) on the Court.   On the other hand, President Nixon nominated three Protestants in succession to take Justice Fortas' place in 1969 and 1970.   Similarly, there were two Catholics on the Court from 1898 to 1921 (Edward D. White and Joseph McKenna), but in 1949 President Truman nominated a Protestant to succeed Justice Frank Murphy.   The next Catholic appointee was William J. Brennan in 1956.

siderations in filling Constitutional Court judgeships. In contrast to this pattern, in Italy the Constitutional Court has tended to overrepresent Sicily and the region south of Rome, an overrepresentation that occurs throughout the Italian judiciary. The Irish follow a custom of having one Protestant among the five Supreme Court justices and one among the seven high court judges. Because of the peculiarities of Swiss politics, allowing each major party to choose a share of Constitutional Court judges provides representation for German-, French-, and Italian-speaking groups, as well as for Protestants and Catholics and, to some extent, for geographic areas.

In India geographic factors as well as ethnic and religious considerations play a part in judicial selection. So far, at least one member of the Court has been a Moslem and, as George H. Gadbois, Jr., has shown, a candidate's regional affiliation is critical: " More often than not, vacancies are filled by men from either the same High Court, or from the same region, as the man whose slot is being filled."[15]

Backgrounds of Judges

Judges of most constitutional courts share much the same kind of social background. All have had far better educations than most people in their countries, usually even than most attorneys. Although there are exceptions like William O. Douglas, whose widowed mother took in washing to support her family, or Arthur Goldberg, whose father was a pushcart peddler, most of these judges have come from middle- or upper-class families. According to John R. Schmidhauser, a " collective portrait " of the American Supreme Court would show:

> The typical Supreme Court justice has invariably been white, generally Protestant with a penchant for high social status denomination, usually of ethnic stock originating in the British Isles, and born in comfortable circumstances in an urban or small town environment. In the earlier history of the Court, he very likely was born in the aristocratic or gentry class, while later he tended to come from the professionalized upper middle-class.[16]

Kommers sketches a similar, although more middle-class, picture of the West German Constitutional Court during its first sixteen years:

> . . . nine of the thirty-nine judges had fathers in the civil service. Seven judges are the sons of elementary and secondary school teachers; another is the son of one of Germany's most renowned professors of law. Four are the sons of small businessmen, two of large landowners, two of clergymen, two of physicians, one of a high army officer, two of engineers, and one of a chemist. Two are the sons of laboring men, while two had fathers in judicial service.[17]

Torgersen reports that Norwegian judges " come from families in the higher social strata."[18] Gadbois describes the archetype of the Indian

Supreme Court justice as "the product of a socially prestigeful and eco-
nomically advantaged family"; and "a Hindu (most often a Brahmin), [who]
was educated at one of the better Indian universities or in England. . . ."[19]
British judges share these general characteristics. According to one study
thirty of the fifty-five High Court judges on the bench in 1964 were graduates
of Oxford, eighteen of Cambridge, and two of the University of London.[20]
More than three out of four of the county judges were also "Oxbridge"
alumni. Most of these men had not studied law at their universities but had
been more narrowly trained, primarily at the Inns of Court and in private
cram courses. Before going to the bench, almost all of them had been
successful in private practice and had been selected for the honorary title
of Queen's Counsel, the British equivalent of the Irish Senior Counsel.

To some extent, since they are all lawyers, constitutional court judges
also share experience in at least a minimal amount of common professional
socialization, although in many countries that training is oriented toward
the practice of law rather than a career on the bench. West Germany,
Italy,[21] and Japan,* however, have judicial professions separate from the
practicing bar. In each nation candidates for all branches of the legal
profession go through an intense program of training. At the end of this
period a fledgling lawyer usually decides whether to become a judge, a
prosecutor, an administrator, a professor, or a practicing attorney. If a
man elects to become a judge, he in effect embarks on a career much like that
of the civil service. Promotion depends on a combination of seniority and
satisfactory performance of duties. As we have already noted, six of the
sixteen members of the West German Constitutional Court must be drawn
from the ranks of career judges. The Japanese requirements are somewhat
more flexible and the Italian even more so. Still, about one-third of Japanese
Supreme Court justices have been professional judges; the proportion is
slightly smaller in Italy. About 70 percent of Norwegian Constitutional
Court judges have had previous judicial experience, although they were not
necessarily professional judges in the West German, Italian, or Japanese
sense. It is also true that many constitutional court judges in common law
countries have had some previous judicial experience—about 25 percent in
Australia, 50 percent in Canada and the United States, and 70 percent in
Ireland.†

---

* Since the end of World War II candidates for all branches of the Japanese legal profession have
gone through the same training, but before World War II judges and prosecutors underwent a
more rigorous educational program than did attorneys who chose private practice. See Takaaki
Hattori, "The Legal Profession in Japan: Its Historical Development and Present State," and
Hakaru Abe, "Education of the Legal Profession in Japan," both in Arthur T. von Mehren
(ed.), *Law in Japan: The Legal Order in a Changing Society* (Cambridge, Mass.: Harvard University Press, 1963).

† The American figure is misleading because many of the justices served only briefly on the bench
before coming to the Supreme Court.

In a way, the tradition of choosing judges solely from among barristers equips constitutional court judges in Australia and Ireland with training and career patterns that are somewhat different from those of the bulk of lawyers —who in fact become solicitors. At first glance, it appears that the American political system hobbles along with almost no socialization process for judges beyond the general law school education shared by all attorneys. But as Grossman has noted, that part of the socialization process that seems to begin with a judge's appointment to a court also can function as an informal socialization process for future judges in that they can see and imitate the career patterns that the successful candidate followed.[22] Two facts stand out about the backgrounds of U.S. Supreme Court justices—and frequently of state supreme court justices as well. First, these men have almost always been members of the party of the chief executive who nominated them. Second, they have usually had considerable political experience, either as presidential confidants, such as John Jay, Roger B. Taney, Louis D. Brandeis, Felix Frankfurter, Fred M. Vinson, and Abe Fortas, or, more commonly, as holders of public office—for instance, William Paterson, Charles Evans Hughes, and Earl Warren as governors; Levi Woodbury, Edward D. White, George Sutherland, James F. Byrnes, Harold Burton, Sherman Minton, and Hugo Black as senators; Taney, Joseph McKenna, James C. McReynolds, Harlan Stone, Frank Murphy, Robert H. Jackson, and Tom C. Clark as attorneys general; and John Marshall and Vinson as congressmen and cabinet members. Frequently, these men have had another kind of political experience as well, in that they have come from politically active families.

Given the power of judges, one should not be surprised that appointing officials would want only "right-thinking" men on the bench, would use party allegiance as one indication of that quality, and would also like to have ideological commitments tested through a period of political apprenticeship. Lincoln stated both the problem and a widely accepted solution when he was deciding whom to nominate as Chief Justice: "We cannot ask a man what he will do, and if we should, and he should answer us we would despise him for it. Therefore we must take a man whose opinions are known."[23]*

In Ireland previous political experience has at times been almost equally as evident as in the United States. In 1967 four of the five Supreme Court

---

* Lincoln's experience here shows how fallible the appointing process can be. After this discussion he chose Salmon P. Chase because Chase was "right" on the questions of emancipation and paper money. When he was confirmed as Chief Justice, however, Chase proceeded to write the opinion of the Court holding paper money unconstitutional—despite the fact that he had helped draft the Legal Tender Acts and, as Secretary of the Treasury, had been responsible for administering the legislation. When the Court changed its position—after President Grant selected two new justices who were really "right" on paper money—Chase stuck to his views that the statutes were invalid. Hepburn v. Griswold, 8 Wallace 603 (1870); Legal Tender Cases, 12 Wallace 457 (1871). For the background of the nominations by Grant, see Sidney Ratner, "Was the Supreme Court Packed by President Grant?" 50 *Political Science Quarterly* 343 (1935).

justices were former attorneys general, a not very subtle demonstration of a tradition that gives the attorney general first claim on a vacancy on the High Court or the Supreme Court.*

"The most distinguishing feature," Donald Kommers has written about West German judges, is "that prior to their elevation to the Constitutional Court they functioned very close to the centers of political influence, while a few of the judges were at the apex of power in Bonn or in the states."[24] In Australia direct political experience is prevalent, though not so obvious as in Germany, Ireland, and the United States. The Australian Liberal and Country party coalition has virtually always appointed its own partisans to the bench, but the Labour party, whether because of a shortage of Labour barristers, acceptance of courts as the domain of conservatism, or an effort to appear less selfish, has recruited many judges from outside its own ranks. Canadian Supreme Court justices have also been drawn from among political activists. As Peter H. Russell reports:

> Of the 49 lawyers who have served on the Court only 10 had not previously been either members of a federal or provincial legislature or members of the bench of a provincial superior court. And even among the 10 exceptions, two . . . served as Deputy Ministers of Justice in Ottawa, which would bring them well within the inner circle of legal men of influence in the federal government. We should further note a considerable amount of overlap between those who were promoted from the provincial courts and those who had been actively engaged in party politics: 11 of the 27 Supreme Court judges who were promoted from the provincial courts had been either federal members of Parliament or members of a provincial legislature before being appointed to the provincial courts.[25]

Japanese judges have typically had less visible and probably less important political careers. In Norway Constitutional Court judges have frequently been administrators in the civil service, but only occasionally have held elective office.

In India Supreme Court justices stand at the opposite end of the spectrum from their American peers. Only a very few Indian judges have ever been actively involved in politics—before going to the Court, that is. This is no accident. Debates in the assembly that drafted the Indian Constitution reflected the belief that judges could be kept out of politics by removing their appointments from the influence of political parties—thus the provisions for appointment by the President and for consultation with sitting judges were devised. Indeed, the justices of the Federal Court—the predecessor of the

---

* By 1970, however, the Irish Government had appointed three new justices. None of these men had been prominent in politics, and one had even been a member of the larger of the two opposition parties.

Supreme Court—and the justices of the high courts had suggested to the constituent assembly that former government ministers should be ineligible to become judges.[26] Although the assembly did not write this suggestion into the fundamental law, not a single justice had, as of 1970, been a prominent national or even a state political leader. Either as a carry-over from British rule or as a result of bringing other judges formally into the recruiting process or both, the tendency in India has been to promote high court judges to the Supreme Court; only one of the first thirty-six justices had not been a member of a high court. To what extent the stormy history of judicial review in India will politicize the recruiting process remains to be seen, but it would be surprising if, after the energy displayed by the Supreme Court in striking down national legislation,[27] the Government did not begin to scrutinize carefully the ideology of candidates.

To be sure, prior experience and party allegiance need not be determining factors in judicial selection. Members of other parties may also think "correctly" on important issues. Their appointment may swing votes from one party to another or attract votes from independents by creating an impression that the administration in power is above petty matters of partisanship. Both as President and Chief Justice, Taft put these latter considerations above party regularity, provoking the gibe that if he were Pope he would appoint a Protestant to the College of Cardinals. One of the more commonly offered explanations for Eisenhower's giving William J. Brennan an interim appointment to the Supreme Court just three weeks before the 1956 election was that the Republicans were trying to woo Catholic voters. Whether or not Brennan's appointment had any relation to the electoral outcome, in that year the Republicans for the first time in a presidential race won a majority of the Catholic vote.

A judicial appointment can also be used to further higher ends of the state. Shortly before American involvement in World War II, for instance, Franklin D. Roosevelt nominated Harlan Fiske Stone to be Chief Justice. Stone had been a prominent Republican, a member of Coolidge's cabinet, and a confidant of Hoover; and he had himself frequently been mentioned in the 1930s as a possible presidential candidate. His nomination was a part of Roosevelt's larger efforts to play down party divisions and to unite the country for the war he saw coming.

Another important variable affecting the work of judges is length of service. In Switzerland members of the Constitutional Court serve only for six-year terms; in Italy their terms run for twelve years, and they are ineligible for immediate reappointment. Prior to the law of February 3, 1971, the professional judges of the West German Constitutional Court served during good behavior and their colleagues for eight-year, renewable terms. Now, however, all German Constitutional Court judges are elected to twelve-year terms without the possibility of reelection. Argentine justices supposedly have tenure during good behavior, but revolutionary and counter-revolutionary regimes have at times construed bad behavior as having been appointed by the previous Government. Several Latin American countries have regularized the practice, terminating the tenure of constitutional court judges with the life of the Government. In Honduras, Nicaragua, and Venezuela the legislature elects judges for terms that run concurrently with those of the legislators.

In most countries the terms of office of constitutional court judges are also limited by mandatory retirement provisions. Australia and the United States* are exceptions to this rule. In Canada the compulsory retirement age is seventy-five, in Ireland seventy-two, in Japan and Norway seventy, in West Germany sixty-eight, and in India sixty-five.

Forced retirement has a number of consequences for the political system. First, it reduces, although it by no means eliminates, the danger of having senile judges on the bench. It does so, however, at the price of losing many judges while they are still in their prime. Fazl Ali of the Indian Supreme Court retired at sixty-five and became governor of one of the states; Ivan Rand, one of the most able of all Canadian judges, had to retire from the Supreme Court while he was still active enough to become dean of the law faculty at the University of Western Ontario. Had the United States employed the Norwegian and Japanese rule of retirement at seventy, John Marshall would have served ten years less than he actually did, Roger Brooke Taney seventeen years less, Oliver Wendell Holmes twenty-one years less, Charles Evans Hughes nine years less, and Louis D. Brandeis and Earl Warren eight years less. Hugo L. Black would have been forced off the bench in 1956 and William O. Douglas in 1970.

Second, when coupled, as in Japan, India, and to a lesser extent in Ireland, with a tradition of promotion that brings a man to the constitutional court late in life, compulsory retirement means that a judge will have a relatively short time to familiarize himself with the work of the court before he is forced out of office. This situation has been most marked in Japan. As a result of the extreme importance of age and hierarchy in Japanese society, Supreme Court Justices have usually been in their early sixties when appointed, giving them but a few years of service. In India the typical Supreme Court judge serves only about seven and one-half years. In Ireland one justice stayed on the Court for twenty-eight years, but the average for the others has been only nine years as compared with fifteen in the United States and twenty in Australia and Canada. Somewhat surprisingly, the West German practice of choosing a minimum of 37 percent of its Constitu-

---

* The American Congress has done much to induce federal judges to retire by age seventy. If a federal judge has served ten years on the bench, he may retire at full pay when he reaches seventy. In addition, if he is in ill health, both the age and service requirements may be waived. Still, few federal judges retire at that age. The old quip that Supreme Court justices never retire and seldom die is as appropriate as ever.

TABLE 4.1

Age and maximum terms of constitutional court judges

Country	Average age at appointment	Maximum years could serve
Australia	53	*
Canada	55	20
India	57	8
Ireland	61	11
Japan	61	9
United States	53	*
West Germany	51	12

* No mandatory retirement age.

tional Court members from professional judges has not turned the Court into an institution staffed by old men nearing retirement.

A third set of effects of compulsory retirement is related to the second. Lines of judicial decisions are likely to be less set as membership is more fluid. So, too, blocs are apt to be less stable as judges frequently come and go. Moreover, judges who come to the bench with only a short time to serve may be—we have little data on this point—less energetic and imaginative in using their power. Judges who have relatively little opportunity to accrue experience on a constitutional court may also be less sure of themselves and more ready to defer to the judgment of other public officials, just as a judge who comes to the bench at an early age may have great advantages in building up practical experience with both technical and policy problems. Again, we do not know.

Fourth, forced retirement provides appointing officials with more frequent opportunities to influence the course of judicial decision making by replacing sitting judges. In addition, appointing officials have more rewards—constitutional court judgeships—to bestow on their followers, although the value of those rewards may decline along with the decrease in expected length of service and chances of exercising real power in shaping constitutional development.

Table 4.1 summarizes some of the data just discussed on the age and tenure of constitutional court judges in several countries.

Social Background and Judicial Decisions

There can be no doubt that patterns of judicial training and recruitment are intriguing, but their importance has to be demonstrated. At a micro-level of analysis it is relatively easy to show that it makes a difference who is on a court.   A Holmes or a Brandeis would—and did—decide issues and write opinions in a way vastly different from a Sutherland or a McReynolds. Certainly the course of American constitutional history would have been changed if Thomas Jefferson had had an opportunity to replace John Marshall with Spencer Roane.   Canadian constitutional history would have been different had the Supreme Court been staffed with men who fully accepted either the liberal views of Ivan Rand or, on the other hand, the conservative ideology of Robert Tascherau.   So, too, the restrictive, states' rights decisions of Edmund Barton, Samuel Griffith, and Richard O'Connor etched out a different kind of Australian Commonwealth than did the decisions of H. B. Higgins and Isaac Isaacs in favor of national power.

At a macro-level it is difficult to prove but plausible to argue that training and recruitment influence "the tone and temper of judicial decision-making."[28]   The similar social and educational backgrounds we have noted across national boundaries lend support for Geoffrey Sawer's assertion that judges are likely to become if not to be "Establishmentarians."[29]   If to begin with they are not from that group now commonly, although very vaguely, called "the Establishment," their co-option into the midst of that rather small number of men who make important policy decisions for society may turn them into defenders of the existing system.   Even associations with power that are peripheral and ceremonial may strengthen their commitment to the maintenance of the system.

Being born into the upper half of society, enjoying a comfortable childhood, receiving an excellent education, undergoing an intensive and usually conservative professional training, and edging slowly up the ladder of a major political party or up the judicial hierarchy hardly forms the stereotyped background for a revolutionary.[30*]   And one would be hard put to find revolutionaries or, by standards of the extreme left or right, even radicals among constitutional court judges.   Occasionally, judges are quite outspoken in their support of social causes, but they have almost invariably preached reform of the system rather than its overthrow.   Even in his controversial book *Points of Rebellion*, William O. Douglas speaks like a fervent old-line Progressive, not like a revolutionary.   One could reasonably expect very different kinds of behavior from judges who were chosen according to different criteria, say from young non-lawyers who had been members of the Students for a Democratic Society in college or from older lawyers who were members of the John Birch Society.

It may not be social origins that are critical here—for a self-made man can become the most rock-ribbed defender of the status quo—but rather the

---

* The fact that such a large number of radical leaders among American college students, despite protestations of class solidarity with "the workers," come from upper- or upper-middle class families may indicate that the popular stereotypes of the revolutionary need drastic revision.

long years of professional training and association. Like traditions generally, those of both bench and bar tend to be conservative. Lawyers as a group may be less conservative than political scientists have thought,[31] but men like Louis Brandeis, Clarence Darrow, and Ralph Nader have undeniably been mavericks in their profession. In practical politics as well, there are usually close limits on the extent to which a young man can flout existing rules—and this is no less true in radical and liberal parties than in conservative organizations. In the Communist party of the U.S.S.R., as in many Marxist groups, the revolutionary spirit has become institutionalized to the point where advancement depends basically on seniority and adherence to organizational norms.[32]

It must be kept in mind, though, that we have been describing typical judges, not all judges. Even within the limits of the spectrum along which they are trained and from which they are selected, there has been a considerable range of background and career patterns. Whatever the general tendencies, at any given time a collegial court may include members from widely different social, political, and career backgrounds. More fundamentally, despite overall similarities in social background, professional training, and kinds of political experience, judges frequently differ among themselves both in their votes and in the reasons they give to justify those votes. Furthermore, those differences can have significant effects on the polity. Just how many of the differences in judicial behavior can be accounted for by social, professional, and political background characteristics is a question that has long fascinated scholars.

Because of real and imagined difficulties of obtaining data in other countries, and because many American political scientists in the past treated courts in the United States as unique institutions, efforts to connect background with actual behavior have been largely confined to the American setting.[33] Although these studies have been painstaking, on the whole the results have been disappointing to those who had hoped to discover strong and direct relationships between behavior and background characteristics. From an analysis of a sample of 298 state and federal Supreme Court justices, Stuart S. Nagel found that Democratic and Catholic judges were more likely than Republican and Protestant judges to vote for liberal results—for example, to vote to protect civil rights and criminal defendants or to favor government regulation of business, and employees over employers.[34] These relationships, however, were weak.

Sheldon Goldman analyzed a sample of 2,055 nonunanimous cases decided by the eleven U.S. Courts of Appeals during the period from 1961 to 1964 and discovered no significant differences between the votes of Catholic and Protestant judges except in cases involving taxation and eminent domain.[35] Other background characteristics, such as age, previous judicial experience, urban-rural origins, and prestige of law school attended, were even less helpful. Party affiliation turned out to be the variable most strongly associated with voting, but it provided no passkey. It correlated significantly with voting behavior in economic issues, but not in civil liberties and criminal justice disputes.

After examining fifty-two U.S. Supreme Court cases involving sectional rivalry during the period from 1837 to 1860, Schmidhauser found party background to be an important variable in accounting for divisions among the justices.[36] Since the four justices with the most consistent records of voting for Southern regional interests were all Southern Democrats and the two justices with the strongest pro-Northern records were Northern Whigs, one cannot separate out the effects of region and party on them. But every judge who participated in more than ten of these fifty-two cases can be ranked by party, regardless of regional background. All the Whigs, including James M. Wayne of Georgia, were at least moderately pro-Northern, and all the Democrats were either neutral or pro-Southern. Even Robert Grier of Pennsylvania and Samuel Nelson of New York were moderately pro-Southern.

Several doctoral dissertations have also noted the significance of party identification in voting on state supreme courts. Jerry K. Beatty[37] concluded that party was the most important variable in accounting for differences among Iowa Supreme Court judges in the 1960s. James F. Herndon,[38] analyzing nine state supreme courts, found that divisions among the judges, at least on the issue of workmen's compensation, were likely to reflect the intensity of competition between the parties; that is, in states where party competition was sharp, party background was an important element in explaining divisions among the judges. Where competition in electoral politics was less severe, party was less helpful in accounting for differences among the judges.

John D. Sprague, after examining seventy years of U.S. Supreme Court decisions involving questions of federalism, conceded that background characteristics like party affiliation or urban-rural origins could not tell us much either about specific cases or about a number of decisions over a short time span. But he added, "*in the aggregate*, the party variable and the urban-rural variable *are* related to judicial outcomes, at least for the federalism cases that have been analyzed here."[39]

In separate studies of the Michigan Supreme Court, Glendon A. Schubert[40] and S. Sidney Ulmer[41] found marked differences between the voting behavior of Democratic and Republican judges on labor issues. Indeed, there were strong indications of party blocs within the Court. David W. Adamany, on the other hand, used data from the Wisconsin Supreme Court and concluded that on issues similar to those examined by Schubert and

Ulmer there was evidence neither that judicial blocs had formed along party lines nor, more fundamentally, that party background could account for much of the difference in the way individual judges voted.[42]*

Adamany suggested that the discrepancy between his findings and those of Schubert and Ulmer might result from the effect of partisanship within a political milieu on the tendency of judges to differ along party lines. Insofar as elected judges have to be sensitive to the views of their constituents—and Ulmer quotes a Michigan Supreme Court justice to the effect that a judge who hopes to stay in office must keep a finger on the pulse of his constituency much as a legislator does—the sharpness of party differences in electoral politics may affect the propensity of judges of different parties to go separate ways. Thus Adamany, somewhat along the same lines as Herndon, explains the relative lack of party cohesion among Wisconsin judges as due in part to the differences in partisanship between the two states. Wisconsin judges are not, as are their colleagues in Michigan, nominated by party conventions; and they face an electorate that is less bitterly divided between the two parties. Adamany does not say so explicitly, but a corollary of his thesis is that a less partisan atmosphere will encourage lawyers who are not party regulars—and who are, therefore, probably less committed along lines of traditional party cleavages—to run for judicial office.

In perhaps the most methodologically sophisticated of the social background studies, D. R. Bowen tabulated the decisions, unanimous as well as nonunanimous, of 373 judges in the U.S. Courts of Appeals and on American state Supreme Courts in the year 1960. He then used multivariate analytical techniques to isolate the effects of six individual variables—age, religion, region, party, length of service on the bench, and educational qualifications—from each other and then to measure the total amount of variance in the voting behavior of these judges that could be accounted for by combining the explanatory power of the six characteristics.[43] Bowen, too, found that party affiliation was the most valuable item in explaining the differences among judges, but it was still not a powerful predictor of votes. "A final inescapable conclusion," he wrote, "about the explanatory power of the sociological background characteristics of these judges is that they are generally not very helpful."[44]

Still, the feeling will not down that somehow background experiences

---

* We should stress that none of these scholars who found party to be useful in explaining judicial behavior claimed that any judge voted a "party line." What they did assert, either implicitly or explicitly, was: (1) Before going to the bench, judges had tended to become Democrats or Republicans because these parties promoted or symbolized certain values that judges cherished; and/or (2) during their pre-Court careers the party affiliations of these judges had tended to bring them into close contact with men who shared certain values, and these contacts cultivated similar values in the judges; and/or (3) as party activists before going to the bench, judges had over a period of years become more intensely committed to those values by the very fact of having had to articulate and defend them.

do filter through a maze of professional training and official beliefs about proper judicial conduct.* It may be, as Lon L. Fuller has suggested, that students of judicial behavior have not been imaginative in their choice of which background characteristics to use as independent variables or wise in their choice of votes as dependent variables.[45] We shall discuss the limitations of votes as indices of values shortly. Here we would note that bolder choices of background characteristics have not been feasible in studying most judges. Few scholars would deny today that a jurist's relations with his parents and siblings, his inner sense of security, the state of his health, and the functioning of various glands could be important factors in shaping his reactions to the problems he faces in the courtroom. But a scholar is not likely to have access to these intimate details of the mental and physical states of a broad sample of judges. Even biographers are frequently unable to discover any such information about a single judge; and when they do, the evidence they gather often turns out to be merely second-hand, impressionistic opinions of people who are not experts on such matters.† There have been several useful psychological studies of statesmen,[46] most notably Woodrow Wilson[47] and James Forrestal;[48] but despite the availability of rich collections of data in the private papers of American justices, there have been no such full-length investigations of judges[49] and only a few shorter analyses.[50]

   Certainly, a broad conclusion from literature on social background and voting behavior is that given the kinds of information social scientists are likely to obtain about the lives of judges, the model pictured in Figure 4.1 so oversimplifies the real world as to be of slight use. From everyday experience one would expect that very similar life histories would have very different effects on the attitudes and behavior of different men, especially on the behavior of sophisticated men who take pride in their individuality.[51]

   Perhaps treating background characteristics that can be discovered as important factors, but factors operating indirectly rather than directly on judicial votes, might lead to more intricate and, so, less easily applied models, like the one in Figure 4.2. In this model " values " would include not only

* One huge reservoir of data on voting behavior of American judges is still largely untapped. The Administrative Office of U.S. Courts compiles a detailed set of records on each of the thousands of cases handled annually by federal district judges. These records are punched into IBM cards and after five years turned over to the Inter-University Consortium for Political Research at Ann Arbor, Michigan. The way these data are coded poses some problems for scholarly use, but they do provide a wealth of voting material that might be used to correlate masses of votes with background characteristics. (As far as we are aware, the only study to utilize these data is Stuart S. Nagel's " Disparities in Criminal Procedure," 14 *U.C.L.A. Law Review* 1272 [1967].) Biographical information about district judges can easily be obtained from publications like *Who's Who*, newspaper reports, and hearings of the Senate Committee on the Judiciary. More subtle biographical data are no easier to obtain for judges than for other public officials.

† There have, however, been occasional exceptions. See, for instance, Harold D. Lasswell, *Power and Personality* (New York: Norton, 1948), esp. pp. 65–88.

FIGURE 4.1

Social Background ─────────▶ Votes

broad policy preferences, such as free speech over privacy or individual freedom over social security, but also the concepts that a judge holds about his proper role. Here part of the influence of social background would be channeled through professional training, and both background and training would interact with hereditary factors in shaping values and role perceptions. In turn, values and role perceptions would interact to bring about, when the stimulus of a case presented itself, a vote.

FIGURE 4.2

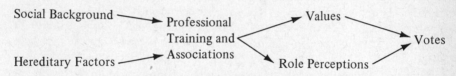

More complex still would be the model in Figure 4.3. Here values would be dynamic, active agents, rather than passive givens.[52] They might change as a judge's life history changed—for instance, when he ceased to be a practitioner, a professor, a senator, or an attorney general and became a judge. His values as well as his perceptions of reality might also change while he was on the bench as he heard the views of his colleagues and saw what was happening in the world about him—happening perhaps, in part, as a result of his previous votes as a judge or his earlier work in another branch of government. The minds of men past middle age may be less malleable than those of children, but judges are not necessarily ineducable. One should not, of course, overestimate the probability of change. In one

FIGURE 4.3

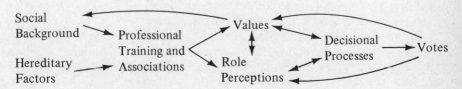

respect, votes and, even more, published opinions represent public expressions of commitments, and by that fact alone they strengthen a judge's attachment to a policy by grappling it to his ego.

There is a further problem and an important one. With rare exceptions, analysts have treated votes as if they comprised a three-point scale: yes, abstain, no. But this can be a gross oversimplification. A judge may be opposed to a particular value; but if he thinks he might lose on the merits, he might actually vote for it on a procedural point in the hope of avoiding a worse defeat. Conversely, a judge on the other side may think it more prudent to accept a sure although limited victory now, rather than delay in the hope of a bigger victory later. Or a judge might prefer to have a case decided on narrow grounds to reduce the likelihood that it would develop into a precedent of major consequence. Numerous other possibilities present themselves. For some years now annual tabulations of U.S. Supreme Court voting prepared by the Commission on Law and Social Action of the American Jewish Congress have distinguished broad votes favoring civil liberties from narrow votes. Joel Grossman recently went much further and developed a fifteen-point scale for measuring the voting response of Supreme Court justices to defendants' claims in a set of eighty-one sit-in cases.[53]

Equally fundamental and more serious from the point of view of operational research, voting is only one form of political behavior open to judges, other public officials, and private citizens. An illustration from the legislative process in the United States will make the basic point clear: In 1958 congressional foes of the Warren Court were on the brink of passing a series of measures aimed at reversing the effects of specific decisions and at curbing the Court's jurisdiction. As each of these bills came up, one influential Southern senator duly voted for it; occasionally he made speeches in favor of a particular proposal and against the Supreme Court. But this senator did not use his position on a powerful committee to whip up votes for the anti-Court alliance, and he even avoided making personal pleas to uncommitted colleagues. At the crucial moment, when it seemed that the conservative Republican–Southern Democratic coalition might succeed, this senator whispered to Lyndon B. Johnson, who was then majority leader of the Senate, how the Court foes could be beaten.[54] The senator's voting record shows that in every instance but one—and that exception was on a procedural question—he voted against the Court. Yet, in fact, by not drumming up support for the conservative coalition and by short-circuiting their strategy, he played a decidedly pro-Court game.

Much like a legislator, a judge has a whole range of activities open to him that go far beyond voting.[55] His choices include questioning counsel during argument; making formal presentations at official conferences; sending memoranda to one, several, or all of his colleagues; having private conversations with fellow members of the court; and, if permitted on his tribunal, writing a dissenting or concurring opinion. Moreover, some U.S. Supreme Court justices have taken their fight to other forums and lobbied to try to get Congress to pass or defeat a bill or the President to support or veto legislative action. When vacancies have occurred on the bench, some justices have also pressured Presidents to select men who thought as they did. The contents of all these messages can include emotional as well as intellectual appeals, and without a doubt, friendship can smooth the path of communication.

As with votes, analysis is complicated by the notions that a judge holds of what he may properly do. Some U.S. Supreme Court justices have felt it improper to try to sway a colleague's vote and in conference will do little more than indicate how they see the basic issues and will vote. These justices seldom, if ever, will lobby with other judges. Other justices— William Howard Taft and Felix Frankfurter are among the clearest examples—spent much of their time trying to drum up support for their views among relatively uncommitted colleagues. Taft was also a frequent lobbyist both on Capitol Hill and at the White House. While Frankfurter also managed to apply a few hundred pounds of pressure and supply many cubic yards of advice, he worked more quietly than the Big Chief, generally operating through friends in the executive branch.

Thus if we restrict ourselves to votes as measures of commitment to values, even if we use more complex schemes of classifications, such as those suggested by Grossman, we ignore a sizable portion of the decisional choices actually open to judges. Table 4.2 provides a graphic illustration of some —though not all—of the options a judge may exercise. The range is considerably broader than yes, abstain, no.

Judicial papers, when they are available, and interviews, if they are possible, may help fill in some of the missing data needed to construct the kind of range of choices shown in Table 4.2. Sometimes neither source is open, however. Then an analyst has no option but to rely heavily on votes, but he can usually supplement them with evidence from opinions and perhaps off-the-bench statements by judges. In any event, when he has to depend primarily on votes, he should do so understanding that his yardstick is only grossly calibrated.

The social background studies—and we hope this analysis—should emphasize that the interrelationships among votes, values, and formal and informal decision-making processes are exquisitely complex. In the next two chapters we shall examine a few of the substantive and methodological problems that have concerned political scientists who have tried to measure the influence of individual values on judicial choice.

TABLE 4.2

*Choices actually open to a judge to support particular values**

For claim

Value	Choice
+50	Vote for, write opinion for, lobby for with colleagues, and lobby for outside court
+40	Vote for, write opinion for, and lobby for with colleagues
+30	Vote for and write opinion for
+20	Vote for and speak for at conference
+10	Vote for but do nothing else

Neutral

Value	Choice
0	Abstain

Against claim

Value	Choice
−10	Vote against but do nothing else
−20	Vote against and speak against at conference
−30	Vote against and write opinion against
−40	Vote against, write opinion against, and lobby against with colleagues
−50	Vote against, write opinion against, lobby against with colleagues, and lobby against outside court

* Anticipating some of the discussion in chapter 7, we would note that we do not make any effort to justify our assignment of these particular numbers to choices. One might reasonably conclude that lobbying outside the court is sufficiently unusual for that option to be assigned a value (negative or positive, depending on the situation) that more accurately indicates intensity; perhaps 100 or 150 or some other number can be justified. For discussions of this problem, see the articles by Tufte and by Robert P. Abelson and John W. Tukey, in Edward R. Tufte (ed.), *The Quantitative Analysis of Social Problems* (Reading, Mass.: Addison-Wesley, 1970).

NOTES

1. Wallace S. Sayre and Herbert Kaufman, *Governing New York City: Politics in the Metropolis* (New York: The Russell Sage Foundation, 1960), p. 538.

2. Ulf Torgersen, "The Role of the Supreme Court in the Norwegian Political System," in Glendon A. Schubert (ed.), *Judicial Decision-Making* (New York: Free Press, 1963), p. 232.

3. David J. Danelski, "The People and the Court in Japan," in Joel B. Grossman and Joseph Tanenhaus (eds.), *Frontiers of Judicial Research* (New York: Wiley, 1969).

4. Fred L. Morrison, "The Swiss Federal Court: Judicial Decision-Making and Judicial Recruitment," in Grossman and Tanenhaus, supra note 3.

5. Donald P. Kommers, "The Federal Constitutional Court in the West German Political System," in Grossman and Tanenhaus, supra note 3; see also Kommers, "The Federal Constitutional Court of West Germany: Some Exploratory Considerations," a paper delivered at the 1967 Meetings of the Midwest Conference of Political Scientists.

6. David J. Danelski, *A Supreme Court Justice Is Appointed* (New York: Random House, 1964).

7. Harold W. Chase: "Federal Judges: The Appointing Process," 51 *Minnesota Law Review* 185 (1966); "The Johnson Administration—Judicial Appointments—1963–1966," 52 *ibid*. 965 (1968).

8. Joel B. Grossman, *Lawyers and Judges: The ABA and the Politics of Judicial Selection* (New York: Wiley, 1965).

9. Richard A. Watson and Rondal G. Downing, *The Politics of the Bench and the Bar: Judicial Selection under the Missouri Nonpartisan Court Plan* (New York: Wiley, 1969).

10. Japan, *Constitution*, Art. 80.

11. India, *Constitution*, Art. 217.

12. *Ibid*., Art. 124.

13. *Ibid*.

14. See R. MacGregor Dawson, *The Government of Canada* 4th ed., revised by Norman Ward (Toronto: University of Toronto Press, 1963), p. 429.

15. George H. Gadbois, Jr., "Indian Supreme Court Judges: A Portrait," 3 *Law and Society Review* 317, 329 (1968); see also Gadbois, "Selection, Background Characteristics, and Voting Behavior of Indian Supreme Court Judges, 1950–1959," in Glendon A. Schubert and David J. Danelski (eds.), *Comparative Judicial Behavior; Cross Cultural Studies of Political Decision-Making in the East and West* (New York: Oxford University Press, 1969).

16. John R. Schmidhauser, "The Justices of the Supreme Court: A Collective Portrait," 3 *Midwest Journal of Political Science* 1, 45 (1959).

17. Kommers, in Grossman and Tanenhaus, supra note 3, p. 96.

18. Torgersen, in Schubert, supra note 2, p. 232.

19. Gadbois, "Indian Supreme Court Judges," supra note 15, p. 317.

20. Brian Abel-Smith and Robert Stevens, *In Search of Justice* (London: Penguin, 1968), pp. 174–178. See also Abel-Smith and Stevens, *Lawyers and the Courts: A Sociological Study of the English Legal System 1750–1965* (Cambridge, Mass.: Harvard University Press, 1967).

21. For an excellent discussion of the Italian legal professions, see Mauro Cappelletti, John Henry Merryman, and Joseph M. Perillo, *The Italian Legal System* (Stanford: Stanford University Press, 1967), chap. 3.

22. Grossman, supra note 8, pp. 19–20. For a consideration of the socialization of U.S. federal district court judges see Robert A. Carp, "The Function, Impact, and Political Significance of the Federal District Courts: A Case Study" (unpublished Ph.D. dissertation, University of Iowa, 1969).

23. Quoted in David M. Silver, *Lincoln's Supreme Court* (Urbana: University of Illinois Press, 1956), p. 208.

24. Kommers, in Grossman and Tanenhaus, supra note 3, p. 97.

25. Peter H. Russell, *The Supreme Court of Canada as a Bilingual and Bicultural Institution* (Ottawa: Queen's Printer for Canada, 1969), p. 72.

26. Granville Austin, *The Indian Constitution: Cornerstone of a Nation* (London: Oxford University Press, 1966), p. 181.

27. See the discussion in chapter 3 regarding Golak Nath's case.

28. Schmidhauser, supra note 16, p. 49. See also Joel B. Grossman, "Social Backgrounds and Judicial Decision-Making," 79 *Harvard Law Review* 1551 (1966); Grossman, "Social Backgrounds and Judicial Decisions: Notes for a Theory," 29 *Journal of Politics* 334 (1967); Sheldon Goldman, "Backgrounds, Attitudes, and the Voting Behavior of Judges: A Comment on Joel Grossman's 'Social Backgrounds and Judicial Decisions,'" 31 *Journal of Politics* 214 (1969); and Grossman, "Further Thoughts on Consensus and Conversion: Reply to Professor Goldman," 31 *Journal of Politics* 223 (1969).

29. Geoffrey Sawer, *Law in Society* (London: Oxford University Press, 1965), p. 91.

30. Of course, it is not at all clear what does contribute to the making of a revolutionary personality. See E. Victor Wolfenstein, *The Revolutionary Personality: Lenin, Trotsky, Gandhi* (Princeton, N.J.: Princeton University Press, 1967); Paul Roazen, *Freud: Political and Social Thought* (New York: Knopf, 1968); Fred I. Greenstein, *Personality and Politics: Problems of Evidence, Inference, and Conceptualization* (Chicago: Markham, 1969); and Harold D. Lasswell, *Psychopathology and Politics* (Chicago: University of Chicago Press, 1930), especially chaps. 6–7.

31. See Walter F. Murphy and Joseph Tanenhaus, "The Supreme Court and Its Elite Publics," a paper presented at the 1970 Meetings of the International Political Science Association at Munich.

32. See Robert C. Tucker's essay "The Deradicalization of Marxist Movements" in his *The Marxian Revolutionary Idea* (New York: W. W. Norton, 1969). On the permanence of elites, even of radical groups, see Roberto Michels, *Political Parties* (New York: Dover, 1959, originally published in 1911), translated by Eden and Cedar Paul.

33. Among the exceptions is Takeyoshi Kawashima, "Individualism in Decision-Making in the Supreme Court of Japan," in Schubert and Danelski, supra note 15.

34. Stuart S. Nagel, "Political Party Affiliation and Judges' Decisions," 55 *American Political Science Review* 843 (1961); "Ethnic Affiliations and Judicial Propensities," 24 *Journal of Politics* 92 (1962); "Testing Relations Between Judicial Characteristics and Judicial Decision-Making," 15 *Western Political Quarterly* 425 (1962).

35. Sheldon Goldman, "Voting Behavior on the United States Courts of Appeals, 1961–1964," 60 *American Political Science Review* 374 (1966).

36. John R. Schmidhauser, "Judicial Behavior and the Sectional Crisis of 1837–1860," 23 *Journal of Politics* 615 (1961).

37. Jerry K. Beatty, "An Institutional and Behavioral Analysis of the Iowa Supreme Court—1965–1969" (unpublished Ph.D. dissertation, University of Iowa, 1970).

38. James F. Herndon, " Relationships Between Partisanship and the Decisions of the State Supreme Courts" (unpublished Ph.D. dissertation, University of Michigan, 1963).

39. John D. Sprague, *Voting Patterns of the United States Supreme Court: Cases in Federalism 1889–1959* (Indianapolis: Bobbs-Merrill, 1968), p. 146.

40. Glendon A. Schubert, *Quantitative Analysis of Judicial Behavior* (New York: Free Press, 1959), pp. 129–142.

41. S. Sidney Ulmer, "The Political Party Variable in the Michigan Supreme Court," 11 *Journal of Public Law* 352 (1962).

42. David W. Adamany, "The Party Variable in Judges' Voting: Conceptual Notes and a Case Study," 63 *American Political Science Review* 57 (1969).

43. D. R. Bowen, "The Explanation of Judicial Voting Behavior from Sociological Characteristics of Judges" (unpublished Ph.D. dissertation, Yale University, 1965).

44. *Ibid.*, p. 201.

45. Lon L. Fuller, "An Afterword: Science and the Judicial Process," 79 *Harvard Law Review* 1604, 1608–1609, 1623 (1966).

46. Fred I. Greenstein, *Personality and Politics: Problems of Evidence, Inference, and Conceptualization* (Chicago: Markham, 1969), pp. 163–167, has a useful annotated bibliography. See also Arnold A. Rogow (ed.), *Politics, Personality, and Social Science in the Twentieth Century: Essays in Honor of Harold D. Lasswell* (Chicago: University of Chicago Press, 1969).

47. Alexander L. and Juliette L. George, *Woodrow Wilson and Colonel House* (New York: John Day, 1965). The study by Sigmund Freud and William C. Bullitt, *Thomas Woodrow Wilson, Twenty-Eighth President of the United States: A Psychological Study* (Boston: Houghton Mifflin, 1967), is more of a fiasco.

48. Arnold A. Rogow, *James Forrestal: A Study of Personality, Politics, and Policy* (New York: Macmillan, 1963).

49. Betty Glad's *Charles Evans Hughes and the Illusions of Innocence: A Study in American Diplomacy* (Urbana: University of Illinois Press, 1966) is, as the subtitle indicates, restricted to Hughes as a diplomat rather than as a judge. Many of Glad's insights, however, can be used to interpret Hughes' careers on the Supreme Court.

50. In addition to Lasswell's *Power and Personality* cited in the footnote to p. 108, see the discussion in Danelski, supra note 6, chap. 11, although what Danelski says refers more to the personalities of Warren Harding and Harry Daugherty than to William Howard Taft and Pierce Butler.

51. Grossman discusses this problem in his "Social Background and Judicial Decisions: Notes for a Theory," supra note 28.

52. See the much more complete, and complex, chart developed by M. Brewster Smith, "A Map for the Analysis of Personality and Politics," 24 *Journal of Social Issues* 15, 25 (1968), and the discussion of this chart in Greenstein, supra note 46, pp. 25–31.

53. See Grossman supra note 51 and his "A Model for Judicial Policy Analysis: The Supreme Court and the Sit-In Cases," in Grossman and Tanenhaus (eds.), supra note 3.

54. The incident is from Walter F. Murphy, *Congress and the Court* (Chicago: University of Chicago Press, 1962), chap. 9.

55. The same point is made at greater length in J. Woodford Howard, Jr., "On the Fluidity of Judicial Choice," 62 *American Political Science Review* 43 (1968), and Walter F. Murphy, *Elements of Judicial Strategy* (Chicago: University of Chicago Press, 1964), especially chaps. 3, 7, and 8.

5
Judicial Decision Making: The Individual Phase

In chapter 1 we pointed out that during the 1920s and 1930s the message of the Legal Realists, both in law schools and political science departments, was that judges had considerable freedom in their decision making and that their choices were more the product of individual values and policy preferences than of automatic applications of legal principles. Oliver Wendell Holmes had stated the basic thesis as early as 1881:

> The life of the law has not been logic: it has been experience. The felt necessities of the time, the prevalent moral and political theories, intuitions of public policy, avowed or unconscious, even the prejudices which judges share with their fellow-men, have had a good deal more to do than the syllogism in determining the rules by which men should be governed.[1]

Forty years later Benjamin Cardozo, then serving on the New York Court of Appeals, said that he took "judge-made law as one of the existing realities of life."[2] He explained that in making law judges not only looked at precedents but also weighed one interest against another and one notion of justice against another. The judge, he wrote, "must get his knowledge just as the legislator gets it; from experience and study and reflection; in brief, from life itself."[3] That knowledge and experience, Cardozo conceded, were deeply personal and, to an extent, even idiosyncratic: "We may try to see things as objectively as we please, none the less, we can never see them with any eyes except our own. . . . We cannot transcend the limits of the ego and see anything as it really is."[4]

Karl Llewellyn,[5] Jerome Frank,[6] Thomas Reed Powell,[7] Charles G. Haines,[8] and Edward S. Corwin[9] drove these lessons home time and again. At least in the world of the political scientist, the statement that a judge's votes are heavily influenced by his values has become one of the givens. Most professional attention in past decades has focused on two sets of questions, one substantive, the other methodological. The substantive questions have been aimed at exploring the specific values and policy preferences that are at work, the relative weight they carry within the framework of an individual judge's jurisprudence, and how these weights differ among judges. The methodological inquiries have centered on how scholars can go about discovering judges' values and measuring their intensity.

Essentially, there are two analytically separate processes of decision making on juries* and appellate courts. First there is an individual phase in which a judge or juror turns over in his mind the specific issues and the broader societal context of the case as he perceives them; the legal principles that seem relevant to him; and the implications he believes possible decisions might have for the litigants, for more general interests, for the course of legal and policy development, and perhaps for the court and for himself personally. In the group phase the members of the court or jury interact and try at least to justify a particular choice, if not to persuade others that it is the best of all possible alternatives. The final decision may be, as it usually is on the Australian High Court, the sum of the individual decisions; or it may be, as it frequently is on the U.S. Supreme Court, a completely new entity shaped in large part by group action.

We take up the individual phase of decision making in this chapter and the group phase in the next chapter. Since either the conclusion or the assumption—and sometimes both—of most of the professional literature has been that judges are heavily influenced by their value preferences,

---

* Because of limitations on our space we have not included a discussion of juries and jurors. There is an abundance of literature on this aspect of judicial decision making, at least in the United States. See the bibliography in Harry Kalven, Jr., and Hans Zeisel, *The American Jury* (Boston: Little, Brown, 1966).

we shall organize this part of our discussion around approaches and methods, rather than around substantive findings.

Opinion Analysis

Analyzing opinions is one obvious way of searching out the values influencing a judge—at least it is an obvious way in those countries, unlike West Germany, where opinions are frequently signed.   Over the years historians as well as lawyers and political scientists have done a great deal of such work on the U.S. Supreme Court, and this approach is still relatively common fare in American law reviews.   This method involves the reading of many, though not necessarily all, of a judge's opinions and picking out strands of thought and weaving them into a more or less coherent jurisprudence.   Sometimes the result has been a lifeless summary of a vital program for action; sometimes, as when a Thomas Reed Powell[10] is at work, it has been a slashing intellectual vivisection that in a kinder age would have brought into existence a Society for the Prevention of Cruelty to Judges.   Usually, the result has been a set of useful, although highly subjective, insights.[11]

Opinions, like other documents, can also be studied by a cluster of techniques called content analysis.   In general terms content analysis refers to the systematic search through written or oral communications for the presence and patterns of carefully specified data.   Pritchett employed a simple variety of content analysis when he classified cases by subject matter for *The Roosevelt Court*, and most scholars in public law who have tinkered with cumulative scaling—which we shall discuss later in this chapter—or the statistical techniques presented in chapter 7 have had to use content analysis in a similar, if not more refined, fashion.

Other varieties of content analysis can facilitate subtle efforts to explore systematically the values reflected in judicial opinions.   Glendon Schubert, for example, used a panel of three scholars to read each of the more than 300 opinions that Justice Robert H. Jackson had written while on the U.S. Supreme Court.   The panel then scored each opinion for the presence or absence of a set of thirteen items: expressions for or against certain policy courses such as state control of civil liberties, easily identifiable groups such as lawyers or judges, or ideal policy goals such as the public interest.[12] The panel next totaled the frequencies of verbal expressions for and against these items.   Then Schubert counted Jackson's votes in these cases, scoring them in five categories: for political liberalism, for political conservatism, for economic liberalism, or for economic conservatism.   The fifth category was residual, including votes in cases that did not involve either political or economic issues.   Schubert then used multivariate techniques of analysis, which we shall describe in chapter 7, to discover and help account for the relationships between Jackson's votes and verbal statements as well as to measure changes in the justice's views over time. Schubert's substantive findings included conclusions that Jackson was more apt to write in defense of civil liberties than to vote for them, and, conversely, that he was more apt to vote to defend business against governmental regulation than to speak of the virtues of unrestrained economic activity. In terms of time, Schubert found that Jackson had made a sharp and significant shift after World War II to stronger support of economic conservatism.

By far the most sophisticated application of content analysis in the study of judicial opinions is that which Werner Grunbaum has in progress at the time of this writing. Encouraged by the success of other scholars in adapting a computerized system of content analysis to the study of international relations,[13] Grunbaum has developed a computerized dictionary and a set of programs for analyzing opinions of the U.S. Supreme Court.[14] Although it is too early to be entirely certain of the payoff of Grunbaum's work, it holds high promise for charting and measuring judicial values.

A felt need to go beyond legalistically oriented analysis of opinion is not new, of course. There was, for example, an implicit call in much of Oliver Wendell Holmes' writing for some kind of psychological analysis of the work of judges. In 1918 Theodore Schroeder explicitly urged scholars to psychoanalyze judges through their opinions. Every opinion, Schroeder wrote, "is unavoidably a fragment of autobiography," "a confession," and a special plea made in defense of impulses that are largely unconscious. "In the light of genetic psychology the judicial intellect is to be studied, not according to the results of decisions, but according to the conscious and unconscious motivations which predetermined the results...."[15]

Schroeder's suggestions are fascinating; but despite some imaginative work by Harold D. Lasswell,[16] scholars have done little to utilize psychoanalytic techniques when dealing with judges. There are contributing causes in the nature of the available data, problems we shall discuss shortly. But the principal reason for this neglect is that political scientists, historians, and lawyers usually lack the necessary training in psychoanalysis. Psychiatrists themselves have preferred to put judicial writings on their bookshelves rather than on their couches.*

---

* As we noted in chapter 4, this is not necessarily an unmixed evil. Psychoanalyses of some public persons have come off very well; see, for example, Alexander L. and Juliette L. George, *Woodrow Wilson and Colonel House: A Personality Study* (New York: John Day, 1956). On the other hand, others have been intellectual disasters; see, for instance, Sigmund Freud and William C. Bullitt, *Thomas Woodrow Wilson, Twenty-Eighth President of the United States: A Psychological Study* (Boston: Houghton Mifflin, 1967). For a useful bibliography of psychological studies of statesmen, see Fred I. Greenstein, *Personality and Politics: Problems of Evidence, Inference, and Conceptualization* (Chicago: Markham Publishing Company, 1969), pp. 163–167. J. Woodford Howard has a lucid discussion of some of the problems of a "psychological" biography in his "Judicial Biography and the Behavioral Persuasion," a paper delivered to the 1969 meetings of the American Political Science Association.

Opinions as mother lodes from which judicial values can be mined—whether by traditional impressionistic means or systematic content analysis or more subtle examination of the shadows of a judge's subconscious—suffer from a number of intrinsic limitations. First, in most civil law countries, such as Germany, Italy, and Switzerland, opinions are usually issued anonymously. Some judges, most likely ex-professors, may have written enough before going to the court to permit skilled content analysts to identify or at least exclude them as authors. As yet, however, this goal has not been achieved. In the future one may be able to program computers to act as electronic psychiatrists and read a judge's personality from his opinions, but such sophisticated techniques are not now available to scholars. And if they were, they might not be able to overcome the next limitation on opinion data.

The second restriction is that even where constitutional courts, like those of Argentina, Canada, Ireland, Japan, and the United States, use "opinions of the court," those opinions are frequently group products. They are, indeed, usually drafted by one author—in Argentina and Japan, unlike in Ireland and the United States, he remains anonymous—but his colleagues and his staff may well play important roles in shaping both the final language and the thought. Holmes used to complain that his colleagues "cut the genitals" out of some of his best work. Chief Justice Tanaka of Japan made the same point, albeit less pungently, when he explained that judges on his Court "have always striven to agree on a common reasoning by compromising, by sacrificing in some degree the particularity of their opinions."[17] In the same vein, a retired Japanese justice told an interviewer: "We collaborated to harmonize our views; that is what we all wanted."[18]

This second disadvantage may be offset somewhat by a judge's having written a number of separate opinions. Concurring and dissenting opinions are not uncommon in Argentina, Canada, Ireland, Japan, and the United States. The problem of group authorship of opinions hardly exists in Australia, where there is a tradition of each judge's writing his own opinion. Still, it may be that the judge under study has not written many separate opinions in cases where certain important kinds of value conflicts are most evident.

There is also a third restriction on the utility of opinions as repositories of individual values. Even where, as in Australia, one can count on opinions to be solely the work of the author, one must keep in mind that judges often—perhaps almost invariably—use opinions as justifications for decisions rather than as explicit descriptions of their own value preferences or even of their personal decision-making processes. Thus there may be other values than he is himself conscious of. Indeed, judges may strenuously deny that they are influenced by any values other than "the law" itself, and in fact there may be occasions when a statute or constitutional clause may remove any opportunity for choice. Judges claim these occasions are frequent.

Biography and Private Papers

With the potential of techniques such as content analysis and psycho-analysis still largely unexplored, political scientists, whether out of wisdom or ignorance, have turned to other kinds of data to use instead of or in addition to judicial opinions. The principal sources have been unpublished judicial papers, votes on cases, and social background characteristics of the judges themselves.

Until the mid-1950s American political scientists most commonly used judicial biography to examine a particular judge's values. Among the purposes of a judicial biography is usually an examination of the structure and functioning of the judge's value hierarchy—most biographers would prefer to say his jurisprudence—and scholars have used, not always systematically, the three kinds of materials listed in the preceding paragraph in addition to analyses of published opinions. All biographers have attempted to obtain and use private papers and, if contemporaries were alive, interviews to supplement data from published sources. Albert J. Beveridge in his four volumes on John Marshall,[19] Carl B. Swisher in his works on Stephen J. Field[20] and Roger Brooke Taney,[21] and Charles Fairman in his *Mr. Justice Miller* all made some use of private papers as well as published material.

Thus there were ample precedents when in 1956 Alpheus T. Mason published his *Harlan Fiske Stone: Pillar of the Law.* Nevertheless, Mason's book constituted a breakthrough both in the extent to which it utilized private judicial papers and in the timing of the publication. The backbone of the other biographies had been the historical settings of important cases, the temper of the times, and the competing legal and political doctrines revealed in official opinions. Information from private papers of judges had provided a bit of sauce, but not the meat. Moreover, all the judges involved were long dead. Mason, on the other hand, structured his book around Stone's private papers; doing so was both natural and easy since the Chief Justice, like William Howard Taft[22] and Frank Murphy,[23] had had many of the instincts of a pack rat and had carefully preserved carbons of his opinions and chatty correspondence about the Court as well as the thousands of memoranda and slip opinions, complete with editorial comments from his colleagues, that had been circulated among the justices.

Mason's skillful use of these revealing sources and his publication of them while five of Stone's colleagues were still on the Court caused great concern among judges and lawyers, and he was subjected to considerable abuse for "eavesdropping on justice."[24]   The vehemence of criticism was closely related to how badly Mason's data had exploded pet theories or had trodden on favorite judges.   Underpinning much of this criticism was also a sentiment that the judicial process was a sacred rite, too holy to be viewed by non-lawyers.

There are, of course, intellectual problems, legal and ethical, in a scholar's using private papers, but there are different and more serious problems behind a judge's decision to leave his papers to a library.   For judges the most acute problem is how frank their colleagues will be with each other if they know that their comments may be published in their lifetimes.   A countervailing consideration is that, in American political culture at least, there is apparently a high regard for open as opposed to secret proceedings. Thomas Jefferson's protest against "opinions huddled up in conclave"[25] is probably a more specific objection than most Americans would voice, but there does seem to be an ingrained suspicion that proceedings in camera are not very candid.   "Open covenants openly arrived at," however naïve as a norm for international relations, is still congruent with insistence on public trials, free speech, access to legislative debates, and, more particularly, disclosure of stock holdings by administrative officials.   Scrutiny of the decision-making processes of a court might build up public confidence. And nothing in Mason's book or in any other scholarly work published since that makes use of judicial papers has even hinted that members of the U.S. Supreme Court have been guilty of any misconduct in their duties as judges.

Whatever the dangers to scholarship in the use of such papers[26]—and the scholar always has to keep in mind that he is looking at documents that may present only one side of a controversy, that may have been edited or even planted, and that at best those documents depend on fallible human reasoning and memory—there are now about a dozen sets of papers of twentieth-century judges open to the scholarly public.   Those of Frank Murphy, William Howard Taft, Sherman Minton, Felix Frankfurter, and Harold Burton, and of Judge Charles Clark of the U.S. Court of Appeals for the Second Circuit are especially valuable, as are those of Chief Justice Stone.

For the purpose of this chapter, we can say that papers do often reveal judges weighing one value against another.   A single example will have to suffice.   *Martin v. Struthers* contested the constitutionality of an ordinance of an industrial suburb that outlawed doorbell ringing to protect the sleep of "swing-shift" workers during World War II.[27]   The workers' right to privacy and their right to have that privacy protected by the state clashed with the right of Jehovah's Witnesses to practice their free speech by summoning residents to the door.   Anyone reading Justice Hugo Black's majority opinion holding the ordinance unconstitutional would have thought that in his value hierarchy free speech towered over the right to privacy. Twenty years later some surprise was voiced when Black in several sit-in cases suddenly came out against free expression and in favor of a kind of privacy.[28]

Frank Murphy's papers show that deciding between these conflicting values was not easy for Black.[29]   In fact, he first voted that the ordinance was constitutional, and as senior majority justice (the vote was 5 to 4) he assigned to himself the task of writing the opinion of the Court.   That opinion quickly dismissed as insubstantial the counterclaims of free speech. Black, however, was apparently troubled by what he had written or by the reactions he received from other members of the Court, for he soon withdrew his opinion, switched his position, and provided the fifth vote to hold the ordinance unconstitutional.   Chief Justice Stone, who had now become the senior member of the majority, graciously assigned Black the task of rewriting the opinion of the Court; and he proceeded to dispatch the claims of privacy as firmly as he had earlier dismissed the claims to free speech.

Two points emerge from Murphy's papers on this case.   First, both values apparently meant a great deal more to Black than one would have gathered from his final vote or published opinion.   His earlier and later panegyrics about the primacy of free speech in a democratic society[30] had not automatically, quickly, or, given his behavior two decades later, permanently convinced him that the right to communicate ideas should always be dominant over privacy.   Second, Black's literary style shielded his close relative weighing of the two values.   As a powerful advocate who knows how to drive his arguments home, he wrote—both for and against free speech —as if no doubt about the absolute validity of his conclusion could ever have crossed the mind of a rational man.

Counting Votes

Papers of American judges are seldom available, and rarely, if ever, have judges from courts outside the United States preserved their correspondence for scholarly use.   One, therefore, usually has to utilize other data.   In all the countries we have been referring to, with the exception of Italy, Norway, and West Germany,* votes are plentiful, and, except in Australia, a judge's votes usually greatly exceed the number of opinions he writes.   Whereas a judge in the United States, Japan, or Ireland may seldom write an opinion on a particular issue, he may over a period of years cast a dozen or more votes in cases raising that issue.   The surprising thing, when one looks back on American political science and the close attention that it has

---

* The second senate of the West German Constitutional Court now publishes the division on cases (8–0, 7–1, 6–2, and so forth) and has begun to identify dissenting judges.

historically paid to the U.S. Supreme Court, is that analysts came so seldom —and so late—to recognize the utility of the vote as a potential key to understanding judicial values.

In his pioneering study " General Observations of the Effects of Personal, Political, and Economic Influences on the Decisions of Judges" Charles G. Haines used as part of his illustrative material the decisions of forty-one different trial judges on the magistrate's court in New York City. "In 1916, " he reported,

> 17,075 persons were charged before the magistrates with intoxication. Of these, 92 per cent were convicted. But the examination of the record of individual judges showed that one judge discharged 79 per cent of this class of cases. In cases of disorderly conduct one judge heard 566 cases and discharged one person, whereas another judge discharged 18 per cent; another 54 per cent.[31]

Over the next twenty years a number of other scholars interested in public law also tried their hands at using quantitatively oriented approaches.[32] These studies were useful in the general sense of substantiating the belief that judges were influenced by something besides formal legal principles. These early works, however, did little either to specify the values that might be influential or to measure the intensity of their impact on judicial decision making; neither did they succeed in making a deep intellectual impact on political scientists generally.

As noted in chapter 1, the breakthrough came with the publication in 1948 of Pritchett's *The Roosevelt Court.* That book formed a watershed in the study of public law. Pritchett combined an acute feel for politics with careful reading of opinions and simple but effective statistical analyses of votes. He classified cases in a straightforward way as involving such value-laden issues as governmental regulation of the economy, civil liberties (freedom of speech, press, association, travel, and religion), and criminal justice; and then he ranked justices in terms of how often they had voted for and against the contending values in nonunanimous decisions.

Table 5.1 is taken from *The Roosevelt Court* and shows how over a six-year period the justices were divided over claims involving rights of defendants in criminal trials. The last column shows the frequency with which the justices voted for a libertarian result. Frank Murphy and Wiley Rutledge were obviously the most pro-defendant in their voting behavior, leading Black and Douglas by substantial margins and, of course, giving preference to radically different values from those of Stanley Reed, Owen Roberts, Harold Burton, and Fred Vinson.

Table 5.1 also shows, as Pritchett explained, that for every judge a case did not necessarily involve a clash of only two values, such as defendants' rights versus public safety. Federalism might be an important variable,

TABLE 5.1

*Alignments of justices in nonunanimous cases
involving constitutional rights of criminal
defendants in state and federal prosecutions,
1941–1946 terms*

| | No. cases | Decisions for defendant | | |
		State cases	Federal cases	Total
No. cases		18	33	51
Majority	51	28%	48%	41%
Murphy	50	94	88	90
Rutledge	41	93	88	90
Black	51	83	55	65
Douglas	51	78	55	63
Stone	34	42	45	44
Frankfurter	51	11	55	39
Jackson	32	18	40	28
Reed	51	22	30	27
Roberts	26	0	47	27
Burton	25	14	17	16
Vinson	10	0	0	0

Source: C. Herman Pritchett, *The Roosevelt Court: A Study in Judicial Politics
and Values, 1937–1947* (New York: Macmillan, 1948), p. 162.
Copyright, 1948, by C. Herman Pritchett. Reprinted by permission.

and as Pritchett later spelled out in greater detail, so might a judge's concept
of his proper role. Table 5.1, for instance, shows Frankfurter to have
been much more willing to reverse federal rather than state convictions,
supporting avowals in his opinions about the high value he put on federalism.

What Pritchett demonstrated was that, at least with the U.S. Supreme
Court in a particular time period, one could rank judges along certain value
dimensions. These statistics showed that, no matter what other values
might be present, Justice Murphy was far more willing to vote to support
defendants' claims than was Justice Frankfurter, and Justice Frankfurter
was more willing to do so than was Justice Reed. These statistics do not
indicate that Justice Reed was either more or less willing to vote to protect
libertarian results than anyone who was not on the Court during this period,
nor that Reed, the man, was not as sympathetic as Murphy, the man, to
defendants' claims.

Like Mason's biography of Stone, published eight years later, *The
Roosevelt Court* evoked boos as well as cheers. More serious than the

implicit and perennial assertion that somehow the sanctity of the judicial tabernacle was being violated by one not properly prepared—that is, not licensed as a member of the bar—to perform that holy ritual were charges that the kind of statistical analyses Pritchett used distorted what actually transpired in the processes of decision making. The bill of particulars included charges that (1) counting votes as equal in all cases is patently erroneous, since some cases are intrinsically more important than others; (2) classifying cases in such categories as civil liberties or economic regulation imposes vague and highly subjective criteria on the work of judges, because a judge may have perceived a case as involving a clash of federal versus state power, not as one of laissez faire versus government control of business; and (3) classifying cases as involving dichotomous choices oversimplifies the complex of values that may be in conflict.[33]

Pritchett himself was aware of these potential pitfalls and had sought to avoid them by combining this voting analysis with careful examinations of published opinions, by weighing the importance of cases in his discussion as well as counting decisions in his tables, by recognizing that because a final decision can be categorized as for or against a particular value does not mean that the judge saw this value as present or that this was the only value set that was influential,[34] and by displaying a cautious skepticism about the objective nature of any classification of cases. His own claims for his novel techniques were modest:

> I am fully aware of the limitations of statistical methods in dealing with the materials of the kind involved here. The greater precision and certainty which such methods appear to yield may, under the circumstances, be in part illusory. Nevertheless, I am convinced that the counting and the charting have a positive contribution to make to the understanding of the motivations of the present court.[35]

Whatever the merits, general or specific, of the criticism leveled at the use of quantitative techniques, that criticism did not succeed in dampening interest, though perhaps it did delay further innovation. In any event, along with the criticism of *The Roosevelt Court* went heavy praise and frequent imitation.

Scaling

A decade after the publication of *The Roosevelt Court*, the controversy over the utility of statistical methods had not yet died down. But it was now widely accepted that quantitative techniques were useful tools for understanding judicial behavior, and a new group of scholars was moving beyond the nominal statistics Pritchett had employed. A shinier mousetrap had come on the scene, an ordinal instrument variously referred to as "cumulative scaling," "Guttman scaling," or "scalogram analysis." Jessie Bernard, a sociologist, published the first application of cumulative scaling to judicial voting behavior in 1955,[36] and by 1960 scalogram analysis had become the register key, as it were, on some professional clarinets.

Scaling was one product of a long series of attempts to transform ostensibly nominal data into ordinal and interval scales.* Early work by such people as E. S. Bogardus[37] had been superseded in the late 1920s and early 1930s by the scaling methods of Louis L. Thurstone[38] and Rensis Likert.[39] These latter approaches seemed to some at the time to offer promise of attaining the Holy Grail of interval measurement. But growing uneasiness that the Thurstone and Likert scales might not even be ordinal— because there was no certain way of showing that the objects scaled fell along a single dimension and hence constituted a single well-structured set of behavioral responses—led to renewed efforts to establish demonstrably ordinal scales. A breakthrough came when Louis Guttman, a mathematical sociologist, developed the cumulative scaling technique that sometimes bears his name.[40]

A simple illustration can provide a general notion of what unidimensional cumulative scaling is all about. Suppose that a dozen people are asked to answer each of the following questions:

1. Do you think that you weigh more than 135 pounds?
2. Do you think that you weigh more than 160 pounds?
3. Do you think that you weigh more than 175 pounds?
4. Do you think that you weigh more than 200 pounds?

Table 5.2, called a scalogram, presents an imaginary set of answers of the sort we might reasonably expect. This response set satisfies the conditions

---

* In this context "nominal," "ordinal," and "interval" refer to the ways in which we can classify and measure data. Nominal data are classifiable in regard to one or more specified characteristics. For instance, either a Supreme Court case involves an issue of civil liberties (assuming one can define civil liberties in an operationally acceptable manner), or it does not; a judge is a Democrat, or he is not; he is a Protestant, or he is not; he is willing to go along with the majority when he is outvoted, or he is not. Ordinal data can be classified in this way, but can also be ranked in terms of the amount of a particular characteristic they contain. When data are nominal, they can be categorized in such a fashion as to help answer the question, "To which of these classes does an item belong?" But when the data are ordinal, they permit an attack on an additional question: "Does one item in a class contain more or less of the characteristic used to determine class membership than each of the other items in the class?" Sometimes even this second question does not exhaust our knowledge of the data. We point out in chapter 7 that if we can pin numbers on data in a defensible manner, we open the doors to some of the most sophisticated statistical techniques available for studying a variety of interesting problems in public law.

To meet interval requirements, data in a class must not only be numbered in a defensible manner but numbered in such a way that the distances between items bear the same relationships as intervals do in a numerical system. Not only is five less than ten and ten less than fifteen, but the interval between five and ten is the same as that between ten and fifteen. This does not imply, however, that ten is twice as large as five or that fifteen is three times as large, as does the structure of cardinal numbers. Standard multivariate statistical techniques almost never presuppose a scale more demanding than interval measurement.

TABLE 5.2

Model of a scalogram

Respondent identification	Questions about estimated weight			
	(+ 135 lbs.)	(+ 160 lbs.)	(+ 175 lbs.)	(+ 200 lbs.)
A	Y	Y	Y	Y
B,C,D	Y	Y	Y	N
E,F	Y	Y	N	N
G,H,I,J	Y	N	N	N
K,L	N	N	N	N

for ordinal measurement indicated in the footnote on page 127; that is, each item must share a basis for classification with every other item in the group, and each item must have an equal, lesser, or greater amount of the matter classified than every other item under analysis. Each of the questions relates to a single basis for classification—the attribute of weight. In addition, an answer to each question can be ranked unambiguously vis-à-vis an answer to every other question. An affirmative answer to question 4 requires a higher estimate of one's weight than does an affirmative answer to questions 3, 2, and 1; an affirmative answer to question 3 requires a higher weight estimate than an affirmative answer to 2 and 1; and an affirmative answer to 2 requires a higher estimate than an affirmative answer to 1. Hence a "yes" in response to question 2 implies a "yes" to question 1 as well, just as a "yes" to question 4 implies the same response to 3, 2, and 1. The responses are thus *cumulative*: An affirmative answer to any specific question implies an affirmative answer to all questions ranked below it.

The quality of cumulativeness leads us to another important quality: reproducibility. Once we know a respondent's scale position—the point at which his affirmative answers cease and his negative answers begin—we can reproduce his entire set of responses. The scale position for respondents B, C, and D in Table 5.2 is 3 because question 3 represents the largest weight class to which they offer affirmative answers. If an individual's answers are entirely consistent, we can reproduce all of them correctly when we know his position on a scale. Knowing that respondents E and F hold scale position 2 enables us to reproduce their responses to all four questions correctly. A perfect scale like the model in Table 5.2 has perfect reproducibility because we would not make even a single mistake in predicting the entire set of forty-eight responses from the scale positions of the twelve members of the group. The array is *unidimensional* because a single scale can adequately account for the entire response set.

Now let us replace question 2, Do you think that you weigh more than

160 pounds? with the query, Do you think that in its decisions the Supreme Court of the United States favors any particular group or groups in this country? Since we have no plausible basis for believing that feeling about the Court's impartiality is in any way related to how much people think they weigh, we would expect the responses to the substituted question to disrupt the response pattern in Table 5.2. All four items no longer share a common attribute. We could not reasonably expect to reproduce correctly the answers a respondent provides to the questions about his weight from his answer to the item about the impartiality of the Supreme Court.

Suppose that we substitute still another item for question 2. This time let us replace, Do you think that you weigh more than 160 pounds? with Do you think that you weigh more now than you did a year ago? Unlike the first substitution, this one seems to have something in common with questions 1, 3, and 4: All involve an estimate by each respondent of the magnitude of his present weight. Nevertheless, a moment's reflection removes any expectation that the scale will remain intact. By the time virtually all educable persons have reached the age of six or seven, they have been conditioned to think routinely of weight as a continuum expressed in cardinal numbers, a unit of measurement that satisfies ordinal requirements. Our original set of questions required each individual to compare his present weight to the same baseline—several well-defined and firmly fixed reference points that stand in ordinal relationship to one another on the weight continuum. Hence the responses of the group to these questions would necessarily result in a unidimensional ordinal scale. But in asking each of several respondents to compare his weight of a year ago, the basis for comparison becomes variable and the data points for last year's weight can have no fixed relationship to the points on the weight continuum defined in questions 1, 3, and 4. How an individual responds to the question involving a comparison of present to former weight will thus be entirely independent of his answers to the original questions; such a response can no more be expected to help us reproduce correctly his answers to questions 1, 2, and 4 than could his reaction to the item about the Supreme Court's impartiality.

When scholars in public law use scaling techniques,[41] judges are the respondents; cases pose the questions; and votes cast by judges provide the answers. After selecting a set of cases in accordance with a plausible basis for classification—such as civil liberties, economic regulation, taxation, or federalism—scholars have categorized judges' votes in each case as favorable or unfavorable and then have sought to arrange them in a matrix similar to that in Table 5.2. All this seems simple enough, but why bother?

The reasons why one might want to scale judicial votes can be better appreciated if we compare what can be done with a given set of votes by treating them in a nominal fashion and then attempting to scale them

TABLE 5.3

Twenty-one federal criminal defendants' claims
cases, U.S. Supreme Court, 1946–1952 terms
(selected justices only)

Justice	Favored claim		Opposed claim		Total	
	N	%	N	%	N	%
Murphy	13	100	0	0	13	100
Douglas	17	85	3	15	20	100
Frankfurter	16	80	4	20	20	100
Jackson	12	60	8	40	20	100
Clark	1	14	6	86	7	100
Burton	3	14	18	86	21	100
Reed	2	10	19	90	21	100
Vinson	0	0	21	100	21	100
Minton	0	0	7	100	7	100

Data source: C. Herman Pritchett, *Civil Liberties and the Vinson Court*
(Chicago: University of Chicago Press, 1954), *passim.*

cumulatively.   Table 5.3 reports the votes of selected U.S. Supreme Court
judges in a set of twenty-one nonunanimous federal criminal defendants'
cases decided during the 1946–1952 terms.   In this table, which is the type
used by Pritchett for aligning judges on a policy value, each judge is positioned
in accordance with the percentage of his total votes favoring defendants'
claims.   The differences among the justices are striking.   Murphy supported
the defendants in every case in which he participated.   Vinson and Minton,
on the other hand, did not cast a single vote in behalf of a criminal defendant.
The remaining justices upheld claims in 10 to 85 percent of the cases in
which they participated.   These data provide prima facie evidence for
contending that the justices can be ranked as they appear in Table 5.3 in
regard to the strength of their commitment to the rights of criminal defendants.

As we pointed out earlier in this chapter, however, there is a prickly
problem inherent in drawing firm conclusions from this kind of data: We
have no assurance that every justice considered the claim made by the
defendant a central, or even an important, issue in every case.   Furthermore,
not every justice participated in all twenty-one cases.   Only three—Burton,
Vinson, and Reed—voted in all of them, whereas Clark and Minton took
part in only one case in every three.   Putting the first problem aside for the
moment and assuming that each judge viewed the claim itself as central to
every case in which he voted, let us see how far the data in Table 5.3 permit
us safely to proceed in comparing the solicitude for criminal defendants
displayed by these nine Supreme Court justices.

Once we assume that every judge treated defendants' rights as a principal parameter, we have no difficulty in ranking those who voted in all twenty-one cases in accordance with their partiality for defendants' rights. Burton is unquestionably more supportive than Reed (Burton > Reed), who is, in turn, more supportive than Vinson (Reed > Vinson). Justice Jackson participated in twenty cases and favored the claims in twelve of them. Even if his missing vote had been unfavorable, he would have been more partial to the defendants than Burton, Reed, and Vinson (Jackson > Burton > Reed > Vinson).

The position of Frankfurter can be determined in similar fashion. He also cast twenty votes, sixteen of them favorable. His missing vote, even if it had been unfavorable, would still have left him more partial to the defendants than Justice Jackson. Furthermore, Douglas, who is also missing only one vote, can be ranked vis-à-vis Frankfurter. Taking the information in the table at face value, we can consider Douglas slightly more supportive of federal criminal defendants than Frankfurter. Frankfurter's and Douglas' relative positions would not have changed had the missing vote for each justice been identical, whether positive or negative. But if Douglas' missing vote had been unfavorable and Frankfurter's favorable, then both justices would be tied, with scores of 17 to 4. Hence, Douglas cannot be less favorable to criminal defendants than Frankfurter and may be more so (Douglas ≥ Frankfurter). It follows that six of the nine judges may be ordered from the data in Table 5.3 alone: Douglas ≥ Frankfurter > Jackson > Burton > Reed > Vinson.

Comparing the remaining judges with these six is more hazardous. Justice Murphy, although he supported the defendant every time he voted, did not participate in eight cases. Had as many as six of these eight missing votes been favorable, Murphy would necessarily have ranked first, because every other judge in the table opposed the defendants at least three times. On the other hand, had all of Murphy's missing votes opposed the claims, then Douglas, Frankfurter, and possibly also Clark and Minton would have ranked above him. Similarly, Minton, who opposed the defendants each of the seven times he participated, might conceivably have cast all fourteen of his missing votes favorably and hence might have ranked above everybody except Douglas and Frankfurter—or he might have cast them negatively and thus tied with Vinson for the lowest ranking. Justice Clark presents the same kind of problem. He, like Murphy and Minton, cannot be ranked with any confidence from the data provided in Table 5.3.

By making fuller use of the data employed in constructing Table 5.3, we can refine our analysis somewhat, even without resorting to scalogram analysis. Table 5.4 is an array containing the complete voting record of the judges in the twenty-one cases reported in Table 5.3. We have ordered the cases in the array chronologically and the judges, as in Table 5.3, by the

TABLE 5.4

Votes cast by selected U.S. Supreme Court justices in nonunanimous criminal defendants' cases (1946–1952 terms)

Justices (ordered by percentage of support)	Cases (ordered chronologically)																					Number of votes
	1	2	3	4	5	6	7	8	9	10	11	12	13	14	15	16	17	18	19	20	21	
Murphy	+	+	+	+	+	+	+	+	+	+	+	+	+	0	0	0	0	0	0	0	0	13
Douglas	+	−	+	+	+	+	+	+	+	+	+	+	−	0	+	+	+	−	+	+	+	20
Frankfurter	−	+	+	+	+	+	+	+	+	−	+	+	+	+	−	+	+	+	0*	+	+	20
Jackson	+	+	+	+	+	0	−	+	+	−	−	0	+	+	−	+	−	−	−	0	−	21
Clark	0	0	0	0	+	0	0	0	0	0	0	0	0	−	0	+	−	−	−	−	−	7
Burton	+	−	+	−	+	−	−	−	−	−	−	0	−	−	−	+	+	−	−	−	−	21
Reed	+	−	+	−	+	−	−	−	−	−	0	0	−	−	−	−	−	−	−	−	−	21
Vinson	−	−	−	−	0	0	0	−	−	−	0	0	0	−	−	−	−	−	−	−	−	21
Minton	0	0	0	0	+	0	0	0	0	0	0	0	0	0	−	0	−	−	−	−	−	7

Legend + = favored claim
  − = opposed claim
  0 = not participating
  * = technically speaking, Frankfurter participated in this case; but he refused to take a stand in regard to the defendant's claim

Data source: C. Herman Pritchett, *Civil Liberties and the Vinson Court* (Chicago: University of Chicago Press, 1954), *passim.*

percentage of support for criminal defendants' claims. Table 5.4 enables us to compare the voting behavior of two or more judges in every case in which they jointly participated. We can now rank Justice Murphy with greater precision than before. Murphy and Douglas, who participated jointly in thirteen cases, disagreed twice. In both instances of disagreement Murphy supported the defendants and Douglas refused to do so. Thus we may infer that Murphy should be ranked above Douglas (Murphy > Douglas). Since the analysis of Table 5.3 indicates that Douglas ≥ Frankfurter, we would expect Table 5.4 to show that Murphy should also be ranked above Frankfurter. A comparison of joint Murphy-Frankfurter participations confirms this expectation. On each of the three occasions when they disagreed, Murphy favored claims by the defendants and Frankfurter opposed them.

The data in Table 5.3 permitted the conclusion that Douglas should be ranked at least equal to Frankfurter and perhaps above him (Douglas ≥ Frankfurter). The data in Table 5.4 warrant a more precise statement of their relationship. Douglas and Frankfurter disagreed seven times, with Douglas supporting the defendants on four occasions and Frankfurter on only three. Table 5.4 thus indicates even more strongly than Table 5.3 that Douglas may be ranked above Frankfurter (Douglas > Frankfurter).

Our analysis, however, bogs down with Clark and Minton. Although Justice Minton disagreed with Douglas, Frankfurter, Jackson, and Burton —he ranks below all of them—he cannot be compared with Murphy, with whom Minton never served, nor differentiated from Reed, Vinson, and Clark, with whom he never disagreed. We run into the same sort of difficulty with Justice Clark. Still the array in Table 5.4 enables us to rank seven of the nine justices: Murphy > Douglas > Frankfurter > Jackson > Burton > Reed > Vinson. This ranking of the judges, although certainly an improvement over that justified by Table 5.3, is less than fully satisfying. But if the array in Table 5.4 can be converted into a scalogram, analysis can take several giant steps. Table 5.5 represents an attempt to rearrange the data in Table 5.4 to form a unidimensional cumulative scale resembling the model presented in Table 5.2.

In positioning both judges and cases in Table 5.5, we have shuffled the rows and columns about so as to minimize the number of inconsistent votes cast. An inconsistent vote, as may be recalled from the discussion of the model scale in Table 5.2, occurs whenever a "minus" appears to the left or a "plus" to the right of a respondent's scale position (denoted for each justice by the vertical thrusts in the solid, steplike line that meanders across the array from its lower-left to its upper-right corners). We used seven justices and nineteen cases in defining the structure of the array. Justices Clark and Minton participated in too few cases to provide useful data in its construction, and cases numbered 19 and 20 are missing key

TABLE 5.5

Scalogram of votes cast by selected U.S. Supreme Court justices in nineteen federal criminal defendants' cases (1946–1952 terms)

Justices \ Category	I		II					III					IV				V			Number of votes	Errors	Possible errors	Unclassifiable cases 20	19
Identification number	3	1	16	5	6	8	14	9	18	4	2	13	7	12	17	21	15	10	11					
Murphy	+	+	0	+	+	+	0	+	0	+	+	+	+	+	0	0	0	+	+	13	0	0	0	0
Douglas	+	+	+	+	+	+	0	+	⊖	+	⊖	⊖	+	+	+	0	+	+	+	18	3	3	+	+
Frankfurter	⊖	+	+	+	+	+	0	+	+	+	+	+	+	+	+	+	+	+	+	19	1	4	+	0
Jackson	+	+	+	+	+	+	+	+	+	+	+	+	−	−	⊕	+	−	−	−	19	0	7	0	−
Burton	+	+	+	+	−	−	−	−	−	−	+	+	−	−	−	−	−	−	−	19	1	4	−	−
Reed	+	+	+	−	−	−	−	−	−	−	−	−	−	−	−	−	−	−	−	19	0	2	−	−
Vinson	−	−	−	−	−	−	−	−	−	−	−	−	−	−	−	−	−	−	−	19	0	0	−	−
																				126	**5**	**20**		
Clark	0	0	0	0	0	0	−	0	−	0	−	0	0	0	0	−	−	0	0				−	−
Minton	0	0	0	0	0	0	−	0	−	0	0	0	0	0	0	−	0	0	0				−	−

CR = .961
S = .750

Data source: C. Herman Pritchett, *Civil Liberties and the Vinson Court* (Chicago: University of Chicago Press, 1954), *passim.*

134

votes necessary for determining with adequate precision where these controversies belong.

The array resulting from our positioning of the 127 votes by seven judges in nineteen cases does not constitute a perfect scale because we would make five errors in reproducing the judges' votes from their scale positions. These errors, one apiece for Frankfurter and Burton and three for Douglas, are circled in Table 5.5. Perfect consistency cannot, to be sure, be expected in most areas of human endeavor, and certainly not in adjudication, where competing interests are almost always involved.

How much inconsistency can be tolerated without destroying the fundamentally cumulative character of a scale? Two methods conventionally used by students of judicial behavior for determining whether a set of votes has been cumulatively scaled on a single dimension are the Coefficient of Reproducibility (CR) and the Coefficient of Scalability (S). When CR exceeds .90 and S exceeds .60, many scholars consider an attempt to scale successful.

As its name implies, CR is a measure of the extent to which an array can be reproduced accurately from the scale positions of the respondents. Since we can correctly reproduce 122 of the 127 votes cast by the seven judges in the nineteen cases used to structure the array in Table 5.5, its CR is .961, that is, 122 divided by 127.

The proportion of potentially inconsistent votes that turned out to be consistent is measured by S. For example, in every case Vinson voted against the defendants and Murphy for them. Thus neither judge could have cast even a single inconsistent vote, whereas Jackson, who voted for the defendants twelve times and against them seven times, could have cast a maximum of seven inconsistent votes (in cases numbered 7, 12, 17, 21, 15, 10, and 11). Reed could have voted inconsistently no more than twice (in cases numbered 3 and 1), Douglas three times (in cases numbered 18, 2, and 13), and so on. All told, the 127 votes cast by the seven judges in the nineteen cases could have contained no more than twenty errors, the sum total of the smaller number of each judge's votes. S, therefore, is .750, or 15 divided by 20.

Both CR and S for Table 5.5 are substantially above the minimum levels conventionally employed by students of public law for establishing the existence of a unidimensional cumulative scale. Although there is some professional exception taken to the adequacy of these measures for demonstrating scalability, for present purposes we may and do assume that the array in Table 5.5 constitutes a valid scalogram.

The scalogram in Table 5.5 enables us to carry the analysis of the voting behavior of these U.S. Supreme Court justices far beyond what proved possible with these same data as portrayed in Tables 5.3 and 5.4. First, and perhaps most important, scalogram analysis enables us to determine whether a set of data can actually be scaled in accordance with a hypothesized dimension. The scalogram in Table 5.5 appears unidimensional and thereby supports what Tables 5.3 and 5.4 left as an untested assumption—that the judges actually treated defendants' claims as the central issue in the entire set of cases. It would be more cautious to say that the scalogram demonstrates that whatever went on in the judges' minds, an analyst who treated these cases as involving defendants' claims could account for the judges' votes with remarkable accuracy.

The scalogram also indicates that the data are cumulative. As the cases are analyzed here, they fall into five categories ordered in such a way that positive votes in a higher category imply positive votes in all cases ranked in lower categories. Thus we can plausibly infer that a less intense commitment to civil liberties is required for a favorable response to category I cases (numbered 3 and 1) than for category II cases (numbered 16), as, in turn, a less intense commitment is required to respond favorably to a category II case than a category III case (numbered 5, 6, 8, 14, 9, 18, 4, 2, and 13), and so forth. The behavior of every justice, as represented by the data in Table 5.5, is consonant with this attitudinal structure.

A third advantage of the scalogram in Table 5.5 over Tables 5.3 and 5.4 is that the scalogram increases our ability to assuage the trauma caused by missing votes. We now know how Murphy voted in every category of cases. We can, therefore, predict with a considerably smaller risk of error that he would have voted for the defendant in each case in which he did not take part. The scalogram even carries us a fair distance toward defining the scale positions of Clark and Minton. Clark, who belonged to the same scale-type as Justice Burton, did not support claims less intensive than those in category II. We also know that Minton did not support category III claims, but we do not have sufficient information to predict how he would have reacted in cases belonging to category II. Missing data remain somewhat troublesome, though to a lesser degree than in Tables 5.3 and 5.4.

The partial resolution of missing data problems leads to a fourth advantage of the scalogram in Table 5.5. We can now rank the justices in regard to their sensitivity to claims by federal criminal defendants with greater accuracy and precision than before. The improved ranking is Murphy = Douglas > Frankfurter > Jackson > Burton = Clark > Reed > Vinson. Where Minton belongs remains unresolved.

A final advantage of scalogram analysis—assessing the impact of personnel change on a court—can be more effectively illustrated if we supplement the data in Table 5.5 and simplify its format as in Table 5.6. The voting patterns of all members of the Court during its 1946–1952 terms appear by case category. This scalogram indicates that if a judge like Murphy (scale position = category V) were replaced by a judge like Burton (scale position = category II), the majority in favor of category IV claims

TABLE 5.6

Summary scalogram of voting patterns:
Nineteen nonunanimous federal criminal
defendants' cases, U.S. Supreme Court
(1946–1952 terms)

Justices	Case category				
	I	II	III	IV	V
Murphy	+	+	+	+	+
Rutledge	+	+	+	+	+
Douglas	+	+	+	+	+
Black	+	+	+	+	+
Frankfurter	+	+	+	+	−
Jackson	+	+	+	−	−
Burton	+	+	−	−	−
Reed	+	−	−	−	−
Vinson	−	−	−	−	−
Court division	8–1	7–2	6–3	5–4	4–5
Clark	0	+	−	−	−
Minton	0	0	−	−	−

Data source: C. Herman Pritchett, *Civil Liberties and the Vinson Court* (Chicago: University of Chicago Press, 1954), *passim.*

would be lost. If, in addition, a second justice occupying scale position V were also replaced with yet another man like Burton, then the majority for category III cases would be lost as well. In fact, this is just what happened when Clark and Minton filled the seats vacated by Murphy and Rutledge in 1949. Clark's voting pattern—which has been entered together with Minton's beneath the scalogram proper—shows that his appropriate scale position is identical to Burton's, that is, to category II. Minton's position, although not precisely defined, is certainly no more favorable to criminal defendants in federal trials than are those of either Burton or Clark and may be even less so. Hence the data in Table 5.6 reveal that once Clark and Minton had replaced Murphy and Rutledge, defendants could no longer win category III and category IV cases when all nine justices participated.

Scalogram analysis is by no means confined to the U.S. Supreme Court but can be used to study any court for which two conditions are met. First, the court must consist of at least five judges, each of whom participates in most of a sizable set of nonunanimous decisions. Second, the votes cast must be reported. The highest appellate courts in several American states— Colorado, Iowa, Wisconsin, and Michigan among them—and constitutional courts in Australia, Canada, India, Ireland, and Japan satisfy these requirements. An earlier version of the present chapter used data on the

Supreme Court of Japan (presented by Dr. Takeo Hayakawa in the references cited in footnote 41 of this chapter) to illustrate cumulative scaling, but we replaced it with material on the U.S. Supreme Court because unfamiliar names made the argument more difficult to follow. An appendix to this chapter contains a revised version of part of his original scalogram prepared expressly for this book by Professor Hayakawa. From the appended Table 5.8 the reader can replicate much of the argument that appears in the previous several pages.

Cumulative scaling of judicial voting behavior, as we earlier hinted, has not been free from dispute. Bones of contention include the adequacy of the conventional tests for unidimensionality and scalability, methods for positioning the columns and rows of the scalogram matrix, the designation of cutting points when several seem equally appropriate, the handling of missing data, and the frequent impossibility of developing a unique solution for a given set of data. Anyone passionately enough interested in pursuing the "not-so-niceties" of this rather acerbic controversy can do so in the professional literature. There is no need here to pick our way through that heavily shell-pocked battleground. The central issue, however, is one that we cannot well avoid: Are the scalogram matrices developed by judicial behavioralists really cumulative scales?

Let us recall the original weight illustrations, mentioned previously. Each respondent was asked to compare his own weight with each of a series of indisputably ordinal reference points. The assumption was that if a series of items constitute an ordinal scale, responses to those stimuli would be reproducible. Now consider what the judicial analyst typically does. He shuffles the votes cast in a set of legal cases so that the responses of the judges are reproducible—and then he assumes, if his efforts prove successful, that he has developed an ordinal scale. Observe the reversal in reasoning.

From: If a series of items constitutes an ordinal scale, then responses to these items will be reproducible.

To: If a set of responses can be ordered in a reproducible fashion, then the items triggering the responses constitute an ordinal scale.

The logical statement "If *A*, then *B*" has been transformed to the very different proposition "If *B*, then *A*." The hazard in such a reversal is patent. The most one can properly claim is that an ordinal scale may be involved if a set of judicial votes can be arranged in reproducible fashion.

How can we tell whether a scalogram is spurious? It is impossible to know for certain. Most social scientists who are committed to cumulative scaling seek to devise a set of items—frequently by trial and error—that results in a high degree of reproducible responses when administered repeatedly to different groups of people. Once a set of items has been shown, time and again, to trigger reproducible responses, the set is assumed to constitute a valid scale. But a set of items is not assumed to form a scale until *after* repeated applications to many groups have resulted in response patterns that satisfy the conventional criteria for reproducibility and scalability.

The public law analyst cannot follow this painstaking procedure because the number of relevant judges is almost always too small. As a result, he has tended to assume that the conventional tests can be applied to any given set of judicial votes to determine the existence of a cumulative scale. These tests, however, have no standard error; that is, there are no tests to tell us the probability that any given set of votes could be expected to satisfy them. There is also reason to suspect that the minimum criteria of CR and S are all too readily met by the more common judicial scaling techniques. We certainly do not argue that all judicial scales are spurious, merely that the conventional tests per se are far from satisfactory guides in separating the wheat from the chaff. The CRs and Ss, like the blood test for paternity, can eliminate certain hypothesized sets of relationships as clearly incorrect, but cannot establish the existence of true ones.

Although the judicial behavioralist may not be able to adopt the more defensible procedures used by many other cumulative scalers, his standards for evaluating his scales could be tightened. For example, he could begin by drawing a sample from the universe of relevant cases, such as those concerned with civil liberties, and seek to scale the votes contained in the sample. If his efforts to scale the sample cases met conventional criteria, he could then articulate the characteristics that presumably render the cases in the sample ordinal. Next the analyst could classify the remaining cases in the civil liberties universe in accordance with the characteristics identified. Finally, these cases could be randomly assigned to subsets and the cases in each subset arranged in the order taken in the original scalogram by cases with comparable characteristics. If the matrix for each of the subsets were to yield sufficiently high CRs and Ss, confidence in the validity of the original scale would be substantially enhanced. Such procedures are laborious, but validity, like chastity, is a demanding virtue.

A final comment on scaling is necessary. We have deliberately avoided discussing what has been called multidimensional scaling because of the conceptual confusion growing out of this term: (1) Scholars have occasionally constructed several scales to handle different sets of cases, and sometimes this kind of analysis is called multidimensional scaling. (2) There is a computer routine called Multiple Scalogram Analysis that can be used to extract different sets of scales for the same data, which is also sometimes called multidimensional scaling. (3) Some scholars have tried to cope with cases that simultaneously present several different kinds of stimuli by using techniques such as factor analysis or discriminant function analysis. A list of some of the basic literature in public law using different kinds of multidimensional scaling will be found in the Notes section.[42]   Although each of these techniques has its own peculiar problems, they do allow analysis to proceed on the basis that litigation may provide judges with several different stimuli rather than merely one.

Role Analysis

In addition to raising questions about such substantive problems as civil rights, national versus local authority, or the legitimacy of economic regulation, cases may also present judges with problems about their proper role in a government system.   Unhappily, the term "role" has many meanings. In chapter 2 we used the word to refer to the actual behavior of judges. In that context we outlined some of the implications for a political system of various judicial roles as interpreting rules, defining boundaries, supervising, legislating, representing, stabilizing, and educating.   In this chapter we shall use "role" in a normative sense to refer to a set of notions about the proper way for a person who holds a particular position or status to behave.*   We shall restrict our discussion to the position of constitutional court judges and to the ideas that these judges themselves have of what is proper behavior for them.   What lawyers, legislators, or members of the general public may deem fitting will be omitted, though those beliefs lurk in the background.†

This normative concept of role has been developed by sociologists[43] and used with some success by political scientists in other fields, most notably in the legislative process.[44]   It is a pleasing notion in that it immediately explains in an intuitive manner much of the conflict that has occurred among judges.   Oliver Wendell Holmes' dissent against the Social Darwinism of his colleagues was not basically grounded on substantive policy differences —for in his own way and for his own reasons Holmes was a believer in the gospel of laissez faire.   Rather the nub of the dispute lay in competing sets of notions about what judges, as judges, should and should not do.   Holmes firmly believed that if the touchstone of due process of law was reasonable-

---

* Wahlke and his associates have offered a useful definition, although one not universally or uniformly used by social scientists, or even by political scientists: "a coherent set of 'norms' of behavior which are thought by those involved in the interactions being viewed, to apply to all persons who occupy the position" under study.   John C. Wahlke, Heinz Eulau, William Buchanan, and LeRoy C. Ferguson, *The Legislative System: Explorations in Legislative Behavior* (New York: Wiley, 1962), p. 8.

† Not only are judges apt to differ among themselves on what is or is not proper role behavior, but members of other groups are likely to disagree with each other and with judges.   Conflicting role expectations can thus be an important variable in accounting not only for judicial decisions but also for the course of judicial-legislative relations and for changing public attitudes toward a court.

ness, then judges ought not to read any particular economic theory into the Constitution. "The Fourteenth Amendment," he said in 1905, "does not enact Mr. Herbert Spencer's *Social Statics*."[45] A year earlier he had reminded his colleagues that "legislators are ultimate guardians of the liberties and welfare of the people in quite as great a degree as the courts."[46] In 1930 he commented bitterly, "I cannot believe that the [Fourteenth] Amendment was intended to give us carte blanche to embody our economic or moral beliefs in its prohibitions."[47]

In the 1930s Harlan Fiske Stone's long debate with George Sutherland and the other Four Horsemen who fought the New Deal was over the same fundamental issue of role, not substantive policy. For while the New Deal was undoubtedly more repulsive to Sutherland than to Stone, it was not at all attractive to Stone's brand of Republicanism. But, like Holmes, Stone thought there were strict limits on how far judges should go in imposing their views about economic regulation on legislators and on the country. "Courts," he warned, "are not the only agency of government that must be assumed to have capacity to govern."[48]

Political scientists have frequently used the concept of role to analyze judicial decisions, but—like judges—until recently, they typically used the word in a general sense, not in the rigorous fashion of sociologists. In *Civil Liberties and the Vinson Court* Pritchett tried to employ the idea of role more systematically. His working hypothesis, he explained, was that in civil liberties cases there were two primary influences on a judge's decision. First was his sympathy toward libertarian claims. Second was the judge's concept of his role, of his obligations and freedom as a judge.

> Every justice in deciding a case must give some thought to what is appropriate for him as a judge to do. The pressures which bear upon him are many, and they are mostly toward a pattern of conformity—conformity with precedents, conformity with the traditions of the law, conformity with public expectations as to how a judge should act, conformity toward established divisions of authority in a federal system based on the principle of separation of powers. While no justice can be oblivious to these pressures, they are not self-enforcing and he is free to make his own interpretations of their requirements.[49]

Pritchett found that this normative concept of role accounted for much of the variance in the way that Justices Murphy, Rutledge, Douglas, and Black, on the one hand, and Justice Frankfurter, on the other, voted in cases involving civil liberties. As manifested in their opinions and votes, the first four justices were "result oriented"; they saw protection of individual freedom as among the chief goals of a judge—if not as *the* chief goal. Precedents and procedural rules had to take second place to the purpose of securing substantive justice. Frank Murphy neatly summed it up: "The law knows no finer hour than when it cuts through formal concepts and transitory emotions to protect unpopular citizens against discrimination and prosecution."[50]

Justice Frankfurter professed even more vehemently and frequently than the four activists his passion for freedom. But echoing Holmes' doctrine on economic issues, he said there were tight restrictions on what it was proper for him as a judge—more particularly as a federal judge—to do to protect freedom. Prescribing a role more narrow and more technically legally oriented, he asserted that precedents and procedural rules should have a seriously inhibiting effect on a judge's range of choice. "After all," he dissented in a criminal justice case in which the majority had reversed a state supreme court on grounds that he thought had not been argued before that court, "this is the Nation's ultimate judicial tribunal, not a super-legal-aid bureau."[51] In another case he protested, "This is a court of review, not a tribunal unbounded by rules. We do not sit like a kadi under a tree dispensing justice according to considerations of individual expediency."[52]

Testing Frankfurter's statements against his votes, Pritchett decided that, by and large, the justice's conduct conformed to his role concepts. As

TABLE 5.7

*Voting records of Supreme Court justices for
civil liberties claims in nonunanimous cases
decided during the 1946–1952 terms (in
percentages)*

	All cases	State cases	Federal cases
Murphy	100%	100%	100%
Rutledge	96	100	89
Douglas	89	98	78
Black	87	89	85
Frankfurter	61	40	83
The Court	35	36	35
Jackson	31	11	54
Clark	24	26	20
Burton	22	22	22
Minton	14	20	9
Vinson	14	19	9
Reed	13	19	7

Number of cases = 113

Data source: C. Herman Pritchett, *Civil Liberties and the Vinson Court* (Chicago: University of Chicago Press, 1953), pp. 190, 225. Copyright 1954 by The University of Chicago. Copyright 1954 under the International Copyright Union.

Table 5.7 shows, in all nonunanimous decisions on civil liberties issues during the 1946–1952 terms, Frankfurter voted for those claims much less often than did Murphy, Rutledge, Douglas, or Black. The picture, however, changes when the cases are subdivided into those coming from state courts, in which only constitutional issues were present and in which the role restraints Frankfurter preached should have been at their peak, and those coming from federal courts, in which, according to Frankfurter's avowed norms, the Supreme Court's discretion was wider. In state cases he still supported civil liberties claims more often than did the Court majority, but with nothing approaching the frequency of the Libertarian Four. In federal cases, with role restraints loosened, Frankfurter moved solidly into the libertarian camp, ranking slightly ahead of Douglas as a defender of individual freedom.

Examining a wide variety of cases decided during the U.S. Supreme Court's 1958 and 1959 terms, Joel B. Grossman broadened and refined Pritchett's analysis by using scalograms to measure the effect of Frankfurter's announced role restraints on his voting.[53] The results corroborated the importance of role in Frankfurter's behavior, but the evidence from these two terms was less substantial than it had been when the earlier civil liberties cases were decided.

Pritchett and Grossman depended on statements in opinions to identify the content of a judge's role concepts and on votes to measure the impact of those norms on actual behavior. Other political scientists, notably Theodore L. Becker and Kenneth N. Vines, have in separate studies used interviews in their efforts to discover judicial notions about role. After questioning Hawaiian judges about a hypothetical case, Becker concluded that for a number of jurists the norm of following precedents overrode personal policy preferences.[54] These judges had been fundamentally sympathetic to a claim against a hospital by a patient injured through the negligence of a hospital employee, but when informed that there was a clear precedent in favor of hospitals in such situations, they said that they would decide against the plaintiff.

Vines' studies, not all of which have been reported, are more elaborate and are based on interviews with state supreme court justices in Louisiana, Massachusetts, New Jersey, and Pennsylvania.[55] He has sought to distinguish a variety of role sectors, one of which he refers to as decision-making roles—whether a judge should interpret law or make law in deciding cases. On this basis Vines classified his respondents in three categories: (1) those who said that their task was to interpret the law, (2) those who reported that they inevitably make law, and (3) pragmatists who saw both functions as part of their decision-making job. As one of these pragmatic judges said, "You're interested in having a just result. You can call it law making or law interpreting. It's a combination of all these things."

Although—surprisingly perhaps—Democratic judges in this sample were more apt to report that they saw their job as law interpreting, Vines could not establish any strong associations between perceptions of decision-making roles and actual voting behavior. This failure may have resulted from the particular sample of judges studied, from the narrow time span involved (only one year), or from the character of the role categories employed. In any event, several unpublished doctoral dissertations contain more encouraging findings.[56] Furthermore, role may turn out to be a valuable tool in cross-national analyses. Part of the problem may lie in the fact that the role concepts of American judges, although different from each other, are too close to provide a sensitive gauge. Across national lines, however, role concepts may differ with sufficient sharpness to supply a much more useful instrument to help understand the individual phase of judicial decision making.

APPENDIX TO CHAPTER 5

TABLE 5.8

Votes cast by selected justices in nonunanimous criminal cases involving civil liberties, grand bench, Japanese Supreme Court, 1957–1960 (cases ordered chronologically, judges by percentage of support for civil liberties claims)

Justices									Cases												
	1	2	3	4	5	6	7	8	9	10	11	12	13	14	15	16	17	18	19	20	21
Kotani	+	−	−	+	+	+	+	−	+	+	−	−	+	−	+	+	−	+	−	+	+
Fujita	−	+	−	0	−	+	+	0	−	+	−	−	+	−	+	+	+	+	+	−	−
Kawamura, M.	−	0	−	+	−	+	+	−	−	+	−	+	−	−	0	+	−	+	−	+	+
Tarumi	+	+	−	−	−	+	+	−	+	+	−	+	−	−	−	+	−	+	−	−	−
Shima	−	+	−	−	−	+	+	−	+	+	−	+	−	−	+	+	−	+	−	+	+
Irie	−	+	−	−	−	−	−	−	+	+	−	+	−	−	+	+	−	+	−	+	+
Ikeda	−	−	−	+	+	−	−	+	0	−	−	−	−	+	−	0	−	−	−	−	−
Saito	−	−	−	−	−	−	−	−	−	+	−	−	−	−	0	+	−	−	−	−	−
Tanaka	−	−	−	−	−	−	−	0	0	+	−	−	−	−	−	−	−	−	−	−	−

Legend   + = favored claim
         − = opposed claim
         0 = not participating

Source: This table, which was prepared expressly for this volume by Professor Hayakawa, constitutes a revision of some of the data that originally appeared in Takeo Hayakawa, "Legal Science and Judicial Behavior, with Particular Reference to Civil Liberties in the Japanese Supreme Court," 1962 *Kobe University Law Review* 1; reprinted in Glendon A. Schubert (ed.), *Judicial Behavior: A Reader in Theory and Research* (Chicago: Rand McNally, 1964).

NOTES

1. Oliver Wendell Holmes, *The Common Law* (Boston: Little, Brown, 1881), p. 1.

2. Benjamin Cardozo, *The Nature of the Judicial Process* (New Haven, Conn.: Yale University Press, 1921), p. 10. See also Louis L. Jaffe, *English and American Judges as Lawmakers* (Oxford: Clarendon Press, 1969).

3. Cardozo, *op. cit.,* p. 113.

4. *Ibid.,* p. 13.

5. See especially Karl Llewellyn, *The Bramble Bush: On Our Law and Its Study* (New York: Oceana Publications, 1951, originally published in 1930), and the essays collected in his *Jurisprudence: Realism in Theory and Practice* (Chicago: University of Chicago Press, 1962); for his final statement, see *The Common Law Tradition: Deciding Appeals* (Boston: Little, Brown, 1960).

6. For Jerome Frank's contribution see especially *Law and the Modern Mind* (New York: Brentano's, 1930), and *Courts on Trial: Myth and Reality in American Justice* (Princeton, N.J.: Princeton University Press, 1950).

7. See chapter 1, note 26.

8. See chapter 1, notes 10, 15, and 16.

9. In addition to the works cited in chapter 1, notes 17 and 18, see the bibliography of Corwin's writings collected in Alpheus T. Mason and Gerald Garvey (eds.), *American Constitutional History: Essays by Edward S. Corwin* (New York: Harper & Row, 1964), pp. 216–229.

10. See, for instance, Thomas Reed Powell, "The Judiciality of Minimum Wage Legislation," 37 *Harvard Law Review* 545 (1924); his "Commerce, Pensions, and Codes," 44 *ibid.* 1 and 193 (1935); and the literature cited in chapter 1, note 26.

11. See, for example, the essays collected in 10 *Vanderbilt Law Review* (February 1957) under the title "Studies in Judicial Biography," and in 18 *ibid.* (March 1965) under the same title; Allison Dunham and Philip B. Kurland (eds.), *Mr. Justice* (Chicago: University of Chicago Press, 1956); Joel Francis Paschal, *Mr. Justice Sutherland: A Man Against the State* (Princeton, N.J.: Princeton University Press, 1951); Fowler V. Harper, *Justice Rutledge and the Bright Constellation* (Indianapolis: Bobbs-Merrill Company, 1965); John P. Frank, *Justice Daniel Dissenting* (Cambridge, Mass.: Harvard University Press, 1964); and many of the biographies listed by John R. Schmidhauser, "The Justices of the Supreme Court: A Collective Portrait," 3 *Midwest Journal of Political Science,* 1, 50–57 (1959). For an overview see J. W. Peltason, "Supreme Court Biography and the Study of Public Law," in Gottfried Dietz (ed.), *Essays on the American Constitution* (Englewood Cliffs, N.J.: Prentice-Hall, 1964).

12. Glendon A. Schubert, "Jackson's Judicial Philosophy: An Exploration in Value Analysis," 59 *American Political Science Review* 940 (1965). See also David J. Danelski, *A Supreme Court Justice Is Appointed* (New York: Random House, 1964), pp. 180–190, and Fred Kort, "Content Analysis of Judicial Opinions and Rules of Law," in Schubert (ed.), *Judicial Decision-Making* (New York: Free Press, 1963).

13. For example, Robert C. North *et al., Content Analysis: A Handbook with Applications for the Study of International Crisis* (Evanston, Ill.: Northwestern University Press, 1963).

14. Werner Grunbaum, *St. Louis Supreme Court Dictionary and Programmer's Guide* (mimeographed, 1969).

15. Theodore Schroeder, "The Psychologic Study of Judicial Opinions," 6 *California Law Review* 89, 94, 96 (1918).

16. Harold D. Lasswell, *Power and Personality* (New York: W. W. Norton, 1948), pp. 65–88.

17. Chief Justice Kotaro Tanaka, "Dissenting and Concurring Opinions," in Julius J. Marke and John G. Lexa (eds.), *International Seminar on Constitutional Review* (New York: New York University School of Law, mimeographed, 1963), p. 298.

18. Quoted by David J. Danelski, "The Supreme Court of Japan: An Exploratory Study," in Glendon A. Schubert and Danelski (eds.), *Comparative Judicial Behavior* (New York: Oxford University Press, 1969).

19. Albert J. Beveridge, *The Life of John Marshall*, 4 vols. (Boston: Houghton Mifflin, 1916–1919).

20. Carl B. Swisher, *Stephen J. Field: Craftsman of the Law* (Washington, D.C.: Brookings, 1930).

21. Carl B. Swisher, *Roger B. Taney* (New York: Macmillan, 1935).

22. Alpheus T. Mason used the Taft papers in his *William Howard Taft: Chief Justice* (New York: Simon and Schuster, 1964), as did David J. Danelski in his "The Influence of the Chief Justice in the Decisional Process," in Walter F. Murphy and C. Herman Pritchett (eds.), *Courts, Judges, and Politics* (New York: Random House, 1961), and Murphy in his *Elements of Judicial Strategy* (Chicago: University of Chicago Press, 1964), and *Wiretapping on Trial* (New York: Random House, 1965).

23. J. Woodford Howard, Jr., used the Frank Murphy papers in his *Mr. Justice Murphy: A Political Biography* (Princeton, N.J.: Princeton University Press, 1968), as did Murphy in the latter two books cited in note 22.

24. Edmond Cahn, "Eavesdropping on Justice," *The Nation* (January 5, 1957), p. 14.

25. Thomas Jefferson to Thomas Ritchie, December 25, 1820, in Andrew A. Lipscomb (ed.), *The Writings of Thomas Jefferson* (Washington, D.C.: The Thomas Jefferson Memorial Association, 1903), XV, 297–298.

26. See comment by J. Woodford Howard, Jr., that history may be a series of tricks the dead play on the living: "Judicial Biography and the Behavioral Persuasion," a paper delivered at the 1969 Meetings of the American Political Science Association.

27. Martin v. Struthers, 319 U.S. 141 (1943).

28. For example, Barr v. Columbia, 378 U.S. 146 (1964); Bouie v. Columbia, 378 U.S. 347 (1964); and Bell v. Maryland, 378 U.S. 226 (1964).

29. The Murphy papers, Michigan Historical Collections, Ann Arbor, Michigan.

30. See especially Hugo Black's separate opinions in Milk Wagon Drivers Union v. Meadowmoor Dairies, 312 U.S. 287 (1941), and New York Times v. Sullivan, 376 U.S. 254 (1964); his speech "Absolutes, Courts, and the Bill of Rights," 35 *New York University Law Review* 865 (1960); and a so-called public interview, "Justice Black and First Amendment 'Absolutes,' " 37 *ibid.* 549 (1962).

31. Charles G. Haines, "General Observations on the Effects of Personal, Political, and Economic Influences in the Decisions of Judges," 17 *Illinois Law Review* 96, 105 (1922).

32. See Albert Somit and Joseph Tanenhaus, *The Development of American Political Science* (Boston: Allyn and Bacon, 1967), Part III.

33. C. Herman Pritchett discusses some of these criticisms in *Civil Liberties and the Vinson Court* (Chicago: University of Chicago Press, 1953), pp. 186–192; see also Wallace Mendelson, "The Neo-Behavioral Approach to the Judicial Process: A Critique," 57 *American Political Science Review* 593 (1963).

34. C. Herman Pritchett, *The Roosevelt Court: A Study in Judicial Votes and Values, 1937–1947* (New York: Macmillan, 1948), pp. 255, 262, 266.

35. *Ibid.*, p. xv.

36. Jessie Bernard, "Dimensions and Axes of Supreme Court Decisions," 34 *Social Forces* 19 (1955).

37. E. S. Bogardus, "Measuring Social Distances," 9 *Journal of Applied Sociology* 299 (1925); *Immigration and Race Attitudes* (Boston: Heath, 1928); "A Social Distance Scale," 17 *Sociology and Social Research* 265 (1933).

38. Louis L. Thurstone: "The Method of Paired Comparisons for Social Values," 21 *Journal of Abnormal and Social Psychology* 384 (1927); "Theory of Attitude Measurement," 36 *Psychological Bulletin* 222 (1929); Thurstone and E. J. Chave, *The Measurement of Attitude* (Chicago: University of Chicago Press, 1929).

39. Rensis Likert, *A Technique for the Measurement of Attitudes* (New York: Archives of Psychology, Monograph No. 140, 1932).

40. Louis Guttman, "The Cornell Technique for Scale and Intensity Analysis," 7 *Educational and Psychological Measurement* 247 (1947); Guttman in Samuel Stouffer *et al.*, *Measurement and Prediction* (Princeton, N.J.: Princeton University Press, 1950), chaps. 2, 3, 6, 8, and 9.

41. The literature using scaling is rather large. Glendon A. Schubert laid down some tentative rules in his *Quantitative Analysis of Judicial Behavior* (New York: Free Press, 1959), chap. 5; he indicated later that he felt some of these rules should be changed—in his "Ideologies and Attitudes, Academic and Judicial," 29 *Journal of Politics* 3 (1967). Although he has used unidimensional scaling, Schubert has placed greater reliance on a version of multidimensional scaling. See infra note 42.

A sampling of the scaling literature would include: S. Sidney Ulmer: "Supreme Court Behavior and Civil Rights," 13 *Western Political Quarterly* 288 (1960); "The Analysis of Behavior Patterns in the United States Supreme Court," 22 *Journal of Politics* 629 (1960); "Scaling Judicial Cases: A Methodological Note," 4 *The American Behavioral Scientist* 31 (1961); and "Dimensions of Judicial Voting," 13 *Midwest Journal of Political Science* 471 (1969); Harold J. Spaeth, "Judicial Power As a Variable Motivating Supreme Court Behavior," 6 *Midwest Journal of Political Science* 54 (1962); "An Analysis of Judicial Attitudes in the Labor Relations Decisions of the Warren Court," 25 *Journal of Politics* 290 (1963); "Warren Court Attitudes Toward Business: The 'B' Scale," in Schubert, *Judicial Decision-Making*, supra note 12; and "Unidimensionality and Item Variance in Judicial Scaling," 10 *Behavioral Science* 290 (1965); John R. Schmidhauser, "Judicial Behavior and the Sectional Crisis of 1837–1860," 23 *Journal of Politics* 615 (1961); Joseph Tanenhaus, "The Cumulative Scaling of Judicial Decisions," 79 *Harvard Law Review* 1583 (1966); Takeo Hayakawa, "Legal Science and Judicial Behavior: With Particular Reference to Civil Liberties in the Japanese Supreme Court," *Kobe Law Review* 1 (1962), reprinted in Glendon A. Schubert (ed.), *Judicial Behavior* (Chicago: Rand McNally, 1964); Sidney R. Peck, "The Supreme Court of Canada, 1958–1966: A Search for Policy Through Scalogram Analysis," 45 *Canadian Bar Review* 666 (1967); "A Scalogram Analysis of the Supreme Court of Canada, 1958–1967," in Glendon A. Schubert and David J. Danelski, supra note 18; and the contributions by Donald E. Fouts, George H. Gadbois, Jr., and Abelardo G. Samonte in the volume edited by Schubert and Danelski, supra note 18; and Frank N. Stein, "Some Epistemological Assumptions Underlying the Metaphysical Paraparameters of Judicial Scaling," 7 *International Yearbook of Psychotheology* (1972) (in press).

42. Glendon A. Schubert, "A Solution to the Indeterminate Factorial Resolution of Thurstone and Degan's Study of the Supreme Court," 7 *Behavioral Science* 448 (1962), reprinted under the title "A Psychological Model of Supreme Court Decision-Making," in his *Judicial Behavior*, supra note 41; Schubert, "The 1960 Term of the Supreme Court: A Psychological Analysis," 56 *American Political Science Review* 90 (1962); Schubert, *The Judicial Mind: Attitudes and Ideologies of Supreme Court Justices, 1946–1963* (Evanston,

Ill.: Northwestern University Press, 1965); S. Sidney Ulmer, "Dimensions of Judicial Voting," 13 *Midwest Journal of Political Science* 471 (1969). For discussions of several other kinds of multidimensional scaling, see Clyde H. Coombs, *A Theory of Data* (New York: Wiley, 1964), and Ledyard R. Tucker and Samuel Messick, "An Individual Differences Model for Multidimensional Scaling," 28 *Psychometrika* 333 (1963). Neither of these last two works is concerned with judges in particular or public law in general.

43. Much of the literature is discussed in Neal Gross, Ward S. Mason, and Alexander W. McEachern, *Explorations in Role Analysis* (New York: Wiley, 1958), especially chaps. 2–5, and Bruce J. Biddle and Edwin J. Thomas (eds.), *Role Theory* (New York: Wiley, 1966).

44. See especially John C. Wahlke *et al.*, *The Legislative System: Explorations in Legislative Behavior* (New York: Wiley, 1962), and Ralph K. Huitt, "The Outsider in the Senate: An Alternative Role," 55 *American Political Science Review* 566 (1961).

45. Lochner v. New York, 198 U.S. 45, dissenting opinion, 75 (1905).

46. Missouri, Kansas, and Texas Railway v. May, 194 U.S. 267, dissenting opinion, 270 (1904).

47. Baldwin v. Missouri, 281 U.S. 586, dissenting opinion, 595 (1930).

48. United States v. Butler, 297 U.S. 1, dissenting opinion, 87 (1936). Sutherland's dissent in West Coast Hotel v. Parrish, 300 U.S. 379 (1937), is largely an effort to meet Stone's argument in United States v. Butler.

49. Pritchett, supra note 33, pp. 191–192.

50. Falbo v. United States, 320 U.S. 549, dissenting opinion, 556 (1944).

51. Uveges v. Pennsylvania, 335 U.S. 437, dissenting opinion, 449–450 (1948).

52. Terminiello v. Chicago, 337 U.S. 1, dissenting opinion, 11 (1949). Frankfurter discussed his concept of the judicial role at greater length in his article "The Judicial Process and the Supreme Court," 98 *Proceedings of the American Philosophic Society* 233 (1954), reprinted in Philip Elman (ed.), *Of Law and Men: Papers and Addresses of Felix Frankfurter, 1939–1956* (New York: Harcourt, Brace & World, 1956).

53. Joel B. Grossman, "Role-Playing and the Analysis of Judicial Behavior: The Case of Mr. Justice Frankfurter," 11 *Journal of Public Law* 285 (1962); see also his "Dissenting Blocs on the Warren Court: A Study in Judicial Role Behavior," 30 *Journal of Politics* 1068 (1968).

54. Theodore L. Becker, "A Survey Study of Hawaiian Judges: The Effect on Decisions of Judicial Role Variations," 60 *American Political Science Review* 677 (1966).

55. Kenneth N. Vines, "The Judicial Role in American States: An Exploration," in Joel B. Grossman and Joseph Tanenhaus (eds.), *Frontiers of Judicial Research* (New York: Wiley, 1969). See also Henry Robert Glick and Vines, "Law-Making in the State Judiciary: A Comparative Study of the Judicial Role in Four States," 2 *Polity* 142 (1969). In his article "The Role of Circuit Courts of Appeal in the Federal Judicial Process," 7 *Midwest Journal of Political Science* 305 (1963), Vines uses the concept of role less in the normative sense in which we are using it in this chapter and more in the operational sense in which we used the term in chapter 2. See also Henry R. Glick, "Judicial Decision-Making and Group Dynamics: A Study of Role Perceptions and Group Behavior on Four State Supreme Courts," a paper presented at the Northeast Political Science Association Convention, 1969.

56. For example, J. K. Beatty, "An Institutional and Behavioral Analysis of the Iowa Supreme Court—1965–1969," University of Iowa, 1970; Henry R. Glick, "Judicial Role Perceptions and Behavior: A Study of American State Judges," Tulane University, 1967; Francis M. Rich, Jr., "Role Perception and Precedent Orientation As Variables Influencing Judicial Decision-Making: An Analysis of the U.S. Court of Appeals for the Fifth Circuit," University of Georgia, 1967; Gene L. Mason, "Judges and Their Publics: Role Perceptions and Role Expectations," University of Kansas, 1967. Beatty has a particularly useful discussion and bibliography in chap. 6 of his dissertation.

6
The Group Phase
of Decision Making

The American and Canadian Supreme Courts have nine judges; the Irish and Argentine have five; the Australian High Court has seven members; and each senate of the West German Constitutional Court has eight judges. The Swiss Constitutional Court has twenty-six members, the Indian fourteen, the Italian and Japanese fifteen. American state supreme courts are typically staffed by five to seven judges, and the eleven U.S. Courts of Appeals are manned by three to fifteen jurists. Thus one of the most striking features of these courts is that they are small and, given the average length of judicial service, rather long-lived groups.[1] Trial juries range in size from seven to twelve members in most countries and so share the characteristic of smallness, although not that of persistence over time.

Even the figures we have just listed overstate the number of judges who often work together on a particular case. The Swiss Court typically sits in panels of five judges, as do the Indian and Japanese courts. More often than not, the Canadian Supreme Court hears cases in panels of seven or five or, occasionally, three judges. Even the Irish Supreme Court sometimes divides into panels of three. In Australia

> the High Court acts through a continuously shifting series of ad hoc committees or panels of two to six members; and it infrequently—11 to 12 percent of the time—utilizes *en banc* (or, as Australian lawyers call it, "full Court") decisions of the entire group of seven justices. Panels of five make a majority of the decisions and panels of three are next in popularity. . . .[2]

Although these groups are small, it is still not probable that all of their members will equally cherish the same specific as well as general values, nor when they agree on those values are these judges always likely to concur in their application to complicated pieces of litigation. Since a decision on a collegial court and, on many courts, an opinion justifying that decision depend on at least majority agreement, the influence of interaction among the judges may be important, and it will certainly be continuous. That influence may be only minor, but it is unlikely ever to be totally absent.

A significant point that can easily be overlooked is that judges of major courts have to be concerned not only with offering a solution to a difficult problem but also with composing an opinion explaining and justifying that solution. For although decisions immediately affect only particular litigants, the opinions—since they will be scrutinized and used as guidelines by many lawyers, other judges, legislators, administrators, and even political scientists —can help shape the behavior of large groups of public officials as well as of private citizens. An opinion, for example, reversing the conviction of a condemned murderer because the trial judge erroneously overruled a defense objection on a technical point of law is likely to have a much more limited effect than a reversal based on the proposition that the death penalty is a "cruel and unusual punishment" forbidden by the constitution.

Thus a judge on a collegial court may often face a choice between publicly defending the result he believes to be right and joining a majority whom he thinks to be wrong. He might choose the latter course if by so doing he can shape the opinion and mitigate the harm done. The choice is not quite so easy as it at first seems, for an eloquent dissent may also be persuasive, if not to current colleagues, perhaps to future judges or to influential people outside the court. Without exploring here the options and the attendant costs and benefits open to judges on collegial courts,[3] we simply note that a judge who is committed to particular jurisprudential goals is not apt to see himself as always free to vote or write as he would if he were deciding cases alone.*   The value dimension of his normative role as a judge, which we discussed in the preceding chapter, is further complicated by his being one of a group of judges who are equal in authority.   If he desires to do good—or evil—he must frequently take into account the values as well as the strengths and weaknesses of his colleagues.   He must also realize that he will be dealing with them not once or twice but hundreds, perhaps thousands, of times over the years.

As we pointed out in chapter 3, formal rules of procedure can not only shape the alternatives available to judges and how judges will perceive those alternatives but can also affect the ways in which qualities such as intelligence, eloquence, and determination can be exercised.   Informal rules can also be important.   Any institution develops unwritten norms that can operate with as much force as formal rules.   To use a gross example, a judge who, whenever he was in the minority, appealed to the legislature to overturn the majority decision or to the executive to ignore it would, in all probability, soon be ostracized by his colleagues.

Dissent in itself is considered illegitimate in some countries.   Examples are Italy and Switzerland, although anyone interested in what the Swiss judges are doing can attend the conferences and listen to and watch the judges discuss cases among themselves and vote.   The ban against dissents had been absolute in Germany until early 1971, when the second senate of the Constitutional Court for the first time published a minority opinion. Historically, the prohibition against separate opinions had, if anything, been even stronger in Japan.   Not only did the Japanese adopt the German legal system, but deep in their own culture there has been a reverence for the appearance of consensus.†   As one authority has noted, custom and tradition inhibit many Japanese "from saying what they think and of revealing their real and innermost feelings and thoughts.   The pressure for social harmony and for outward unanimity is too strong."[4]

Article 11 of the post–World War II Constitution broke sharply with Japanese tradition in its authorization of concurring and dissenting opinions. As one would have expected, Supreme Court justices did not immediately

---

* A judge on a court that uses institutional opinions and still allows dissents faces this dilemma most sharply, but all judges may experience it.   Where opinions are given seriatim, a judge might lessen the effect of the majority's decision by agreeing with the result but offering a far more restrictive rationale that might be one step in the direction he thinks right.   So, too, where dissents are not permitted, a judge might be in a more advantageous position to influence the opinion-writer if he were doing so as a fellow member of the majority rather than of the minority.

† Cross pressures are not unique to American culture.   Japanese judges at times experienced a conflict between harmony with their colleagues on the bench and harmony with members of other reference groups, such as law school professors.   Danelski reports that sometimes members of the old court would put their seal upside down on judgments as a subtle indication of dissent. David J. Danelski, "The Supreme Court of Japan: An Exploratory Study," in Glendon A. Schubert and David J. Danelski (eds.), *Comparative Judicial Behavior* (New York: Oxford University Press, 1969), p. 137.

exploit their new freedom, and those who had previously been judges were the slowest to adapt to the new ways.[5]   Still, the transition was on the whole both smooth and rapid, and dissents and concurrences are now fully legitimate and frequently used.   Wistful reminders of the past occasionally pop up, though, as when the Court in the *Sunakawa* decision announced that the ruling was unanimous except for the separate opinions of ten justices.[6]

Like their Japanese brethren, Indian Supreme Court justices have also broken with tradition regarding separate opinions, but with very different results.   The Indian Court has one of the highest records of consensus of any constitutional tribunal on which dissent is a legitimate option.   Gadbois calculated that 92 percent of the 3,272 reported decisions between 1950 and 1967 were unanimous.[7]   This proportion is all the more surprising given both the factionalism that characterizes the rest of Indian politics and society as well as the British legal tradition that prevailed in India before 1950 of seriatim expression of judicial views—a tradition reflected in the work of Australian and Canadian courts, although not in the British Privy Council.[8]   The Indian judges have hit on a way of restricting their public expression of disagreement to the most fundamental issues, such as those raised by Golak Nath's case.[9]   They may have joined in a tacit agreement not to publish dissents except on very basic matters.   In addition, or alternatively, it may be that the procedure of circulating opinions and the sensitivity of Indian judges to their colleagues' wishes plus a desire for consensus may allow most differences to be settled privately by negotiation and compromise.   The explanation that the judges have all seen the issues as being best resolved in the same fashion is implausible in light of the sharpness and depth of differences revealed in the nonunanimous decisions.

Even in the United States judicial attitudes toward dissent have changed from time to time.[10]   Before John Marshall's chief justiceship, each member of the Supreme Court usually wrote his own opinion, although opinions of the Court were sometimes used.   In an effort to mass judicial power, Marshall persuaded his colleagues to accept institutional opinions as the norm.   Soon, as Justice William Johnson explained to Jefferson, a justice had to be cautious about writing separate opinions lest he " become such a cypher in our consultations as to effect no good at all."[11]   Later, members of the Court became more tolerant of dissent, but a vague consensus remained in effect that a judge should prefer teamwork to individual expression of views.   Indicative of the folkways of the Taft Court was the note that Pierce Butler wrote Harlan Stone about an opinion he had circulated:

> I voted to reverse.   While this sustains your conclusion to affirm, I still think reversal would be better but I shall in silence acquiesce.   Dissents seldom aid in the right development or statement of law.   They often do harm.   For myself I say: " Lead us not into temptation."[12]

Even James C. McReynolds, one of the most crusty, ornery, self-willed curmudgeons ever to sit on any court, would occasionally suppress a dissent. As he noted on the slip opinion that Stone circulated in *Sonzinsky v. United States*, upholding the authority of the federal government to use its taxing power to regulate the sale of sawed-off shotguns: "I don't think so; but if all the others do they must prevail though wrong."[13] The U.S. Reports record the decision as unanimous.

After the New Deal fight, the Roosevelt appointees took a much more liberal attitude toward separate opinions, especially concurrences, than had their predecessors. As an associate justice on the Taft and Hughes Courts, Stone had built up a reputation as a dissenter, but the practice of his younger colleagues seemed extreme even to him. He commented several times in private about a breakdown in consensus among the brethren. And he once sent a memorandum to the justices reminding them that "there is considerable scope for self-restraint in the matter of dissent. . . . It is not necessary to play every fly speck in the music. . . ."[14]

The Importance of Interaction

An understanding of the group phase of judicial decision making is critical to an understanding of the judicial process, because judges frequently have both the opportunity and the capacity to influence each other's votes and opinions. Many biographers, especially recent scholars like Alpheus T. Mason in his works on Chief Justices Stone and Taft[15] and J. Woodford Howard, Jr., in his study of Frank Murphy,[16] have shed considerable light on the decisional effects of interaction among judges. Mason and Howard relied heavily on the private papers of their subjects and were fortunate in selecting three men who kept copious records. In the Taft papers one can find memoranda among the justices as well as weekly letters from Taft to his sons or brothers describing what was going on within the Court. Stone and Murphy stored away similar memoranda as well as drafts of opinions marked with the comments of their colleagues. Murphy and, later, Justice Burton also kept longhand notes of what the justices said during the secret conferences at which they discussed the cases, and both judges preserved the docket books in which they recorded the votes at these conferences.

Use of judicial papers in illuminating the group phase of the decisional process is not limited, of course, to biographies. In separate studies, Danelski[17] and Murphy[18] have analyzed the importance of leadership as well as of negotiation and bargaining within the U.S. Supreme Court. On a collegial court all judges may be equal in authority, but they are not likely to be equal in eloquence, intellectual power, social charm, or in the quality that in friends we call resoluteness and in others we call stubbornness. Nor are judges apt to hold each of their colleagues in equal esteem, affection, and respect. The data in judicial papers reveal the decisional process on the U.S. Supreme Court to be far different from the mere voting by nine men of their individual value preferences.

As we have already said, one variable that needs to be measured is the extent to which judges on a collegial court value unanimity.[19] The accuracy of votes as indicators of judicial values on policy questions declines as the importance of unanimity to judges increases. And a judge who places a low value on consensus can sometimes manipulate a judge who places a high value on cohesion. In the 1920s, for instance, Louis Brandeis played on Chief Justice Taft's passion for unanimity. When he was in the minority, Brandeis frequently circulated a dissent and then waited for Taft or another member of the majority to approach him to suggest a compromise. In exchange for concessions in the majority opinion, Brandeis would often agree to withdraw his dissent.[20]

An official conference at which the judges sit down together and discuss a case before voting provides a ready-made forum for leadership and influence. Such meetings are formal, frequent, and important in the United States, Japan, and civil law countries. They tend to be less formal and perhaps less frequent, but not necessarily less important, in Canada, India, and Ireland.

Canadian Supreme Court conferences, Russell says, are "not nearly as extensive or systematic" as those in the U.S. Supreme Court.

> Usually the judges who have sat for a case will hold a brief informal meeting after oral argument is completed. The main purpose of this conference is to see how the judges are generally disposed toward the case and, if there seems to be a fairly clear consensus, to agree among themselves as to which judge will write the Court's opinion.[21]

If no consensus emerges, the judges will probably meet again to clarify their views, perhaps after circulating memoranda and opinion drafts. The Canadian judges may also meet occasionally to discuss the status of some of the more difficult issues the Court is facing. Until fairly recently, Canadian judges tended to follow—as Australian High Court judges still do—the House of Lords' tradition of seriatim opinions. But now the Canadian Supreme Court is about as likely as its American counterpart to settle a case with an institutional opinion. Thus in their discussions and in their comments on draft opinions, the Canadian judges have had to work to find common ground for at least a majority view, although they apparently do not labor as hard for unanimity as do their Indian counterparts.

Since conferences are public in Switzerland—as in Mexico—an interested scholar who is fluent in French and German* can watch efforts at, and

---

* Each Swiss judge is supposed to speak in his own language, but Italian-Swiss judges often use French.

sometimes the effects of, influence.   Morrison's work is partly based on such first-hand observations,[22] and on an occasion when one of the authors of this book sat with him, a judge was seen to change his vote after hearing a colleague speak.

Less vividly but still usefully, judicial papers may sketch the opportunities for influence that a conference presents.   Justice Frank Murphy's papers, for instance, show that by speaking first, Chief Justice Stone—who was by no means a particularly skillful leader—often had a real impact on the final vote.   At the very least, his initial statement of the issues focused the subsequent discussion.   More generally, the votes as recorded in Murphy's docket books are on many occasions different from the opinions that justices first set out when the debate began.

Even when what is said at conference does not shift votes, it may shape views.   The handling of the Harry Bridges case[23] by the U.S. Supreme Court provides an interesting illustration.   After the government had failed under existing law to deport Bridges, a West Coast labor leader who was not an American citizen, Congress in 1940 passed an amendment with the explicit purpose of making it legally possible to expel him because of his alleged Communist affiliations and activities.   Following a fresh set of hearings, the attorney general ordered Bridges deported.   A federal district court and the Circuit Court of Appeals denied Bridges' application for a writ of habeas corpus, but the Supreme Court granted his petition for review.

According to Justice Murphy's notes on the conference, Chief Justice Stone opened the discussion by stating that the issues before the Court were narrow: Did Bridges come under the amended act?   If he did, was there evidence to support the decision of the attorney general?   Since Congress had absolute power to exclude or expel aliens for any reason whatever, Stone could not see that it was relevant that Bridges was being deported for membership in the Communist party.   Several justices said they agreed with Stone, others disagreed, and the conference discussion soon became heated.   One justice asked whether the Court would sustain deportation because of membership in the Democratic or Republican parties.   Another said he seriously doubted that Bridges had had a fair hearing.   A third expressed wonder that the special inspector who conducted the hearing could have allowed in evidence the sort of hearsay testimony used against Bridges. A fourth justice commented that in amending the statute, Congress had done nothing less than pass an ex post facto law.

Even the justices who thought the Court should affirm the lower court decision admitted distaste for the whole business.   One of them baldly stated that the attorney general had behaved like a "damn fool."   Another conceded that Congress had done a shabby thing.   These judges, however, insisted that the issue was one of power, not of wisdom or morality.   Congress had authority to deport aliens for any reason, good or bad, wise or foolish.

As the discussion went on, it became clear that there was a majority to reverse. Felix Frankfurter, who was in the minority, then warned that the implications of the case went far beyond Harry Bridges. Frankfurter feared that if the Court were to restrict the constitutional power of Congress to expel aliens, Congress would limit further immigration, if not completely shut it off. Murphy recorded the justice as saying:

> I have a special appreciation of this, having come in as an alien. I speak from a depth of conviction about this country and its future. If you reverse this [decision] don't write law on books that will embarrass the future of the Congress in this country. I consider the action of the A[ttorney] G[eneral] as unwise and foolish. But I don't reach [a] judgment that will seriously hamper freedom of action of this country. It will be a great injustice to immigrants to this shore. They wanted a freer country. You will be doing a great injustice to future generations because members of Congress will let no one come in.

The justice concluded with a straightforward plea: "I beg of your conscience not to write into law something born out of a special situation." Another minority justice emphasized the same point: "It was a rotten thing Congress did but I would be slow to subject others to greater injustices in [an] effort to save Bridges."

Whether or not it was because of the minority's arguments, the opinion of the Court did not rest on constitutional grounds. Rather, the majority justified the decision on procedural grounds: Testimony that violated basic standards of fairness had been admitted against Bridges. Justice Murphy, in a separate and lone concurrence, branded the amended statute as unconstitutional on its face. Stone, joined by Roberts and Frankfurter, dissented.

The exercise of influence among judges is not restricted to official conferences. Members of the same court are of necessity in frequent contact with each other. An earlier opinion or questions asked counsel during argument may affect another judge's thinking, just as shop-talk and social intercourse may. In any study of influence, a scholar should not restrict himself to purely intellectual transmissions. All human beings—and the data reported in chapter 4 support the hypothesis that judges are human beings—are more or less vulnerable to emotional appeals and to extra-rational persuasion.

Another example from the Murphy papers will illustrate influence exercised outside of an official conference and by arguments that partake as much of flattery and cajolery as of reason. In 1943, when a majority of the U.S. Supreme Court was about to sustain in *Hirabayashi v. United States*[24] some of the wartime restrictions imposed on Americans of Japanese ancestry, Murphy began preparing a blistering dissent condemning the blatant racism that underpinned governmental policy. Hearing of this, Felix Frankfurter pleaded with Murphy:

> Please, Frank, with your eagerness for the austere functions of the Court and
> your desire to do all that is humanly possible to maintain and enhance the
> *corporate* reputation of the Court, why don't you take the initiative with the
> Chief Justice in getting him to take out everything that either offends you or
> that you want to express more irenically?[25]

Even after an exchange of several other notes, Murphy remained adamant
and circulated his dissent, branding the whole program against the Nisei
as "utterly inconsistent with our ideals and traditions" and "at variance
with the principles for which we are fighting." Frankfurter read Murphy's
protest in horror and immediately wrote another impassioned plea:

> Of course I shan't try to dissuade you from filing a dissent. . . . [But] do you
> really think it is conducive to the things you care about, including the great
> reputation of this Court, to suggest that everybody is out of step except
> Johnny, and more particularly that the Chief Justice and seven other Justices
> of this Court are behaving like the enemy and thereby playing into the hands
> of the enemy?[26]

Murphy was moved at least to second thoughts about the implications of his
opinion. Within a few days he had switched his vote and had modified his
dissent into a concurrence, though one that expressed concern over the
"melancholy resemblance" between American treatment of the Nisei and
Nazi treatment of the Jews.

Much more frequent in the United States than negotiations between
majority and minority justices are those among members of the majority
about the wording of particular opinions. This is probably true in all
countries where the court speaks through an institutional opinion. These
courts follow some variant of the U.S. Supreme Court's practice of circulating
every draft to all the judges, majority and minority, for comment. It is
quite common for an opinion of the U.S. Supreme Court to go through five
or six drafts as all members of the majority—and occasionally some members
of the minority—make suggestions for change. Some of these may pertain
only to matters of style, but often they involve matters of substance that
require negotiation and renegotiation. At best, it is difficult for a group of
strong-willed men to agree to a complex document that must be broad
enough—and sometimes vague enough—to encompass all their views and
still tight enough to survive the counterarguments of potential or actual
dissenters. Italian, West German, British Privy Council, and where advisory
opinions or questions about the constitutionality of statutes passed since
1937 are raised, Irish judges face a different set of strictures. We simply
do not know whether the requirement of a public face of unanimity increases
or decreases bargaining within a court, although there are strong indications

that negotiations among the judges are commonplace occurrences within the two senates of the West German Constitutional Court.

While we do not have data on other constitutional courts comparable to those available for the United States, we can make some general inferences about exchanges of influence.   In countries where there is no tradition of or movement toward an institutional opinion, negotiations about the wording of individual opinions are probably unimportant.   But as we have already noted, there still may be opportunities of a more subtle and less formal nature for judges to persuade each other in the way they both vote and write their opinions.   Although we do not know much about patterns of leadership within most courts that do not permit dissent, we have good reason to believe that the British Privy Council was long dominated by two judges, first Lord Watson and later Lord Haldane.[27]   It would be plausible to extrapolate from this experience the hypothesis that similar opportunities exist within courts like those of West Germany, Italy, and Switzerland.

Where judges sit in panels, there is an additional avenue of influence that should not be overlooked: The choice of which judges are to hear which cases can be a critical factor in the outcome.   Prudent use of his assigning authority gave Chief Justice Owen Dixon of Australia far more power than one would have estimated from knowing only the formal prerogatives of his office[28] in a legal system that puts a premium on individual expression of judicial views and practically eschews decisional conferences.

Measuring Influence and Interagreement: Bloc Analysis

To study constitutional courts outside the United States, we have to look at types of evidence other than private papers, since these are rarely available. Once again, interviews are potentially fruitful sources of data.   Danelski in Japan, Kommers in West Germany, and Morrison in Switzerland have demonstrated that judges are willing to give some information while they are still on the bench.   Scholars have also developed analytical techniques to employ where papers are not available and interviews are not likely to be forthcoming.   Opinion analysis can be useful.   A skilled observer can pick out from anonymous opinions lines of reasoning associated with one judge or can identify similar strands in opinions authored by other judges. Occasionally, one can see in a majority opinion a blend of arguments—and a not always logically consistent compound—associated with different members of the majority.[29]   On rare occasions there will be a candid discussion of the difficulties of securing agreement.[30]   As we indicated in the previous chapter, perhaps content analysis, augmented by sophisticated computer programming, will eventually prove helpful here.

The group phase of judicial decision making can also be studied by quantitative analyses of voting behavior.[31]   One frequently used method for doing so—cumulative scaling—is more appropriate for investigating the individual phase of judicial decision making and was fully discussed in chapter 5.   Some scholars have also tried to discern the patterns in which judges join each other's opinions as a means of mapping the contours of interaction and influence.[32]   Other analysts have attempted to employ game theory.[33]   Another widely employed quantitative device suitable for studying the group phase is bloc analysis.

As its name suggests, the purpose of bloc analysis is to identify groups of judges within a court who tend to vote together.   Originally devised for the study of legislative behavior, bloc analysis did not attract much interest among scholars in public law until C. Herman Pritchett adapted it for studying the U.S. Supreme Court.[34]   Although several judicial behavioralists have proposed refinements in Pritchett's techniques, complete agreement on certain important procedures has not yet evolved.   Nonetheless, apart from reliance on the phi coefficient, a statistic to be discussed in chapter 7, the alternative ways of proceeding are rather similar.

Let us begin by selecting a set of cases for which the judges' votes are available and calculating the percentage of agreement in the votes cast by every pair of judges to be analyzed.   A convenient set for illustrative purposes is the forty-two nonunanimous civil liberties cases decided by the Japanese Supreme Court from 1955 to 1960.   Eight justices voted in at least 80 percent of these cases: Fujita, Irie, M. Kawamura, Kobayashi, Kotani, Saito, Shima, and Chief Justice Tanaka.   Since the Chief Justice agreed with Justice Saito in thirty-seven of the forty cases in which they jointly participated, their percentage of agreement is 93 (37/40).   On the other hand, Tanaka agreed with Justice Kobayashi in only 24 percent (11/41).   All told, twenty-eight pairs of agreement percentages must be calculated if the voting records of eight judges are to be compared.   If five judges were involved, ten interagreement scores would be needed; seven judges require twenty-one scores, and nine judges thirty-six scores.

In calculating interagreement scores, the analyst is faced with the same troublesome choices that arise in most attempts to quantify judicial votes—and how one decides among them may affect substantive findings, such as the apparent cohesion and even the apparent composition of blocs.   Does one, for example, use as a base figure the number of cases decided or simply the number of opinions in which judges participate?

When constitutional courts consolidate two or more cases and then dispose of them together by one set of opinions, as the U.S. Supreme Court frequently does, the procedure followed may seriously affect the substantive results.   Similar difficulties arise when one considers whether judges who vote the same way but justify their votes in separate opinions should be

TABLE 6.1

*Matrix of interagreement: Japanese Supreme
Court, 42 nonunanimous civil liberties cases,
1955–1960 (percentages of interagreement for
pairs of judges participating in at least 34 cases)*

Kob	Kot	Fuj	Kaw	Shi	Iri	Tan	Sai	
—	88	83	79	61	57	24	21	Kobayashi
	—	78	84	63	57	27	27	Kotani
		—	81	68	66	32	34	Fujita
			—	77	79	41	40	Kawamura, M.
				—	100	55	65	Shima
					—	65	62	Irie
Court cohesion = 61						—	93	Tanaka
Sprague criterion = 81							—	Saito

Blocs: left—Kobayashi-Kotani-Fujita-Kawamura: Bloc cohesion = 81
center—Shima-Irie: Bloc cohesion = 100
right—Tanaka-Saito: Bloc cohesion = 93

Data source: Takeo Hayakawa, " Legal Science and Judicial Behavior, with Particular Reference
to Civil Liberties in the Japanese Supreme Court," 1962 *Kobe University Law Review* 1; reprinted in Glendon A. Schubert (ed.), *Judicial Behavior: A Reader in Theory and Research* (Chicago:
Rand McNally, 1964).

counted as agreeing or disagreeing. We know from a careful reading of
their opinions that judges who are in fundamental agreement frequently
prefer for tactical or stylistic reasons to express their views individually, and
we know from judges' papers that men who fundamentally disagree may
join in a common opinion, as Black, Stone, and Douglas did in *Korematsu
v. United States.*[35]

Once the procedures to be followed in calculating agreement scores have
been determined, the analyst's next step is to construct a matrix of interagreement scores. Again there is a problem because there is no universally
accepted best way of positioning the judges in such a scheme. Table 6.1
contains a matrix for the twenty-eight pairs of eight Japanese Supreme Court
judges who participated in at least 80 percent of the forty-two nonunanimous
civil liberties cases decided between February 23, 1955, and October 19, 1960.
The criterion we used for ordering the judges from left to right was the
strength of their support for civil liberties claims. Kobayashi had voted to
uphold these claims 85 percent of the time, the highest percentage of support
for any of the eight justices, so we placed him on the extreme left. Kotani
followed with 81 percent, Fujita with 74, Kawamura with 68, Shima with
54, Irie with 45, and Tanaka and Saito with 7 percent each.

Until the publication of John D. Sprague's important book on judicial bloc analysis,[36] matrix construction proceeded, as we have proceeded here, more or less idiosyncratically. Bloc analysis, as a result, was not reliable in the sense that a variety of rather different and equally plausible arrays could often be developed from any given set of data. Sprague devised a method for matrix construction that produces a unique array—except in rare cases when ties can lead to more than one equally valid solution. Central to Sprague's method is the ordering of judges so as to maximize the level of agreement in first-order relationships—those between contiguous individuals in an array. (Higher-order relationships, those between individuals who are separated by one or more other judges, are considered only in the case of ties.) We used Sprague's method in preparing Table 6.2,* which reports the interagreement between all pairs of judges who participated in at least ten of the twenty-three nonunanimous criminal cases decided by the Canadian Supreme Court during the five-year period 1961 to 1965.

The principal advantage of Sprague's method is that it generally results in a unique and hence reliable array. Every analyst who uses the method on a given set of cases will produce an identical matrix. Any system that leads all who follow it faithfully to the same answer has much to commend it. Reliability, however, can sometimes exact heavy costs, a subject to which we shall shortly return.

There is an advantage beyond reliability in using Sprague's method. His rules for matrix construction avoid the necessity for relying on liberalism-conservatism or some other dimension in positioning judges in an array. There is, as Sprague points out, "no a priori reason to suppose that courts divide themselves on a left-right dimension."[37] Moreover, when dealing with a large group of undefined cases, as in Table 6.3, there may be no

---

* When following Sprague's method for ordering a matrix, the first step is to identify the pair (or pairs) with the largest association score. In Table 6.2, the Abbott-Judson pair has an association score of 100, higher than any other pair. Because the first step in Sprague's method always produces at least a simple tie, the second step must be an effort to resolve it. This is done by charting paths. Take the highest pair; place, in turn, one member of the pair in the first position and then the other (Abbott-Judson and Judson-Abbott); and if the absence of ties permits, select the path with the highest association score for the relationship between position 2 and position 3. In this instance, however, a further tie results. Since the association scores for the four possible paths cannot show that any one of them is obviously superior, a still higher order relationship must be examined. As the following figure reveals, the scores for the third and fourth positions remove paths 3 and 4 from contention. Although the initial tie between Abbott

Paths	Positions			
	1	2	3	4
1	Abbott (100)	Judson (88)	Tascherau (87)	Fauteux
2	Judson (100)	Abbott (88)	Tascherau (87)	Fauteux
3	Abbott (100)	Judson (88)	Martland (70)	Ritchie
4	Judson (100)	Abbott (88)	Martland (70)	Ritchie

and Judson is not thereby resolved and, indeed, cannot be for this set of data, Tascherau clearly belongs in position 3 and Fauteux in position 4. Martland follows Fauteux and takes position 5 because none of the remaining judges (Ritchie, Hall, Cartwright, and Spence) agrees with Fauteux as strongly as Martland does. The same procedure is followed in placing each of those remaining judges in the position he occupies in Table 6.2.

TABLE 6.2

Matrix of interagreement: Canadian Supreme Court, 23 nonunanimous criminal cases, 1961–1965 (percentages of interagreement for pairs of judges participating in at least 10 cases)

					Judges ordered by Sprague's method				
						Position			
Unresolved tie		*3*	*4*	*5*	*6*	*7*	*8*	*9*	
Abb	= Jud	Tas	Fau	Mar	Rit	Hal	Car	Spe	
—	100	88	80	88	74	33	21	14	Abbott
	—	88	77	88	74	25	27	43	Judson
		—	87	67	44	13	14	40	Tascherau
			—	63	45	14	00	44	Fauteux
				—	70	00	40	40	Martland
					—	75	53	33	Ritchie
						—	89	80	Hall
							—	80	Cartwright
								—	Spence

Court cohesion = 53

Sprague criterion = 77

Data source: Stephen R. Mitchell, "The Supreme Court of Canada Since the Abolition of Appeals to the Judicial Committee of the Privy Council: A Quantitative Analysis," a paper presented to the Meeting of the Learned Societies and the Canadian Political Science Association, 1967.

plausible basis for postulating a dimension of any sort. Table 6.3 is an interagreement matrix for all Canadian Supreme Court judges who took part in at least 25 percent of the 105 nonunanimous decisions officially reported from 1961 through 1965. We would need to know a good deal more about these cases than we do before we would be justified in ordering the judges in this table in terms of some value-oriented dimension. Sprague's method of matrix construction is ideally suited for situations of this kind.

After constructing a matrix of interagreement, one seeks to identify the existence of one or more "blocs"—a label that in this particular context signifies nothing more than that a group of judges had a specified level of interagreement. Constructing a formula to compute any particular level is easy. What is difficult to justify is why an analyst chose one level of interagreement rather than another as the minimum for inferring the existence of a bloc. In essence, political scientists have tried, with an admitted degree of arbitrariness, to set a level that at least intuitively indicates a frequency of agreement far higher than one would expect as a result of chance alone.

Schubert has suggested a simple procedure that many find attractive: computing a cohesion index by averaging the percentages of interagreement

TABLE 6.3

Matrix of interagreement: Canadian Supreme
Court, all nonunanimous cases (N = 105),
1961–1965 (percentages of interagreement for
pairs of judges participating in at least 38 cases)

Mar	Rit	Hal	Car	Spe	Tas	Fau	Abb	Jud	
—	88	56	53	54	64	69	48	45	Martland
	—	71	61	50	56	59	56	44	Ritchie
		—	79	55	47	47	41	37	Hall
			—	59	31	36	34	34	Cartwright
				—	58	44	45	32	Spence
					—	76	62	71	Tascherau
						—	63	62	Fauteux
							—	88	Abbott
								—	Judson

Court cohesion = 56

Sprague criterion = 78

Data source: Stephen R. Mitchell, " The Supreme Court of Canada Since the Abolition of Appeals to the Judicial Committee of the Privy Council: A Quantitative Analysis," a paper presented to the Meeting of the Learned Societies and the Canadian Political Science Association, 1967.

for what seem to be subgroups in an array. According to Schubert an index score of 70 or greater should be taken to indicate a highly cohesive bloc, and 60 to 69 a moderately cohesive bloc. Sprague has developed a more stringent test, which we shall refer to as " Sprague's criterion." To compute the Sprague criterion, one first determines the level of cohesion for the court as a whole (that is, the average percentage of interagreement for all the pairs of judges to be analyzed). For the array in Table 6.1 the level of court cohesion is 61, and for the array in Table 6.3 it is 56. Then one adds to this court cohesion figure half of the difference between it and 100. Thus for Table 6.1 Sprague's criterion would be determined by adding $(100 - 61)/2$, or 20, to 61 for a criterion of 81. For Table 6.3, $(100 - 56)/2$, or 22, is added to 56 for a criterion of 78. Sprague would designate as a bloc any subgroup with a cohesion index at least as large as his criterion. In Table 6.1 any subgroup with a cohesion index of at least 81 would qualify as a bloc, and in Table 6.3 any set of judges with a cohesion index of 78. The advantage of the Sprague criterion is that it reserves the name " bloc " for subgroups showing substantially greater cohesion than the court as a whole.

We consider it desirable to modify Sprague's procedures in one respect: No judge should be included in a bloc if his average interagreement with other bloc members is lower than Sprague's criterion. Our modification prevents a pair of judges with a very high percentage of interagreement from pulling into a bloc a contiguous judge who agrees with one of them considerably less often than with the other. For this reason, in outlining the blocs in Table 6.1, we included Justice Kawamura in the left bloc, but not in the two-man center bloc. Hence in Table 6.1 we have identified three blocs, none of them interlocking. The four-judge bloc on the left consists of Kobayashi, Kotani, Fujita, and Kawamura; the bloc in the center contains two judges, Shima and Irie; and the bloc on the right also comprises two judges, Tanaka and Saito.

There is no magic, of course, in any of these standards for defining blocs. Cohesion levels falling somewhat short of the Sprague criterion, for instance, need not be automatically cast beyond the pale of substantive interest.

Let us now return to the procedures for positioning the judges in an interagreement matrix. When discussing this matter a few paragraphs earlier, we indicated that the reliability ensured by Sprague's method of matrix construction could entail heavy costs. We can illustrate why this is so by reordering the data on the twenty-three criminal cases decided by the Canadian Supreme Court that are presented in Table 6.2 in the same manner used when preparing Table 6.1—that is, from left to right in accordance with the strength of support of defendants' claims. We have done this in Table 6.4. The arrangement of the judges in Table 6.4 portrays the relationship between Judson, Abbott, Tascherau, Fauteux, and Martland in a more

TABLE 6.4

Judges from Table 6.2 reordered from left to right by percentage of support for defendants' claims

Car	Hal	Spe	Rit	Mar	Jud	Abb	Tas	Fau	
—	89	80	53	40	27	21	14	00	Cartwright
	—	80	75	00	33	25	13	14	Hall
		—	33	40	43	14	40	44	Spence
			—	70	74	74	44	45	Ritchie
				—	88	88	67	63	Martland
					—	100	88	77	Judson
						—	88	80	Abbott
							—	87	Tascherau
								—	Fauteux

Court cohesion = 53
Sprague criterion = 77

Data source: Stephen R. Mitchell, "The Supreme Court of Canada Since the Abolition of Appeals to the Judicial Committee of the Privy Council: A Quantitative Analysis," a paper presented to the Meeting of the Learned Societies and the Canadian Political Science Association, 1967.

TABLE 6.5

Matrix of intragreement: U.S. Supreme Court, all nonunanimous cases, 1939 term (percentages of intragreement for pairs of judges)

	Black	Douglas	Murphy	Frankfurter	Reed	Stone	Hughes	Roberts	McReynolds	
	—	100	100	95	87	81	56	36	8	Black
		—	100	95	87	80	58	37	8	Douglas
			—	95	90	75	55	45	11	Murphy
				—	92	86	61	40	13	Frankfurter
					—	87	66	44	17	Reed
						—	71	50	21	Stone
							—	80	50	Hughes
								—	64	Roberts

Court cohesion = 63
Sprague criterion = 81

Data source: C. Herman Pritchett, *The Roosevelt Court: A Study in Judicial Politics and Values, 1937–1947* (New York: Macmillan, 1948), p. 244. Copyright 1948 by C. Herman Pritchett. Reprinted by permission.

meaningful fashion. These five judges meet Sprague's criterion for bloc definition, even as we have modified it. Nevertheless, Table 6.4 suggests that it is more realistic to treat the five judges as constituting two interlocking blocs, one consisting of four judges (Judson-Abbott-Tascherau-Fauteux) and the other of three (Martland-Judson-Abbott). Table 6.4 is more revealing than 6.2 because it deals more effectively with the higher-order relationships between Martland, on the one hand, and Abbott-Judson, on the other. Much of the time, to be sure, the bloc structures developed by the several methods for matrix construction do not differ appreciably. If, for example, we reconstructed Table 6.1 by Sprague's method, we would find that the positions of several of those Japanese judges would change, but the composition of the bloc structure would remain identical.

Advantages of Bloc Analysis

The advantages of bloc analysis are numerous. At the very least, one can describe in a succinct and precise manner the extent to which subgroups of judges vote together on a court. Armed with that information, a scholar may be able to make more sense out of other data he has obtained and fit various pieces into a more coherent explanation of the problem of how and why judges make choices.

Table 6.5 shows how often the justices of the U.S. Supreme Court agreed with each other in nonunanimous cases in the 1939 term. Note that Black, Douglas, and Murphy voted together in every nonunanimous case. One could hardly ask for a more cohesive bloc. Frankfurter joined this group in 95 percent of these cases to form with Murphy, Black, and Douglas a bloc that would meet most rigorous standards of cohesion, including Sprague's. In almost nine out of ten nonunanimous cases Reed and Stone agreed with each other, and in more than eight out of ten they agreed with Black, Douglas, and Frankfurter. Although Reed and Murphy voted together almost every time, Stone and Murphy had the lowest percentage of agreement (75 percent) of any pair of judges in the six-man bloc.

One might conclude that these five Roosevelt appointees were deliberately joining with Stone, who had been the most active opponent on the bench against what the Supreme Court had been doing over much of the previous decades. Research into the private papers of the justices supports this hypothesis. In fact, not only were the young New Deal judges attracted to Stone as a hero who had vigorously opposed the Supreme Court's opposition to economic reform, but Stone saw them as potential allies. The Court's conferences at which the judges discussed the cases among themselves and voted were then held on Saturdays. These conferences were dominated by

TABLE 6.6

Matrix of interagreement: U.S. Supreme Court, all nonunanimous cases, 1944 term (percentages of interagreement for pairs of judges)

	Black	Douglas	Rutledge	Murphy	Reed	Jackson	Frankfurter	Stone	Roberts	
	—	79	78	74	62	53	47	41	9	Black
		—	78	74	70	57	52	52	20	Douglas
			—	79	63	62	56	47	20	Rutledge
				—	64	57	54	46	25	Murphy
					—	64	67	72	41	Reed
						—	75	67	45	Jackson
							—	74	61	Frankfurter
								—	61	Stone

Court cohesion = 57

Sprague criterion = 79

Data source: C. Herman Pritchett, *The Roosevelt Court: A Study in Judicial Politics and Values, 1937–1947* (New York: Macmillan, 1948), p. 246. Copyright 1948 by C. Herman Pritchett. Reprinted by permission.

Chief Justice Hughes, who often disagreed with Stone. So Stone organized his own allies and held rump conferences at his home on Fridays, inviting the younger judges and frequently Justice Roberts—even though he and Stone had serious disagreements on constitutional issues—to join him in formulating the stands that they would take the following day. Evidence in Stone's papers also indicates that Stone was infrequently persuaded by any arguments that Justice Murphy made, since, in private, Stone had expressed serious reservations about Murphy's intellectual competence. On the other hand, Murphy .was apparently quite open to Stone's persuasion.

Table 6.5 shows that Hughes and Roberts also tended to vote together, agreeing in 80 percent of these cases, just under Sprague's index of 81 for the table. McReynolds, the last of the Four Horsemen who only a few years earlier had waged such a bitter war against the twentieth century, was relatively isolated. He was closest to Roberts, but with a level of agreement well below that found within any of the other groups.

The data in Table 6.5 show that Hughes frequently agreed with Stone. In part this may have been the result of their sharing a more traditional, although in Hughes' case not necessarily a more passive, view of the judicial function. One could also hypothesize, again from material in private papers of the justices, that Hughes' agreement with Stone was in part the result of the interaction of two factors: Stone's ability to lead a six-judge coalition and Hughes' determination to vote, whenever possible in conscience, with the majority. Since Hughes thoroughly edited his papers before his death, it is difficult to ascertain how much of this aversion to being in the minority was due to some personal insecurity, to a concept of the proper role of the Chief Justice, or to a desire to retain control of assigning the task of writing the opinion of the Court. In any event, during his first nine terms as Chief Justice (1930–1938), Hughes had publicly dissented in only 23 out of 1,382 rulings announced by full opinion.

A second advantage of bloc analysis is that, in helping us to identify those judges who vote together on issues that divide the Court, it puts us in a better—though clearly not an ideal—position to draw rough outlines of the most likely positive patterns of interaction. Thus as we just noted, Stone did caucus with the five new appointees in 1939 to build up an influence to counter that which Chief Justice Hughes would be exerting. Stone had less success with Roberts at that time.

Observing blocs over time may tell us even more about what is going on among the judges. We may see that the blocs are relatively permanent. On the other hand, we may find that groups of judges who voted together during one period drift apart as new judges come onto the Court and/or new issues come before them.

Table 6.6 contains Pritchett's data for the U.S. Supreme Court's 1944 term. Hughes and McReynolds had retired by then, and Robert H. Jackson and Wiley Rutledge had joined the Court, with Harlan Stone taking over as Chief Justice. There was still a discernible liberal bloc composed of Black, Douglas, Rutledge, and Murphy, but the percentages of agreement dropped drastically from those of 1939. No pair of judges reached the 80 percent level that in 1939 had made Hughes and Roberts seem to be enjoying only relatively mild togetherness. Stone's alliance with Frankfurter had weakened noticeably but not nearly as dramatically as his alliance with Black, Douglas, and Murphy. The Chief Justice now found himself much more at home in the company of Roberts than with the young liberals who had joined his caucus.

Perhaps the greatest advantages of bloc analysis are the kinds of questions it provokes one to ask. One line of inquiry involves the extent of division and cohesion across a range of issues. For instance, one might see if the same judges vote together on one kind of civil liberties case as on another or on all civil liberties and economic decisions. If the lines of division ran the same way across all issues, and if nonunanimous decisions formed a high percentage of the court's total output, we would be seeing a very different phenomenon than if there were different blocs across different issues, even where the rate of disagreement was equally high. In the first instance, it would be reasonable to hypothesize that the court's division was far more serious in terms of the tribunal's capacity to function as a truly collegial institution. We would probably be witnessing ideologically consistent subgroups of judges confronting one another, rather than persuading each other. Without having any inside information, we would tend to believe not only that the chances for the judges in one group to influence the judges in the other blocs were small but also that such deep and wide divisions were likely, over time, to exacerbate personal relations and so to make positive interaction even more difficult. It would take something like a dangerous threat from the outside or a whole new set of issues or an influx of new personnel to bring the court to a stage where the judges would be influencing one another across bloc lines.

The existence of different blocs for different issues might give us some additional insights into judicial values: as to how, for instance, some judges might be adamantly opposed to governmental regulation of one kind of private action yet perfectly willing to countenance governmental regulation of another kind. Furthermore, we might find some clues about leadership within the court. From the general voting pattern of a particular judge and his opinions in some cases, we might expect him to vote a different way on another set of issues than he, in fact, has. We might find that these unexpected votes occurred when a particular judge in a bloc wrote an opinion or only after a certain judge came onto the court. Such clues, of course, may also come from scalogram analysis and are much more likely to come from an examination of private papers.

A second set of questions is concerned with the characteristics of blocs. How widespread is the bloc phenomenon? As the data in Tables 6.1 through 6.4 show, judicial blocs are by no means confined to the U.S. Supreme Court. Blocs, however, are not inevitable on collegial courts. Sprague found none in nonunanimous federalism cases decided by the U.S. Supreme Court for the years 1903–1906 and 1916–1920, nor did we find any when analyzing all nonunanimous decisions of the Australian High Court for the years 1951–1958.

Do judicial blocs appear only in the civil liberties area? Over the last generation it has been true that judges, like citizens generally, are apt to disagree vehemently on questions of civil liberties. In Canada, for instance, Russell found that blocs were most evident on such issues,[38] but Table 6.3, which includes negligence and tax cases decided by the Canadian Supreme Court, confirms the findings by U.S. Supreme Court analysts that blocs may encompass a wide range of issues.

A third set of questions that bloc analysis, like any kind of intellectually serious study, raises involves explanation. How does a scholar account for what he has found? Some analysts might assume that existence of a cohesive bloc indicates that the judges share the same values. Although this might be a reasonable working assumption if we had no other evidence than votes, we do have other evidence; and as we have already indicated, that evidence makes this a very dangerous assumption. It is not necessarily worthless as an explanation, but it should be tested as such—as a hypothesis —rather than accepted without further investigation. In many instances this hypothesis may account quite well for similar voting patterns. It is quite clear that on the U.S. Supreme Court in the 1940s Black, Douglas, Murphy, and Rutledge shared much the same value hierarchy and that Black, Douglas, Warren, and Brennan did so during the 1950s and early 1960s.

Bloc analysis can also raise some of the questions discussed in chapter 4 about whether certain common social background characteristics might be influencing the perceptions, values, and votes of judges. Because of the small number of judges on a constitutional court at any particular time, one can only suggest hypotheses, but that need not be a small accomplishment. Consider the nine Canadian judges ordered in Table 6.3 from left to right in accordance with their support for the claims of defendants in criminal cases. Three of the four judges who voted least frequently for claims of criminal defendants were from the province of Quebec. One might reasonably wonder whether French Canadian culture in some way influenced judges to be less sympathetic toward such claims than did the contrasting culture of British Canada. Given the disparate assumptions of the civil and common law about matters of criminal justice, it would hardly be shocking to find men trained in the two legal systems differing sharply on these questions.   In any event, this kind of hypothesis can be—and to some extent has been*—tested by further research.

One might suggest a number of other possible explanations for judges' voting together.   The existence, size, cohesion, and stability of blocs may depend on: (1) the size of a court, (2) whether it meets only *en banc* or sometimes in panels, (3) traditions concerning the writing of seriatim opinions and the desirability of expressing individual or group dissent, (4) whether there is forced retirement at a specific age that ensures a turnover in personnel, and (5) regulations or conventions precluding the open expression of dissent in special circumstances or the disclosure of the authorship of majority opinions, as in Argentina and Japan.

A more dynamic explanation might try to account for patterns of change as well as of continuity.   For example, Tables 6.5 and 6.6 show dramatic differences in interagreements among U.S. Supreme Court justices between the 1939 and 1944 terms.   Stone had replaced Hughes as Chief Justice and was more tolerant of dissent.   Moreover, he was a poor leader, and as Mason's biography shows, often got into wrangles with his colleagues. But it is probable that as the new justices became more accustomed to their jobs they would also have grown in self-confidence and that even had Stone been more astute, he, or the most adroit leader, would have found them difficult to control.†

Perhaps most important, the Court from 1944 to 1945 was a different institution than it had been from 1939 to 1940.   In the earlier period the New Deal justices more or less shared the common goal of destroying the constitutional roadblocks that the old Court had set in the path of government regulation of the economy.   None of the new justices wanted the Court to continue to protect laissez faire.   But these young judges were badly, and sometimes bitterly, divided about their roles, both in the behavioral, systemic sense in which we used the term in chapter 2 and in the normative sense in which we employed it in chapter 5.   Like many alliances, that of the Roosevelt appointees was wrecked by its own victory.   Fresh problems caused the old groups to splinter and help breed new approaches and novel judicial ideologies.

* In a study of voting patterns on the Canadian Court from 1950 to 1960, Donald E. Fouts found that the four judges from Quebec who sat during this period—Abbott, Taschereau, Rinfret, and Fauteux—were the least likely members to support civil liberties claims.   See " The Supreme Court of Canada, 1950–1960," in Glendon A. Schubert and David J. Danelski (eds.), *Comparative Judicial Behavior* (New York: Oxford University Press, 1969).   Peter H. Russell's analysis supports this general finding: See *The Supreme Court of Canada as a Bilingual and Bicultural Institution* (Ottawa: The Queen's Printer for Canada, 1969), esp. chaps. 4–5.

† It is fascinating to speculate how a deviant judge like McReynolds can affect analytic measures of interagreement and also substantively affect the solidarity of a court.   If, for example, one removes McReynolds from Table 6.5, the picture changes dramatically.   First of all the number of nonunanimous cases drops sharply, since McReynolds had dissented alone thirteen times. Second, both the index of cohesion and Sprague criterion rise.   One might wonder whether McReynolds' doctrinal isolation and his personal churlishness did not make it substantively easier for the other judges to agree with each other.

Limitations of Bloc Analysis

When discussing the procedures employed in bloc analysis, we considered some of the technical difficulties public law scholars must face. But we did not then deal with the major substantive limitations of this method for studying the group phase of judicial decision making. Let us do so now.

First, we should make clear what bloc analysis cannot do. Obviously, it cannot be used to further understanding of courts that do not publish judges' votes. The technique cannot be used in studying, for instance, the Italian and Austrian constitutional courts or, until dissents become common-place, that of West Germany. Moreover, bloc analysis must be employed only cautiously in dealing with courts in countries like Norway, where dissents are possible but unusual, or Ireland, where only a small percentage of decisions are published. Even the records in the Irish Supreme Court's archives may not always contain a notation of dissenting votes, since the group decision-making process there is less formal than in the United States. Many constitutional courts, however, do publish a large enough percentage of the votes of judges to make the technique of bloc analysis potentially useful in those countries. Among them are Australia, Canada,* India, Japan, and the United States.

A second limitation is that the fact that judges vote together does not of itself demonstrate that those judges ever consulted each other or in any way tend to exert influence on one another. Nor can one be sure that two judges who vote together share either at the conscious or subconscious level the same value preferences unless they join in the same opinions. Many cases present a variety of issues. One judge may vote to reverse a series of convictions by the national government because of strong views on civil liberties, another because he sees such matters as being properly handled only by local authorities. If the cases had involved local prosecutions, the second judge might well have voted the other way. As we saw in the previous chapter, Frankfurter often voted with conservative colleagues against civil liberties claims because of his notions about his proper role as a judge.

A third limitation on bloc analysis is that, since it focuses on non-unanimous decisions, it may exaggerate the divisions on a court. One must constantly discount the importance of blocs by the frequency and significance of the cases in which a particular bloc opposes other groups of judges.

---

* About two-thirds of the Canadian Supreme Court decisions are officially published—enough to allow some solid inferences about patterns of influence. There are some problems of sampling present, however, since it is unlikely that the missing third of the cases constitute a random sample of the universe of decisions.

There is a fourth kind of problem in bloc analysis, one that is raised more by the character of past research than by the nature of bloc analysis itself. The tables used in this chapter have so far indicated how often judges voted together in pairs, not how often all members of a designated bloc actually voted together as a single unit. This can be a significant omission, and one can be badly misled if the court under study has frequent changes in personnel or often sits in panels rather than *en banc*. In Table 6.1 the four members of the left bloc (Kobayashi-Kotani-Fujita-Kawamura) of the Japanese Supreme Court, with a bloc cohesion index of 81, cast identical votes in only 70 percent of the thirty cases in which all four participated. This means that they voted together as a four-man unit in but half of the forty-two cases reported in Table 6.1. Table 6.2 shows a Canadian Supreme Court bloc of Cartwright-Hall-Spence with a cohesion index of 83. Yet all three of these justices actually voted together in only four of the twenty-two cases reported and cast identical votes in but three of these cases.

One can repair this omission quite simply, though not easily, by going beyond the kind of bloc analysis we have been discussing. We can, for instance, further analyze apparent blocs of three or four judges to see if, in fact, they do vote as a unit and, if they do, with what frequency and on what issues they oppose other blocs of judges.[39] Table 6.7 arranges from left to right the votes of the justices of the U.S. Supreme Court in non-unanimous civil liberties decisions in the 1957 term. The interagreement among Douglas, Black, Warren, and Brennan is high, and by using the same raw data on which Table 6.7 is based, we can see that these four judges

TABLE 6.7

Matrix of interagreement: U.S. Supreme Court,
all nonunanimous civil liberties cases, 1957 term
(percentages of interagreement for pairs of
judges)*

Do	Bl	Wa	Br	Ff	Ha	Wh	Bu	Cl	Justice
—	93	86	81	51	38	36	24	4	Douglas
	—	94	81	47	45	43	31	11	Black
		—	86	40	31	43	30	16	Warren
			—	64	57	52	43	22	Brennan
				—	84	64	65	47	Frankfurter
					—	77	73	59	Harlan
						—	80	61	Whittaker
Court cohesion = 54							—	76	Burton
Sprague criterion = 77								—	Clark

* *N* = 56; all justices participated together in forty-nine or more decisions.

TABLE 6.8

Three- and four-man blocs in nonunanimous
civil liberties cases, 1957 term

		Interagreement	Meets Sprague criterion?
Bloc I:	Douglas, Black, Warren	86%; $N = 51$	yes
Bloc Ia:	Douglas, Black, Warren, Brennan	76%; $N = 49$	almost
Bloc Ib:	Douglas, Black, Brennan	78%; $N = 54$	yes
Bloc II:	Frankfurter, Harlan, Whittaker, Burton	52%; $N = 52$	no
Bloc IIa:	Frankfurter, Harlan, Whittaker	62%; $N = 55$	no
Bloc III:	Whittaker, Burton, Clark	58%; $N = 55$	no

voted together in thirty-seven out of forty-nine, or 76 percent, of the non-unanimous cases in which all of them participated. We also find that bloc cohesion increases to 86 percent when we consider Douglas, Black, and Warren as a three-man group. Table 6.8 presents the results of other analyses using the votes recorded in Table 6.7.

Further analysis would show that Bloc Ib in Table 6.8 opposed Bloc IIa in only seventeen out of forty-seven, or 36 percent, of the cases in which all six justices participated, but that Black and Douglas voted together in opposition to Clark in 96 percent of these civil liberties decisions. These two tables and the data on which they are based indicate that although Douglas and Black almost always together opposed Clark on civil liberties issues and that Douglas, Black, and Warren voted together very frequently, as a bloc these latter three justices only met opposition on civil liberties issues from other relatively cohesive groups—in this term they met opposition from Frankfurter, Harlan, and Whittaker—in a little more than one-third of the nonunanimous cases. The Douglas-Black-Warren bloc, incidentally, won only one of the seventeen decisions in which they opposed the latter group.

In summary, if bloc analysis is intelligently and cautiously used, it can help clarify some relations on collegial courts and thus sharpen understanding of the problem to be explained. In addition, bloc analysis can help formulate plausible hypotheses to account for the relationships that we have delineated. When used with other data, such as those found in judicial papers, bloc analysis can become an even more fruitful intellectual tool. One can say of bloc analysis much the same as has been said about the analogous technique of finding legislative alignments and influence by means of roll-call votes: It is hardly the golden key to all our questions, but in some circumstances it may be the only key we have. Its utility clearly increases as we use it in conjunction with other evidence and other analytical techniques.

NOTES

1. For a general discussion of approaches to the U.S. Supreme Court as a small group, see Walter F. Murphy, "Courts As Small Groups," 79 *Harvard Law Review* 1565 (1966). See also Eloise C. Snyder, "The Supreme Court As a Small Group," 36 *Social Forces* 232 (1958).

2. Glendon A. Schubert, "Opinion Agreement Among High Court Judges in Australia," 4 *The Australian and New Zealand Journal of Sociology* 2, 3 (1968).

3. For a discussion see Walter F. Murphy, *Elements of Judicial Strategy* (Chicago: University of Chicago Press, 1964), chap. 3, and David N. Atkinson and Dale E. Neuman, "Toward a Cost Theory of Judicial Alignments: The Case of the Truman Bloc," 13 *Midwest Journal of Political Science* 271 (1969).

4. Nobutaka Ike, *Japanese Politics* (New York: Knopf, 1957), p. 267.

5. Takeyoshi Kawashima, "Individualism in Decision-Making in the Supreme Court of Japan," in Glendon A. Schubert and David J. Danelski (eds.), *Comparative Judicial Behavior* (New York: Oxford University Press, 1969).

6. The *Sunakawa* decision is reprinted in John M. Maki (ed.), *Court and Constitution in Japan: Selected Supreme Court Decisions, 1948–1960* (Seattle: University of Washington Press, 1964), p. 298.

7. George H. Gadbois, Jr., "Indian Judicial Behavior," 5 *Economic and Political Weekly* 149, 151 (1970).

8. For an account of the background and work of the Privy Council, see Edward McWhinney, *Judicial Review* 4th ed. (Toronto: University of Toronto Press, 1969), chap. 2 and literature cited.

9. See the discussion of the *Golak Nath* case in chapter 2.

10. See Karl M. ZoBell, "Division of Opinion in the Supreme Court: A History of Judicial Disintegration," 44 *Cornell Law Quarterly* 186 (1959).

11. Quoted in Donald G. Morgan, *Justice William Johnson: The First Dissenter* (Columbia: University of South Carolina Press, 1954), p. 182.

12. Pierce Butler to Harlan Fiske Stone, *The Malcomb Baxter, Jr.*, file, 277 U.S. 323 (1928), the Stone papers, the Library of Congress, Washington, D.C.

13. Sonzinsky v. United States, 300 U.S. 506 (1937).

14. Harlan Fiske Stone to the Court, January 13, 1944, the Stone papers, the Library of Congress, Washington, D.C.

15. Alpheus T. Mason: *Harlan Fiske Stone: Pillar of the Law* (New York: Viking, 1956); *William Howard Taft: Chief Justice* (New York: Simon and Schuster, 1964).

16 J. Woodford Howard, Jr., *Mr. Justice Murphy: A Political Biography* (Princeton: Princeton University Press, 1968).

17. David J. Danelski, "The Influence of the Chief Justice in the Decisional Process," in Walter F. Murphy and C. Herman Pritchett (eds.), *Courts, Judges, and Politics* (New York: Random House, 1961).

18. Murphy, supra note 3.

19. See especially Atkinson and Neuman, supra note 3.

20. See Alexander M. Bickel, *The Unpublished Opinions of Mr. Justice Brandeis* (Cambridge, Mass.: Harvard University Press, 1957).

21. Peter H. Russell, *The Supreme Court of Canada as a Bilingual and Bicultural Institution* (Ottawa: The Queen's Printer for Canada, 1969), p. 89.

22. Fred L. Morrison, "Judicial Process in Switzerland: A Study of the Swiss Federal Court" (unpublished Ph.D. dissertation, Princeton University, 1966).

23. Bridges v. Wixon, 326 U.S. 135 (1945). See Murphy, supra note 3, pp. 189–192.

24. Hirabayashi v. United States, 320 U.S. 81 (1943).

25. Felix Frankfurter to Frank Murphy, June 5, 1943, *Hirabayashi* file, the Murphy papers, Michigan Historical Collections, Ann Arbor, Michigan.

26. Frankfurter to Murphy, June 10, 1943, supra note 25.

27. See note 8, supra.

28. See Glendon A. Schubert, "Judges and Political Leadership," in Lewis J. Edinger (ed.), *Political Leadership in Industrialized Societies: Studies in Comparative Analysis* (New York: Wiley, 1967); Schubert, "The Dimensions of Decisional Response: Opinion and Voting Behavior of the Australian High Court," in Joel B. Grossman and Joseph Tanenhaus (eds.), *Frontiers of Judicial Research* (New York: Wiley, 1969); and Schubert, supra note 2.

29. For instance, Charles Evans Hughes' opinion for the Court in Home Building and Loan Association v. Blaisdell, 290 U.S. 398 (1934). Mason, *Stone*, supra note 15, pp. 360–365, reconstructs the process by which Hughes grafted onto his opinion some radically different views of Justice Cardozo. Justice Sutherland in dissent had a field day showing how illogical the final product was.

30. For example, Screws v. United States, 325 U.S. 91 (1945), and Abbatte and Falcone v. United States, 359 U.S. 187 (1959). For an "inside" account of the split within the Court over the Screws case, based on Murphy's papers, see J. Woodford Howard, Jr., and Cornelius Bushoven, "The Screws Case Revisited," 29 *Journal of Politics* 617 (1967).

31. See Atkinson and Neuman, supra note 3. Prof. Norman Jacknis of the State University of New York at Stony Brook is also developing a mathematical model to account for patterns of influence through voting records. See, in addition, Edward J. Weissman, "Mathematical Theory and Dynamic Models," in Schubert and Danelski, supra note 5; Alan Sagar, "The Uses of Simulation in the Study of Judicial Processes" (mimeographed, 1970), 38 pp.; Werner F. Grunbaum, "Analytical and Simulation Models for Explaining Judicial Decision-Making," in Grossman and Tanenhaus, supra note 28, chap. 10; and Norman Jacknis, "Theory and Methods for Analyzing Processes of Political Influence and Policy Making" (unpublished Ph.D. dissertation, Princeton University, 1971), chap. 8.

32. See, for example, S. Sidney Ulmer, "Leadership in the Michigan Supreme Court," in Glendon A. Schubert (ed.), *Judicial Decision-Making* (New York: Free Press, 1963).

33. For instance, Glendon A. Schubert, *Quantitative Analysis of Judicial Behavior* (New York: Free Press, 1959), pp. 188–210; and Schubert, "Policy Without Law: The Certiorari Game," 14 *Stanford Law Review* 284 (1962). For a sharp and perhaps premature effort to evaluate the payoff of game theory in the study of public law, see Walter Berns, "Law and Behavioral Science," 28 *Law and Contemporary Problems* 185, 187–195 (1963).

34. C. Herman Pritchett, *The Roosevelt Court: A Study in Judicial Votes and Values, 1937–1947* (New York: Macmillan, 1948).

35. Korematsu v. United States, 323 U.S. 214 (1944).

36. John D. Sprague, *Voting Patterns of the United States Supreme Court: Cases in Federalism, 1889–1959* (Indianapolis: Bobbs-Merrill, 1968).

37. *Ibid.,* p. 32.

38. Russell, supra note 21, chaps. 4–5.

39. See, for example, S. Sidney Ulmer, "Toward a Theory of Sub-Group Formation in the United States Supreme Court," 27 *Journal of Politics* 133 (1965), reprinted in Thomas P. Jahnige and Sheldon Goldman (eds.), *The Federal Judicial System: Readings in Process and Behavior* (New York: Holt, Rinehart and Winston, 1968); and Joel B. Grossman, "Dissenting Blocs on the Warren Court: A Study in Judicial Role Behavior," 30 *Journal of Politics* 1068 (1968).

7
Statistical Methods
in the
Study of Public Law[1]

Since the publication of *The Roosevelt Court*, research in public law has mirrored the increased reliance on quantification characteristic of contemporary social science. In earlier portions of this book we considered devices for analyzing voting alignments and judicial blocs, techniques that required virtually no knowledge of conventional statistics. But certain other modes of analysis, which are increasingly well represented in the literature of public law, cannot be adequately understood without at least an intuitive grasp of some subjects covered in elementary courses in statistics. The goal of this chapter is not to provide a substitute for such courses. Rather, it is to present those unlettered in statistics but dogged in spirit with enough background to cope with much of the quantitative analysis of judicial data that they could not otherwise critically assess. The chapter is divided into four parts. It begins with a

TABLE 7.1

Perceptions of the U.S. Supreme Court,
1964 Survey Research Center Survey

Perceptions	Independent variables						Statistics
	1. Party identification						
	Democratic		*Republican*		*Independent*		
	N	*%*	*N*	*%*	*N*	*%*	
Supportive of the Court	79	32.2	26	16.0	42	36.2	$\chi^2 = 17.47$
Critical of the Court	166	67.8	136	84.0	74	63.8	$P < .001$
Total	245	100.0	162	100.0	116	100.0	

	2. Power of federal government				Statistics
	Too great		*Not too great*		
	N	*%*	*N*	*%*	
Supportive of the Court	36	13.3	76	49.4	$\chi^2 = 65.84$
					$P < .001$
Critical of the Court	235	86.7	78	50.6	$\phi = -.39$
Total	271	100.0	154	100.0	

	3. Public school prayer				Statistics
	Favor		*Oppose*		
	N	*%*	*N*	*%*	
Supportive of the Court	87	21.6	42	55.3	$\chi^2 = 36.83$
					$P < .001$
Critical of the Court	316	78.4	34	44.7	$\phi = -.28$
Total	403	100.0	76	100.0	

	4. Sex				Statistics
	Male		*Female*		
	N	*%*	*N*	*%*	
Supportive of the Court	77	30.1	71	26.1	$\chi^2 = 1.03$
					$P > .05$
Critical of the Court	179	69.9	201	73.9	$\phi = +.04$
Total	256	100.0	272	100.0	

consideration of chi square as a tool for determining statistical significance and then takes up the phi coefficient as a measure of association. In the last two sections attention shifts to numbered data: The third deals with methods for analyzing two variables, and the fourth part consists of brief comments on several multivariate techniques that are too intricate for detailed consideration in this book.

Testing Statistical Significance: Chi Square

When studies are based on samples, as a fair amount of research in public law now has been,[2] a concern should arise about what is called sampling error—the likelihood that the units under analysis do not accurately reflect the larger universe from which those units were extracted. For illustrative purposes we use some of the responses to questions that the Survey Research Center of the University of Michigan asked a sample of 1,450 American adults in 1964. Among these queries were two that directly pertained to the U.S. Supreme Court:

> We are all pretty busy these days and can't be expected to keep up on everything. Have you had enough time to pay any attention to what the Supreme Court of the United States has been doing in the past few years?

The 600 people (41 percent of the sample) who responded affirmatively were then asked:

> Is there anything in particular that it has done that you have liked or disliked? (What is that?) (Anything else?)

Table 7.1 summarizes in a crosstabular form the responses to these questions about the Court and answers to other inquiries. The table classifies each person who offered one or more "likes" but no "dislikes" as supportive of the Court and each respondent who mentioned one or more "dislikes" but no "likes" as critical. The table omits any respondent who gave both "likes" and "dislikes." Now it would be of mild but only passing interest to learn that this particular group of adults responded to these questions as indicated in Table 7.1. What a scholar would deem critical is the validity of generalizing from the views registered by this sample to views held by members of the larger universe, the adult population of the United States.

The Survey Research Center chose this sample on a random basis; that is, every adult American who was not in jail, in a hospital, or in some

other kind of institution had an approximately equal chance of being interviewed. Providing this equal chance minimized the likelihood that the
sample would differ significantly from the larger universe.[3] But minimizing
a difficulty is not the same as eliminating it, and in a world inhabited by
fallible and marvelously variegated human beings, a small sample will never
provide a perfect replica of the population as a whole. This is true even
where the number of possible variations is small. Suppose, for instance,
a man wanted to know if a coin were properly balanced. If he flipped it
100 times he would not expect to end up with precisely 50 heads and 50 tails.
Certainly a record of 48 heads and 52 tails would constitute an intuitively
reasonable indication that the coin was well balanced, for the next set of
100 tosses might well yield 52 heads and 48 tails. If, on the other hand,
90 heads and 10 tails turned up on the first set of 100 tosses, the man would
suspect that there was something wrong with the coin.

The upshot of all of this is that small differences between groups within
a sample may be due to sampling error rather than to real differences within
the universe. How large does the difference have to be before one is justified
in concluding that it is not merely a manifestation of sampling error? The
reply can be precise, clear cut, and all encompassing: It depends. Statisticians use several tests to determine the probability—for one can never be
absolutely certain—that sampling error is at fault. These are called tests
of statistical significance.[4] There is an arbitrary but widely accepted convention that when two subsamples contain differences in an independent
variable* that are small enough to be expected to appear as often as 5 times
in every 100, there is a strong probability that sampling error alone is
responsible for the discrepancies. Conversely, if the differences observed
are so substantial that one would not expect them to happen as often as
5 times in 100, then the accepted convention indicates that these differences
are not likely to be the result of sampling error alone. Thus if a scholar's
findings pass the test of statistical significance, and if, in addition, he has
been meticulous in his work and can reasonably assume that no systematic
errors occurred in the phases of collecting and processing his data, he can
then conclude that real differences exist within the universe on the items he
is analyzing. Whether those differences are important or even interesting
is another question, one to which we return in a few pages.

The test for statistical significance most commonly applied by researchers
in public law is called chi square. It is often appropriate for use with nominal
data, although rarely with ordinal data.† We must leave a full explanation

---

* A dependent variable is a measure of a set of phenomena that we wish to explain (for example,
differing reactions to decisions of the U.S. Supreme Court); and an independent, or explaining,
variable is a measure of a phenomenon that we think might account for the dependent variable.

† For a short working definition of the differences between nominal and ordinal data, see pages
127–128.

of chi square to texts in elementary statistics,[5] but there is some point in showing the standard method for administering the test and in discussing some of its characteristics and limitations. We shall do so with the data in Table 7.1.

For all practical purposes, that table contains two independent, random subsamples, one of people who commented favorably about the work of the Supreme Court and another of those who commented unfavorably. These subsamples are random because of the nature in which the entire sample was drawn; they are independent of each other in the sense that selection of respondents in the second subsample was in no way influenced by the selection of those in the first subsample.

It may help intuitive understanding of the chi square test if we use the analogy of the coin tossing. For the hypothesis that a coin is properly balanced we substitute the hypothesis that the adult population of the United States contains no differences in party identifications between Court supporters, on the one hand, and Court critics, on the other. We would not, as a result, expect to find that differences between the percentages of Democrats, Republicans, and Independents in the two samples reported in Table 7.1 exceed those attributable to sampling error. If the hypothesis of no differences in party identification is correct, the values of chi square for the relationship between party identification and Court perceptions should not exceed 5.99 in more than 5 pairs of Court supporter–Court critic samples in 100. (Almost every elementary statistics text contains a listing for such values of χ^2 for various-sized samples of differing cell arrays.) Should chi square for the data exceed this figure, we would be justified in rejecting the hypothesis of no difference between the party identifications of Court supporters and Court critics.

Chi square actually measures the magnitude of the deviations of sample cell data (observed frequencies) from the data one would expect these cells to contain if they were drawn from a universe that contained no differences. The general formula for computing the statistic is

$$\chi^2 = \sum \frac{f_o{}^2}{f_e} - N$$

where f_o represents the frequencies observed, f_e the frequencies expected, N the number of respondents in both samples, and $\sum$ the conventional symbol for summation.

The observed frequencies appear in Table 7.1, and N is simply their sum. To obtain an estimate of the expected frequencies for each of the six data cells, we determine the proportion in the combined samples of Democrats $(245/523 = .468)$, Republicans $(162/523 = .310)$, and Independents $(116/523 = .222)$ and multiply each of these, in turn, by the respondents in the Court supporters sample (147) and by those in the Court critics sample (376). Thus the expected frequency for Court supporters who identify as Democrats is (.468) (147) = 68.80, and the expected frequency of Court critics who consider themselves Republicans is (.310) (376) = 116.56.

After obtaining the expected frequencies for each of the data cells, it is helpful to construct a table like Table 7.2, which contains all the information necessary for completing the computation of chi square by means of the general formula. Most statistics texts describe several computational short-cuts.

As indicated in the last column of Table 7.1, chi square for the relation-ship between party identification and Court perception is 17.47. Sampling error would not be expected to yield a chi square of such magnitude for six-celled sample data as often as 1 time in 1,000 ($P < .001$). Hence we can confidently reject the hypothesis that the adult population of Court supporters does not differ in party identification from the adult population of Court critics.

When analyzing four-celled data rather than six-celled data, as is the case for each of the other independent variables cross-tabulated with Court perceptions in Table 7.1, the magnitude of chi square necessary to establish statistical significance is somewhat lower: A chi square of 3.84 would be expected to occur by chance in 5 pairs of samples in 100 drawn from a

TABLE 7.2

Party identification of Court supporters and Court critics: 2 × 3 computational table for calculating chi square*

Data cell	f_o	f_e	f_o^2	f_o^2/f_e
Court Supporter–Democrat	79	68.80	6,241	90.71
Court Supporter–Republican	26	45.57	676	14.83
Court Supporter–Independent	42	32.63	1,764	54.06
Court Critic–Democrat	166	175.97	27,556	156.59
Court Critic–Republican	136	116.56	18,496	158.68
Court Critic–Independent	74	83.47	5,476	65.60
Total	523	523.00	60,209	540.47

$$\chi^2 = \sum \frac{f_o^2}{f_e} - N = 540.47 - 523.00 = 17.47$$

$$df = 2$$

* We have listed the party identification categories as Democrat-Republican-Independent rather than as Democrat-Independent-Republican in this and subsequent tables concerned with chi square because we want to avoid any possible implication that chi square is appropriate for ordinal data in tables larger in size than 2 × 2.

universe containing no differences, a chi square of 6.64 in 1 pair of samples in 100, and a chi square of 10.83 in 1 pair of samples in 1,000. The chi squares recorded in the statistics column of Table 7.1 for the differences between the views of Court critics and Court supporters about the power of the federal government and public school prayers are so large that one would not expect them to appear even once in 1,000 pairs of random samples ($P < .001$) drawn from a universe in which Court supporters did not differ from Court critics on these subjects. Sexual differences in the samples of Court supporters and Court critics, on the other hand, yield a chi square small enough so that we would expect to observe it in many more than 5 pairs of random samples in 100 ($P > .05$). It is thus safe to infer that men and women in the adult population do not differ in their perceptions of the U.S. Supreme Court, whereas people who differ about federal power or about public school prayers also differ in their feelings toward the Court.

At this juncture a caveat is very much in order. A relatively weak association between two variables may turn out to be statistically significant when the samples are large. Chi square and similar tests are tests of statistical significance only; that is, they indicate the degree of confidence one can place in a relationship occurring by chance. They tell us nothing about the fundamental importance of that relationship. Showing that random samples contain more Democrats who are Court supporters and Republicans who are Court critics than can reasonably be attributed to chance is a far cry from demonstrating that party identification tells a great deal of substantive importance about perceptions of the Supreme Court.

Reference to the relevant data in Table 7.1 should make this obvious. Although the data reveal that Democrats are somewhat more partial to the Court than are Republicans, these data also indicate that most Democrats, like most Republicans, who can comment on the Court's specific work, do so in critical terms. Thus, knowing a respondent's party identification does help to explain his Court perceptions—but not very much.

The chi square test indicates that the association between Court perceptions and feelings about the power of the federal government is also statistically significant at $P < .001$. Here, however, a glance at the data in Table 7.1 is enough to show that the association between these variables is substantially stronger than that between Court perceptions and party identification. Knowing a respondent's feelings about the power of the federal government provides a much better (if still far from foolproof) basis than does party identification for predicting his perceptions of the Court.

The observant reader will no doubt have noticed that the magnitude of the chi square for the relationship between Court perceptions and attitudes toward federal power is considerably larger than that for the relationship between Court perceptions and party identification. Why then cannot the size of the chi squares be used to indicate the relative strength of the

TABLE 7.3

College graduates' perceptions of U.S. Supreme Court: 1964 Survey Research Center Survey

Perceptions	Independent variables						Statistics
	1. Party identification						
	Democratic		*Republican*		*Independent*		
	N	%	N	%	N	%	
Supportive of the Court	15	45.5	8	23.5	10	45.5	$\chi^2 = 4.32$
Critical of the Court	18	54.5	26	76.5	12	54.5	$P > .05$
Total	33	100.0	34	100.0	22	100.0	

Perceptions	2. Power of federal government				Statistics
	Too great		*Not too great*		
	N	%	N	%	
Supportive of the Court	11	21.6	16	69.6	$\chi^2 = 15.76$
Critical of the Court	40	78.4	7	30.4	$P < .001$
Total	51	100.0	23	100.0	$\phi = -.46$

Perceptions	3. Public school prayer				Statistics
	Favor		*Oppose*		
	N	%	N	%	
Supportive of the Court	17	27.9	13	76.5	$\chi^2 = 13.26$
Critical of the Court	44	72.1	4	23.5	$P < .001$
Total	61	100.0	17	100.0	$\phi = -.41$

Perceptions	4. Sex				Statistics
	Male		*Female*		
	N	%	N	%	
Supportive of the Court	22	42.3	11	28.9	$\chi^2 = 1.69$
Critical of the Court	30	57.7	27	71.1	$P > .05$
Total	52	100.0	38	100.0	$\phi = .14$

association between the several variables reported?* Actually, for these data it can, because the number of cases involved in computing the chi squares in Table 7.1 does not vary greatly. But when the *N*s on which they are based differ dramatically, chi squares cannot be directly compared.

We can see what a vast impact *N* can have on the magnitude of chi square by comparing Table 7.1 with Table 7.3. The former contains data for all respondents with Court perceptions, and the latter, data only for the subset of people who graduated from college. Although the strength of the relationship between Court perceptions and party identification in both tables is in reality almost the same, the chi square for the table with the larger number of cases (Table 7.1) is nearly four times greater than the chi square for the subset of college graduates (Table 7.3). A similar result occurs for the relationship between Court perceptions and attitudes toward federal power. There the relationship of the larger group is slightly weaker than it is for the subset in Table 7.3—even though the chi square for the larger group is more than four times greater.

We cautioned against assuming that a statistically significant relationship is necessarily any assurance of substantive importance. There is also need to warn that the converse may also be true. When the number of cases under study is quite small, a strong association may result in a chi square so tiny that one cannot be confident that the relationship was not caused by the luck of the draw. The strength of the association between Court perceptions and party identification for the subset of college graduates in Table 7.3 is, if anything, a bit stronger than that for the larger group. Yet the chi square for the subset indicates a high probability that the relationship is due to sampling error, whereas that for the entire group of respondents is statistically highly significant.

Perhaps a return to the coin-tossing analogy can facilitate an intuitive understanding of why this is so. Two heads in a pair of tosses of a coin would not lead most people to suspect its fairness; 600 heads in 1,000 tosses of the coin certainly would. Yet the proportion of heads in the 2-toss set (1.00) is far larger than in the 1,000-toss set (.60). Large differences are likely to occur by chance in small sets of tosses, but even fairly small differences are highly unlikely to appear randomly in very large sets.

The implications of all of this are simple. One should always test as best he can the reliability of the relationships among data, but he should not confuse measures of statistical significance with measures of substantive importance. That a given pattern is unlikely to be produced by chance does not mean that the pattern is important or even interesting. On the other hand, a high probability that a pattern is due to chance does not prove that it is, in fact, a result of chance alone. Especially when dealing with

---

* The strength of the association between two variables, as measured by the phi coefficient (ϕ), is discussed in the second part of this chapter.

small samples, relationships may occur that seem substantively important but do not meet the commonly accepted minimum levels of chi square or similar tests.   Under those circumstances it is advisable to treat the findings with the utmost caution, but they need not be ignored.   Perhaps other explanations can account for the data equally as well or better, or perhaps there are more subtle relationships present than one first imagined.   If after second thought an analyst still believes that he has discovered an important relationship, he can try to obtain more data so that he can more satisfactorily test the probability of having uncovered a meaningful relationship.

Measuring Association: The Phi Coefficient[6]

As indicated earlier, chi square is defective as a measure of association because its size varies with the number of cases involved.   Unless differences in sampling size are controlled, even chi squares for 2×2 tables cannot be directly compared.   The phi coefficient (ϕ) can be derived from chi square.*   Phi is independent of sample size and thus useful for comparing correlations between pairs of variables.   Since no measure of association for 2×2 tables is as widely used by public law analysts,[7] phi merits careful attention.

The statistics columns of Tables 7.1 and 7.3 contain the phi's for each 2×2 relationship reported.   These phi's are comparable, and so they warrant a variety of inferences.   For example:

☐ Feelings about federal power are more strongly correlated with the Court perceptions of college graduates than of the population as a whole.

Attitudes toward public school prayer form a much better predictor of the Court perceptions of college graduates than of the general public.

Attitudes toward public school prayer constitute at least as good a predictor of the way college graduates view the Court as feelings about federal power do of the Court perceptions of the entire community.

The sex of a college graduate tells more about his Court perceptions than does the same information for someone who did not attend college.

For college graduates, as for the general public, the best single predictor of Court perceptions is feeling about the power of the federal government.

$$* \phi = \sqrt{\frac{x^2}{N}}$$

In addition to facilitating comparison, the phi coefficient has other desirable properties. One is that the sign of phi tells whether the relationship between the variables is positive or negative. Another advantage of phi is that its range, under certain conditions at least, extends from -1.0, a perfect negative correlation, to $+1.0$, a perfect positive correlation. Finally, phi, whatever its upper limits in any particular set of circumstances, can be interpreted in the same manner as Pearson's product moment correlation, a statistic considered in the third part of this chapter.

Despite these valuable properties, the phi coefficient has several limitations that pose dangers to its use in public law. One limitation already mentioned is that phi can be used only for 2×2 arrays. There are, in addition, real hazards in using phi unless the data are truly dichotomous—unless, for example, one is dealing with males versus females, single-judge versus collegial courts, criminal versus civil cases, judges versus nonjudges, Japanese Supreme Court judges versus Australian High Court judges, unanimous versus nonunanimous cases, or majority versus dissenting votes.

The most serious dangers arise when an analyst uses phi to try to measure correlations in the voting behavior of pairs of judges. An understanding of these dangers will be enhanced if we first describe the usual manner for computing the phi coefficient.

The computational formula for phi, unlike that for chi square, requires that data be converted from frequencies into proportions. Table 7.4 presents in proportional form the data from Table 7.3 for likes and dislikes cross-tabulated with attitudes toward public school prayer. Each cell in Table 7.4 also contains a letter in parentheses, which makes the following formula for computing the phi coefficient self-explanatory:

$$\phi = \frac{ad - bc}{\sqrt{(a + c)(b + d)(c + d)(a + b)}}$$

TABLE 7.4

Attitudes toward public school prayer of Court supporters and Court critics: computational table for calculating the phi coefficient

School prayer	Court perceptions		Marginals
	Supportive	Critical	
Favor	.218	.564	.782
	(a)	(b)	(a + b)
Oppose	.167	.051	.218
	(c)	(d)	(c + d)
Marginals	.385	.615	1.000
	(a + c)	(b + d)	

Expressed verbally, phi equals the difference between the product of the diagonals divided by the square root of the product of the marginals. Applying this formula to the data in 7.4,

$$\phi = \frac{(.218)(.051) - (.564)(.167)}{\sqrt{(.218 + .167)(.564 + .051)(.167 + .051)(.218 + .564)}} = -.41$$

Let us now consider how phi is utilized to measure the correlation of the voting behavior of a pair of judges, whether for use in bloc analysis or for other purposes. In our earlier treatment of bloc analysis we measured the strength of the association between a pair of judges by the percentage of nonunanimous cases in which they voted together. In the 1962 term of the U.S. Supreme Court, for example, Black and Douglas participated jointly in 103 nonunanimous decisions.[8] They voted in unison in 77 of these and disagreed with one another in 26—for an agreement percentage of 75 (77/103). To use phi, however, it is necessary to categorize the votes of a pair of judges proportionately in a 2×2 array. This is done by dividing the 77 common votes into two subsets: The first subset consists of the 68 votes Black and Douglas cast together as members of a Court majority, and the other of the 9 times when they dissented in common. The 26 cases in which Black and Douglas disagreed with each other are also divided into two subsets: the 12 cases in which Douglas joined the majority while Black dissented and the 14 cases in which Douglas dissented while Black stayed with the majority. In the following table this is presented in schematic form convenient for computing the phi coefficient.

		Black		
		+majority	−majority	
Douglas	+majority	.660	.117	.777
		(a)	(b)	(a + b)
	−majority	.136	.087	.223
		(c)	(d)	(c + d)
		.796	.204	1.000
		(a + c)	(b + d)	

Applying the computational formula,

$$\phi = \frac{(.660)(.087) - (.117)(.136)}{\sqrt{(.660 + .136)(.117 + .087)(.136 + .223)(.660 + .117)}} = .25$$

There is an immediate difficulty here. A phi coefficient of .25 does not signify a particularly strong relationship. Yet we know that Black and

Douglas voted together in 75 percent of all the nonunanimous cases in which both participated; and we also recall from arithmetic that that can be considered a rather strong relationship.

Let us see how reliable a measure phi is for all the other justices. In Table 7.5 we have indicated the frequencies of votes cast in all nonunanimous cases by all pairs of U.S. Supreme Court judges during the 1962 term. The frequencies appear below the diagonal. Above the diagonal are both the percentages of interagreement and the phi coefficients for all 36 pairs. The percentages are reported in the upper-left-hand corners of the cells, and the phi coefficients in the lower right. In positioning the judges in the matrix, we used percentages of interagreement.*

Close inspection of Table 7.5 discloses that the phi coefficients differ from the percentages often and traumatically. Percentages identify the 5 most strongly associated pairs as Warren-Brennan (96), Brennan-Goldberg (84), Warren-Black (83), Warren-Goldberg (80), and Brennan-Black (80). Only 2 of these pairs, Warren-Brennan and Warren-Black, are among the pairs with the 5 highest phi coefficients, whereas 2 other pairs, Warren-Goldberg and Brennan-Goldberg, have very low phi's. Moreover, a particular percentage does not always yield the same phi. Both Black-Brennan and Warren-Goldberg have agreement percentages of 80, but their respective phi's are .21 and −.02. An even greater discrepancy occurs with the Goldberg-Douglas and White-Stewart pairs: Although the judges in each pair agreed with one another 74 percent of the time, the pairs have phi's of .09 and .42. It is hardly surprising, then, to find that the bloc structures identified by the two methods of measuring the cohesion between pairs of judges have slight resemblance.

If a phi of +.25 is arbitrarily selected as a cohesion index for identifying a bloc,† only one bloc, Black-Warren-Brennan, is common to both types of analysis. Percentages indicate that Warren-Brennan-Goldberg constitute a second bloc that interlocks with Black-Warren-Brennan. Phi coefficients fail to recognize Goldberg's ties with Warren and Brennan, but they point to four other blocs: a Harlan-White-Stewart bloc that interlocks with a Clark-Harlan-White bloc and a couple of two-man blocs, Goldberg-Stewart and Black-Douglas.

When two methods addressed to the same problem and identical data yield such disparate results, there is obvious cause for anxiety. The reason phi's have so little in common with percentages lies in the differing characteristics of the two measures. Percentages are sensitive only to the distribution

---

* We did not employ Sprague's method because its failure to take higher-order relationships into account results in a less satisfactory arrangement for present purposes than does our intuitive alternative. See pages 162–164 for a discussion of Sprague's method.

† No measure comparable to Sprague's criterion has been developed.

Table 7.5

Bloc structures as revealed by percentages and phi coefficients: all nonunanimous cases, 1962 term U.S. Supreme Court

		Douglas		Black		Warren		Brennan		Goldberg		Stewart		White		Harlan		Clark	
		%	φ	%	φ	%	φ	%	φ	%	φ	%	φ	%	φ	%	φ	%	φ
Douglas	+	—		75	(.25)	75	.07	76	.11	74	.09	46	−.27	62	−.19	20	−.57	43	−.29
	−																		
Black	+	68	14	—		83	(.40)	80	.21	72	−.04	44	−.35	65	−.16	20	−.58	53	−.05
	−	12	09																
Warren	+	73	19	78	19	—	+	96	(.76)	80	−.02	53	−.25	73	−.15	28	−.41	59	−.08
	−	07	03	03	07														
Brennan	+	75	20	78	19	91	04	—	+	84	.12	54	−.23	75	−.14	30	−.36	57	−.01
	−	05	03	04	02	01	05												
Goldberg	+	71	19	71	19	72	08	80	04	—	+	68	(.28)	72	−.15	39	−.03	45	−.32
	−	08	04	10	01	09	08	04	04										
Stewart	+	44	20	44	20	51	02	54	02	60	03	—	+	46	(.42)	64	(.36)	51	−.02
	−	36	03	38	01	38	02	38	00	30	09								
White	+	60	22	63	22	72	17	74	17	71	10	59	03	—	+	51	(.25)	68	(.33)
	−	16	01	16	01	09	00	08	00	10	00	03	14						
Harlan	+	18	19	19	19	27	00	30	00	37	00	31	06	34	02	—	+	57	(.19)
	−	61	02	62	02	01	01	00	00	39	02	30	33	45	15				
Clark	+	40	18	46	12	54	04	55	04	45	00	35	23	52	04	26	32	—	+
	−	39	03	35	07	39	05	42	00	42	00	26	16	27	13	11	31		

Scalogram criterion: 80 percent   Phi criterion (arbitrary): +.25

of votes between the two diagonals, *ad* and *bc*, but not to the way in which votes are divided between *a* and *d* or between *b* and *c*; that is, it makes no difference in computing percentages whether the 77 votes Black and Douglas cast together were all majority votes, all dissenting votes, or any combination of the two. Percentages measure the proportion of cases in which the two judges voted together. Phi, on the other hand, is very sensitive to the distribution of votes in all four cells and thus to whether the judges were in the minority or the majority. If, for example, the *d* cell, which contains a pair's joint dissents, is empty and the other three cells are not (as is the case with 8 of the 36 pairs: Warren-White, Warren-Stewart, Warren-Harlan, Brennan-White, Brennan-Stewart, Brennan-Harlan, Goldberg-White, and Goldberg-Clark), then phi must be negative no matter what percentage of the time the pair voted together. Thus the Warren-White pair has a negative phi (−.15), even though Warren and White cast common votes 73 percent of the time. A nearly empty *d* cell may cause similar incongruities, as the Goldberg-Black and Goldberg-Warren phi's show. Those pairs have agreement percentages of 72 and 80, but the presence in both instances of only a single vote in the *d* cell resulted in negative phi's of −.04 and −.02.*

These characteristics of the phi coefficient considered, is it a suitable statistic for measuring the level of agreement between pairs of judges? In our judgment it is not, because only one variable is actually involved: how often judges vote together. Percentages measure this accurately. But phi, like all simple correlational statistics, assumes measurements on each of two variables. In seeking to develop the data necessary to fill the four cells essential in computing phi, judicial analysts have split majority and dissenting votes into two subsets and treated each as a separate variable. In doing this, they have introduced a second variable (the extent of agreement with the Court's majority) that is irrelevant and conceptually

* Another characteristic of the phi coefficient with serious implications for the desirability of using it to measure the association between pairs of judges is that the magnitude of phi increases as the size of the numerator in the computational formula approaches that of the denominator. Two considerations determine the size of the numerator. It varies directly (1) with the proportion of all votes cast that falls along a single diagonal (whether *ad* or *bc*) and (2) with the equality of the division of the votes between the two cells of each diagonal. When all the votes cast fall along the *ad* diagonal and these votes are evenly divided between the *a* (joint agreement with the majority) and the *d* (joint agreement in dissent) cells, phi is +1.0; when all the votes fall along the *bc* diagonal (containing all disagreements between the judges in a pair) and are evenly distributed between the *b* and the *c* cells, phi is −1.0. The Warren-Brennan pair in Table 7.5 has a high phi coefficient (.76) because of the first consideration—96 percent of their votes are on the *ad* diagonal. Their phi would have been higher still if there had been near equality in the division of *ad* votes between the *a* and the *d* cells instead of a .93 versus .07 split. Warren-Brennan thus satisfied the first consideration much more fully than the second. Harlan-Stewart, on the other hand, with a phi of .36, met the second condition, but not the first. Although the proportion of their votes falling along the *ad* diagonal is only .64, these are almost equally divided between the *a* and the *d* cells. The phi for Harlan-Stewart would have been substantially lower if the division between the *a* and the *d* cells had been more extreme.

confusing.*   The practical results, as we have seen, can be incongruous. Using the phi coefficient to measure the association between pairs of judges is unlikely to instill confidence in the end product.

Numbered Data: Two Variables[9]

When data can be numbered realistically, they can be more fully and precisely analyzed.   Precision is an advantage in almost any kind of analysis, qualitative as well as quantitative.   Only partially utilizing data always leads to some loss of precision.   The consequences are not necessarily damaging, but sometimes they seriously obscure and distort the relationships that are most important.

How can one go about pinning numbers to data?   The ways are many —and occasionally very obvious.   Numbers can clearly represent gradations in age, income, amount of education, length of judicial service, or how often people have moved, voted, married, or picketed courthouses.   Nor is it much less readily apparent that one can tag numbers to dichotomized variables: female = 1 and male = 2; black = 1 and white = 2; no prior judicial experience = 0 and prior judicial experience = 1; rejection of a civil liberties claim = 1 and support for that claim = 2—although, admittedly, the justification for assigning precisely those numbers to the categories indicated is hardly self-evident.

Consider now how numbers might be assigned to the responses to the questions (stated on page 181) about the work of the Supreme Court. When classifying responses to these questions in the discussion of conventional nominal statistics, we did not make full use of the data.   People who made one critical response were squeezed into the same pigeonhole with those who made two or three; Court supporters were also lumped together, whether they made one favorable comment or several.   In addition, we totally ignored both the people who were unable to articulate a single like or dislike (about 60 percent of the entire sample) and those who mentioned both likes and dislikes (12 percent).

If we could pin numbers to the data, alternative methods of classifying the responses would become available. By assigning each comment a weight of 1, we can readily construct a variety of conceptually distinguishable metrics.   One such instrument, a Court visibility scale, could be created by assigning each respondent a number equal to the sum of his total comments. People who offered no comments would receive a 0, those who offered one

---

* As Duncan MacRae has put it, " A good index, measuring some concept, should not depend on considerations irrelevant to that concept."   See " Indices of Pairwise Agreement Between Justices or Legislators," 10 *Midwest Journal of Political Science* 138, 139 (1966).   For a spirited, but to us unpersuasive, rebuttal, see S. Sidney Ulmer, " Pairwise Association of Judges and Legislators: Further Reflections," 11 *Midwest Journal of Political Science* 106 (1967).

comment, a 1, and so on to those with a maximum of three favorable and three critical comments, who would be tagged with a 6. Another measure, which could be termed a specific support scale, combines visibility with evaluation. In constructing the specific support scale, we assigned each respondent who commented on the work of the Court a $+1$ for each favorable comment and a -1 for each critical comment; his final score is equal to the sum of these weightings. Thus two positive responses and one negative $(+1, +1, -1)$ yield a score of $+1$; two negative responses and one positive $(-1, -1, +1)$ yield a score of -1; three positive and one negative $(+1, +1, +1, -1)$ yield a $+2$; and so forth. This scale has a range of $+3$ to -3.

It is important to recognize that the visibility scale differs from the specific support scale in two major ways. First, the visibility scale includes the entire set of respondents, whereas the specific support scale treats only those who offered at least one comment on the work of the Court. Second, the two scales measure different things and, therefore, frequently yield different scores when both are applied to a particular respondent. To illustrate:

Response pattern	Visibility scale score	Specific support score
$+++---$	6	0
$--$	2	-2
$++---$	5	-1
$++$	2	$+2$
$++-$	3	$+1$

Several other, and conceptually different, scales can be constructed from these same data.

Let us now turn to another kind of problem and to another set of questions asked in the survey:

Some people think that the Supreme Court gets too mixed up in politics. Others don't feel that way. How about you? Do you think the Supreme Court gets too mixed up in politics or not? Do you feel strongly about that or not so strongly?

Responses to these items can be tagged with numbers in this manner:

☐ Supreme Court is not too mixed up in politics; feel strongly   1
Supreme Court is not too mixed up in politics; do not feel strongly   2
Yes and no; it depends   3
Supreme Court is too mixed up in politics; do not feel strongly   4
Supreme Court is too mixed up in politics; feel strongly   5

TABLE 7.6

Likert scale of diffuse-support items

| | Assessment of court | | | |
| | Favorable | Neutral | Critical | |
Question set	1 2	3	4 5
Court is too mixed up in politics	No ....Pro/con ....Yes
Court favors groups	No ....Pro/con ....Yes
Court does a good job	Yes ....Pro/con ....No
Court can be trusted more than Congress	Yes ....Pro/con ....No

When several questions have been posed to tap aspects of a broader subject, it sometimes seems desirable to combine the responses into a single index. One rather elementary method for doing so is a variation of the Likert scale.[10] To illustrate, let us take the set of questions on the Court's involvement in politics and add three additional queries: How well does the Court do its job? Does the Court favor particular groups? and Can the Court be trusted more than Congress can? If each of these new questions were scored in the same fashion as the Court-in-politics set (from 1 to 5, with a low score favorable to the Court and a high score critical of it), we would end up with a generalized, or diffuse-support, scale ranging from a low of 4 (a score of 1 per question), extremely favorable, to a high of 20 (a score of 5 per question), extremely critical. Since there are always some respondents who do not answer every question, the analyst would then have to divide each respondent's total score by the number of questions he actually answered in order to make all the scores comparable. Table 7.6 should help clarify the manner of scoring.

At this point it should be stressed that we do not consider any measuring instrument used here for illustrative purposes to constitute ipso facto a defensible assignment of numbers to the data under consideration. Nothing more is intended here than to provide an intuitive notion of some of the ways in which numbers can be assigned to data of this character. Nonetheless, let us for the purposes of exposition *assume* that a plausible case can be made for such scales as these* and proceed directly to a discussion of what can be done with them.

---

* Actually, the indices produced by Likert's methods did not in this instance result in enough unique data points to permit effective exposition of the scatterplot, one of the analytical tools central to the discussion that follows. However, an alternative method of index construction, factor analysis, can create indices that not only correlate highly with those produced by Likert scaling but also contain the profusion of data points desirable for illustrating scatterplot techniques. Hence most of the indices used in the remainder of this chapter are factor, rather than Likert, indices. Although factor analysis is far too complex for detailed consideration in this book, a brief discussion of it appears in an appendix to this chapter.

Returning to a set of subproblems in the study of public attitudes toward the Supreme Court, how do blacks, who as a group benefited most from Supreme Court decisions during the twenty years before these surveys were taken, feel about the Court? And what effect does knowledge about the Court have on their opinions? Relevant data appear in a second poll, one that the Survey Research Center conducted in 1966.

The sample included 133 blacks, of whom 96 (72 percent) provided information rich enough to score them on both diffuse support and on an index of Court knowledge. We developed the Court-knowledge index by factor analytic techniques from a cluster of questions designed to measure how much a respondent knew about the judges sitting on the Court, recent Court decisions, the Court's constitutional responsibilities, and attempts to change the Court or its personnel. Figure 7.1 is a scatter diagram reporting the scores for all 96 black respondents on the pair of indices. Diffuse support is recorded on the vertical (Y) axis and Court knowledge on the horizontal (X) axis. Hence a person with high knowledge–strong diffuse support would be scored in the upper-right-hand corner of the figure, and a respondent with low knowledge–weak support would be represented on the lower left.

The hazards of treating these data as if they were nominal (a practice sometimes defended in the name of conservative and hence desirable procedure) are nicely illustrated if we seek to summarize the contents of this scatterplot in a 2×2 table and then to compute the nominal statistics employed earlier in this chapter. If a diffuse-support score of 3.20 were used as the point separating strong support from weak support and a score of 2.00 were used to distinguish high knowledge from low knowledge, the data in the plot would be categorized as follows:

Court knowledge

Diffuse support	Low	High	
Weak	18	2	$\chi^2 = 1.53$
Strong	59	17	$\phi = +.13$

But if we used a diffuse-support score of 4.50 to separate strong support from weak support and a knowledge score of 1.40 to separate high from low knowledge, the plotted data would take this form:

Court knowledge

Diffuse support	Low	High	
Weak	47	18	$\chi^2 = 9.99$
Strong	12	19	$\phi = +.32$

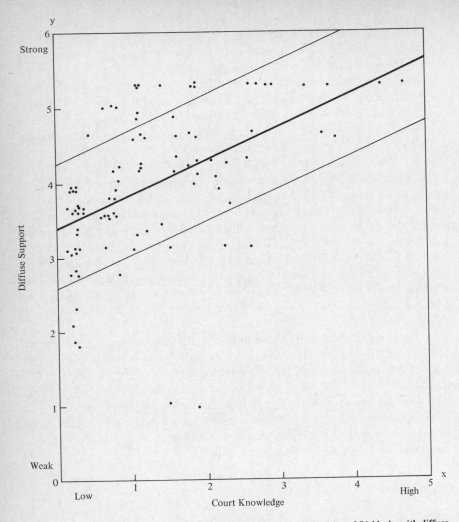

FIGURE 7.1 1966 Survey Research Center Postelection Survey: scatter plot of 96 blacks with diffuse support scored on Y axis, Court knowledge scored on X axis

Still another option would be to use a diffuse-support score of 4.50 and a knowledge score of 1.00 as break points. Then the plotted data would appear as follows:

Court knowledge

Diffuse support	Low	High	
Weak	41	24	$x^2 = 21.21$
Strong	4	27	$\phi = +.46$

One cannot fail to notice that each of these 2×2 tables with its accompanying nominal statistics suggests fundamentally different interpretations of the relationship between diffuse support and Court knowledge. What is more, a variety of other break points would be just as defensible (or indefensible) as those used for illustrative purposes. Thus treating as nominal, data that can be numbered is neither conservative nor radical; it is merely dangerous and misleading.

A more appropriate method for describing the relationship between these measurements of diffuse support and Court knowledge carries the catchy title of bivariate linear regression analysis.[11] With this technique we can determine the functional relationship between two variables by plotting the straight line that best fits* the pattern of the data. In Figure 7.1 the regression line is the bold line running upward from about the center of the Y axis toward the upper-right-hand corner of the plot. The general formula for determining the regression of a dependent variable (Y) on an independent, or describing, variable (X) is

$$Y = a + bX$$

where a is a constant and b is the coefficient of regression, or the slope of the line. Nothing more demanding than ordinary multiplication and division is required to apply the formula in which a and b are calculated from the raw data as follows:

$$b = \frac{N\Sigma XY - (\Sigma X)(\Sigma Y)}{N\Sigma X^2 - (\Sigma X)^2}$$

$$a = \frac{\Sigma Y - b\Sigma X}{N}$$

---

* "Best fit" in this context means that the sum of the squared distances (measured vertically) from the data points to the straight line passing through their midst is less than the sum of squared distances from those points to any alternative straight line.

But these computations are tedious enough to force most scholars to rely on desk calculators or to leave the work to their selfless research assistant, the computer.

Solving the preceding formulas for the data represented in Figure 7.1, we find that

$$a = 3.40$$
$$b = .45$$

Thus a black respondent's diffuse-support score is equal to .45 times his Court-knowledge score plus a constant of 3.40; or completely in algebraic terms,

$$Y = 3.40 + .45X$$

It is now possible to estimate the value of diffuse support for any given Court-knowledge score. For example, if a respondent's knowledge score is 2.00, his diffuse-support score will be 4.30.

Fitting a line carries us a long step forward. From a knowledge of the functional relationship between diffuse support and Court knowledge, we can now predict magnitudes of the former from magnitudes of the latter. These predictions are not, to be sure, completely reliable. If they were, every value of Y would fall precisely on the line of regression, and a glance at Figure 7.1 shows that most of the points are somewhat off the regression line. An accurate indicator of how reliable the predictions actually are is a measure of dispersion called the standard deviation (σ),* which is roughly demarcated by the thin lines that parallel the regression line. These thin lines reveal that more than three-quarters of the Y values lie within .83 of a diffuse-support unit from the regression line. In other words, in predicting diffuse support from Court knowledge, we would not have missed by more than .83 of a diffuse-support unit as often as 1 time in 4—and much of the time we would have come considerably closer than that.

Bivariate linear regression is a powerful analytic tool, but several caveats on its use are necessary. One can fit a regression line to literally any set of points, including the pigeon droppings in the Piazza San Marco. In the absence of a meaningful relationship between a pair of variables, however, the slope is likely to be slight and the standard deviation relatively large. On the other hand, a slight slope and a large deviation do not necessarily imply that there is no meaningful relationship between a pair of variables; a relationship can be strong but nonlinear. Still another

---

* The standard deviation, which is the most widely used and valuable measure of dispersion, may be defined verbally as the square root of the arithmetic mean of the squared deviations from the mean.

hazard stems from the presence of what are called outliers, a tiny number of data points far distant from the main clusters. Because of the nature of the statistical computation involved, regression analysis, as careful attention to the formulas presented for computing the constant (a) and slope (b) will disclose, gives such heavy weight to extreme outliers that their impact (if one is unaware of their presence) may seriously mislead the analyst. The single best way to avoid all such hazards is the scatterplot, since it allows the analyst to "see" his data and to recognize some of the forces at work.

Let us now return to the scatterplot in Figure 7.1. It confirms, to be sure, what regression analysis indicated with greater precision: Knowledgeable blacks tend to be more supportive of the U.S. Supreme Court than blacks who know less about the Court's work. But closer inspection of the scatterplot reveals an interesting pattern that the regression equation and its standard deviation could not by themselves bring to our attention. Most of the dispersion appears at the low-knowledge end of the plot, where knowledge (X) is less than 2.00. Twenty-one of the twenty-three data points lying beyond one standard deviation from the line of regression occur before the knowledge score reaches 2.00. Almost 90 percent of the data points beyond knowledge equal to 2.00 are less than one standard deviation from the regression line. As knowledge rises to 2.65, the upper 40 percent of its range, every data point lies close to the regression line. Moreover, 80 percent of the respondents who score above 2.65 on the Court-knowledge index report the highest diffuse-support levels possible on our index.

What the scatterplot indicates has major substantive implications. The general feelings about the Court expressed by blacks who have a very meager knowledge of it vary over a fairly wide range. Not only do increments in Court knowledge result in sharp increments in diffuse support, but Court knowledge also quickly attains a threshold beyond which diffuse support, as measured by our index, is maximal. Once diffuse support has reached its upper limit, of course, it cannot be further augmented by additional increments in Court knowledge. Only a modest knowledge of the Court is necessary to make the black man its staunch supporter. The linear regression equation may not be a dissatisfying way of describing the data, but it is hardly an ideal way either. With the two circled outliers from Figure 7.1 removed, the curve in Figure 7.2 accounts for substantially more variance in diffuse support than the original regression equation does.*

---

* Among the ways in which such a curve may be described in linear fashion are the following:

diffuse support $= 2.41 - .24$ Court knowledge $+ 3.77 \log_{10}$ Court knowledge
    and
diffuse support $= 3.18 + .94$ Court knowledge $- .13$ Court knowledge^2

The first equation accounts for more variance than the second (51 percent as compared with 38 percent), but it also contains a larger standard deviation.

FIGURE 7.2

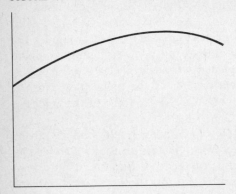

The relationship portrayed here between Court knowledge and diffuse support is, to be sure, dependent on the scales devised to measure them. Differently constructed scales might point to relationships that could be described more effectively by bivariate linear regression than can the data here illustrated. Our purpose in presenting this illustration is to show how a scatterplot can reduce the likelihood that regression will mislead the analyst.

Something more might be said about the problem of outliers, cases that grossly differ from the basic pattern. Two such people are obvious in Figure 7.1. The data points for this pair of black respondents, both of whom were scored as moderately knowledgeable and strongly critical of the Court, are circled in the figure. Fortunately, in this particular instance, the impact of these two outliers was barely noticeable. But because of the nature of the formula used, regression analysis is typically very sensitive to the impact of widely deviant cases. To illustrate how serious a problem outliers can create, let us add two dummy outliers (each with the coordinates $X = 5.20$, $Y = .50$) to the original set of 96 cases. Now the regression equation becomes diffuse support $= 3.74 + .16$ Court knowledge, with a standard deviation of .98, and suggests a substantially different relationship between the two variables.

As deviant cases, outliers may not only alert the analyst to the possibility that the data may be defective, but accounting for them sometimes constitutes an important part of building a theory. In survey research, when the number of outliers is small, one can often find an explanation of the deviance by looking at the actual text of the answers the respondents gave. In this instance we could readily, though in the second instance painfully, account for both deviants. One respondent was a man from St. Louis who, the interviewer had warned in a note attached to the back of the protocol, had been uncooperative and inattentive during the interview. He had been in a hurry to go out and had simply given the quickest answer to each question. Thus we could

put him aside as a "busted interview." The other outlier was a highly educated woman from New York City. She was actually more favorably
disposed toward the Court than her diffuse-support score indicated. Our
coding and scale construction were simply not sufficiently subtle to pick up
the nuances in her replies to the questions.

A further advantage of regression analysis is that one can, if he wishes,
compare the regression equations for two different groups of respondents
for identical variables. We may, for example, compare the regressions of
diffuse support on Court knowledge for the subsample of 96 blacks (diffuse
support = 3.40 + .45 Court knowledge; σ = .83) with a subsample of 200
white Southerners (diffuse support = 3.22 − .38 Court knowledge; σ =
1.23). The Southern whites are almost an inverse image of the blacks.
Increments of Court knowledge reduce diffuse support by Southern whites,
whereas such increments augment support by the blacks. One should note,
however, that the slope of the regression line for the white Southerners is
not quite so steep, nor the reliability of the relationship between the variables
quite so strong, as for the blacks. The reason is that knowledgeable Southern
whites include a number of people who would conventionally be categorized
as liberals, whereas there are almost no conservatives on these issues among
our black respondents.

It is generally not permissible, on the other hand, to compare the slopes
for different pairs of variables, even for a single group of respondents. We
cannot do so because the slope of the line (*b*) describes the extent to which a
pair of variables is associated in terms of the units of the measuring instruments. The Court-knowledge index and Duncan's Index of Socio-Economic
Status (SES) furnish convenient illustrations. Court knowledge is a con-
tinuously distributed scale with a range of .00 to 5.30; Duncan's Socio-
Economic Status Index is distributed in intervals of 1 over a range of 1 to 99.
There is no technical obstacle to computing the regression of diffuse support
on each of these variables for the subsample of 96 blacks, as in Table 7.7,
but to compare them is to be guilty of "illegal statisticizing." The great
differences in the measuring instruments make comparison of the slopes (and
hence computing the regressions) at best unedifying, at worst badly misleading.

In an effort to render relationships based on differing units of measurement comparable, Karl Pearson devised his product moment correlation,
usually indicated by the symbol *r*.* By treating each variable in terms of its
own standard deviation, measuring instruments are standardized so that the
strength of the association between any pair of variables can be expressed
on a scale that ranges from −1.0 to +1.0. If all the data points fall on the

---

* Pearson's *r* is normally computed by means of a formula such as the following:

$$r_{xy} = \frac{N\Sigma XY - (\Sigma X)(\Sigma Y)}{\sqrt{[N\Sigma X^2 - (\Sigma X)^2][N\Sigma Y^2 - (\Sigma Y)^2]}}$$

regression line, *r* is either +1.0, when the slope is positive, or −1.0, when the slope is negative. If the data points are so distributed that the regression line has no slope at all, *r* will be .00. But as long as the regression line has some slope, *r* can assume a wide range of values.

Pearson's *r* has another useful property. When *r* is squared, the resulting measure, called the coefficient of determination, indicates the percentage of the variation about the line of regression accounted for by an independent variable. Thus Court knowledge, as reported in the last column of Table 7.7, can account for 24 percent of the variance in diffuse support for the

TABLE 7.7

1966 Survey Research Center postelection
survey: subsample of 96 blacks scored on diffuse
support

| Independent variables | *Diffuse support* | | |
	Slope (*b*)	Correlation (*r*)	Coefficient of determination (*r²*)
Court knowledge	.45	.49	.24
Duncan SES	.01	.22	.05

subsample of 96 blacks, whereas Duncan's SES cannot account for more than 5 percent. This is why *r*s of less than .20 are usually considered very weak. There are circumstances, however, when a reduction of even 1 percent in otherwise unexplained variance can be extremely important. There are other occasions when learning that two variables are related only weakly or not at all constitutes a real advance in knowledge.

Both bivariate linear regression analysis and bivariate correlation analysis are valuable tools. If one wants to know the functional relationship between *Y* and *X* in terms of their original units of measurement—and this is essential for prediction—then he needs to determine the slope. But if the scholar's concern is to compare the strength of the association among pairs of variables, he must compute their correlation coefficients. For a proper understanding of the relationship between pairs of variables in a data set, one usually must find both their regression equations and their correlation coefficients. Yet even this is not enough. When discussing regression analysis, we warned about certain hazards that may result from the presence of outliers and from nonlinear relationships. These pitfalls are even more serious when *r* is used alone. An endless variety of data sets can yield highly similar correlation coefficients. Moreover, outliers and nonlinearity may mask relationships even when both *b* and *r* are computed. Only scatterplots can assure adequate protection against such dangers.

Numbered Data: Multivariate Analysis[12]

Scatterplots and bivariate correlation and regression analysis are valuable analytical aids. Indeed, they are so valuable that it would be well worthwhile to pin numbers to data, wherever feasible, even if they were the only additional tools that became available as a result. But they are only the simplest of the many devices made possible by numbered data. Unfortunately, multivariate analysis is too complex a subject for more than the most casual treatment in this book. Nevertheless, we can at least illustrate several techniques and the kinds of questions to which they can help us address ourselves.

Partial Correlation

Partial-correlation analysis is a tool for determining the strength of the association between a dependent and an independent variable when the effect of one or more other independent variables is held constant. For instance, in the subsample of 96 blacks, the correlation between the dependent variable, diffuse support, and an index of political partisanship is .25. This means that blacks who prefer the Democratic party tend to view the Court somewhat more favorably than those who prefer the Republicans. But we also know that diffuse support and Court knowledge are rather strongly correlated ($r = .49$). How much of the relationship between diffuse support and political partisanship, we may ask, would remain if the relationship between diffuse support and Court knowledge were held constant?

The answer depends on the degree to which partisanship and Court knowledge are correlated. To the extent that they are correlated, Court knowledge and partisanship overlap and are measuring the same phenomenon. Once we know the correlation between Court knowledge and partisanship ($r = .39$), it is easy to control the overlap by partial-correlation analysis. With the overlap controlled, the correlation between diffuse support and partisanship drops from .25 to .07. Partial correlation also tells us that controlling Court knowledge leaves the relationship between diffuse support and partisanship unaffected for the subsample of 200 Southern whites. We once used this kind of analysis to show that virtually none of the variance in specific comments about the Supreme Court made immediately after the 1964 election need be attributed to support for Senator Goldwater in his 1964 Presidential election campaign.[13]

Multiple Correlation

Although partial correlation reveals the amount of association between two variables when one or more other variables are held constant, it cannot solve a related problem: How much variance in a dependent variable is accounted for when the explanatory power of two or more variables is combined? The statistic that indicates the combined variance accounted for by two or more explanatory variables is multiple correlation. For the subsample of 200 white Southerners, the correlation between diffuse support and Court knowledge is $-.32$ and $-.31$ between diffuse support and attitudes toward civil rights.

We cannot simply add these two correlation coefficients together to find the combined correlation of Court knowledge and attitudes toward civil rights, because Court knowledge and attitudes toward civil rights are themselves related and, therefore, overlap. Since this overlap is actually rather small, the correlation between diffuse support and Court knowledge jumps from $-.32$ to $-.47$ when the contribution of attitudes toward civil rights is added via multiple correlation analysis. When two other independent variables—alienation from government and political partisanship—are also added, the coefficient of multiple correlation (R) becomes $-.54$. For the subsample of black respondents the correlation between diffuse support and Court knowledge (.49) does not increase when either attitudes toward civil rights or political partisanship is added, but R climbs to .55 when the alienation-from-government variable is included.

A major virtue of multiple correlation analysis is that it tells how much variance in the dependent variable remains unexplained. R, when squared, measures the percentage of the variance in the dependent variable that can be attributed to the combination of independent variables. Obviously, much unexplained variance in diffuse support remains for both subsamples after Court knowledge, political partisanship, alienation from government, and attitudes toward civil rights are all taken into account.

Multiple Regression

Multiple regression is related to multiple correlation much as bivariate regression is to bivariate correlation. We use multiple regression analysis to determine the slopes for the regression of a dependent variable on each of two or more predictors used in combination—after the overlap among them has been removed. The regression of diffuse support on Court knowledge for the subsample of 200 Southern whites is

diffuse support $= 3.22 - .38$ Court knowledge

When we utilize multiple regression analysis to add political partisanship, alienation from government, and attitudes toward civil rights, the equation becomes

diffuse support = .01 − .42 Court knowledge − .17 political partisanship − .28 alienation from government − .36 attitudes toward civil rights

Similarly, for the subsample of 96 blacks, the regression of diffuse support on Court knowledge (diffuse support = 3.40 + .45 Court knowledge), after the three other predictors are added via multiple regression analysis, becomes

diffuse support = 2.22 + .48 Court knowledge + .06 political partisanship − .30 alienation from government − .05 attitudes toward civil rights

We can now compare the relative importance of any of these predictors for the two subsamples. Court knowledge and alienation from government are almost equally useful predictors of diffuse support both for Southern whites and for the black respondents, although the effect of Court knowledge on blacks is almost the opposite of its effect on Southern whites. Attitudes toward civil rights tell a good deal about the diffuse-support level of Southern whites, but virtually nothing about that of blacks. Although political partisanship is not particularly helpful in accounting for the diffuse support of either group, it does indicate something more about the diffuse support of white Southerners than about that of blacks.

Residuals

As we pointed out when discussing bivariate regression, the line of regression is the straight line that best fits the data points in the least-squares sense, and many Y values deviate from it to some extent. The distance of a Y value from the regression line is its residual. Respondents with large diffuse-support residuals are those whose diffuse-support scores are least adequately accounted for by the regression equation. These respondents are the deviant cases. The same holds for multiple regression. Take the following linear regression equation for the subsample of 200 Southern whites:

diffuse support = .53 − .41 Court knowledge − .21 political partisanship − .42 attitudes toward civil rights
$\sigma = 1.15$

Of the 200 respondents 13 have residuals greater than 2.00; 9 of these people support the Court far more strongly and 4 far less strongly than the multiple regression equation would have led us to predict.   Since we can easily identify these deviant respondents, analysis can now advance another major stage.   There are several highly rewarding statistical techniques for analyzing residuals, but unfortunately, they tend to be rather complex.* Although often hard to draw, no bow in the armory of quantitative social science is more powerful than residual analysis.

Other Multivariate Techniques

Recent studies in public law have employed other multivariate techniques, such as the analysis of variance, smallest-space analysis, multiple scalogram analysis, factor analysis, and discriminant-function analysis.[14]   All are too intricate for treatment here.   Since, however, some of the indices in this chapter were constructed by factor analytic techniques, an elementary discussion of that widely used tool is appended.[15]

APPENDIX: FACTOR ANALYSIS

Factor analysis is a highly complex, extremely controversial, and somewhat mystical technique, the fundamental purpose of which is to reduce a large number of related variables to a smaller number of variables (or factors) that at least summarize and perhaps underlie the larger set of items.   Because of the complexity of the arithmetic calculations involved, most contemporary varieties of factor analysis can only be run on a computer.

For illustrative material we again turn to the surveys of public opinion about the U.S. Supreme Court.   One of the subsamples was a group of 209 administrative assistants of senators and congressmen.   Included in the questionnaire were eight queries aimed at uncovering respondents' basic political orientations.   The questions asked for views about the power of the federal government, school desegregation, racial intermarriage, broadened Medicare programs, federal aid to education, prayers in public schools, governmental regulation of business, and the behavior of civil rights leaders. It was quite plausible that, since these respondents were highly knowledgeable and sophisticated people who wrestled with such problems as an integral part of their life's work, their answers would be internally consistent.   If this

---

* Sometimes, when the number of cases involved is small, however, residual analysis can be quite simple.   For instance, we merely read the actual texts of the interviews to find out why the outliers on Figure 7.1 were deviants.

hunch—supported by evidence from earlier studies*—was correct, we could treat these answers as an indication of an ideology, one that, given the nature of the questions, could reasonably be labeled liberalism-conservatism. We would then be in a position to test the relationship between that ideology and support for the Supreme Court.

One course open was simply to assume that the administrative assistants had been consistent and to construct an index along the lines of a Likert scale. This kind of measure is often useful, but it leaves untested the assumption that the items (the answers) are really related to each other. Thus a problem similar to that discussed in chapter 5 in the section on cumulative scaling arises. One of several means of probing for consistency would be to construct a correlation matrix, showing exactly how each item was correlated with every other item. The researcher could then build an index in which he could place greater confidence by using only those items that were strongly correlated with each other—if, that is, he could establish an operationally justifiable criterion to distinguish strong from not-so-strong associations.

Factor analysis is another way of both testing the strength with which items are related and creating an index based on those relationships. Factor analysis operates from a correlation matrix and proceeds through several statistical operations to produce "loadings," or "weights," for each item. These loadings are usually computed along the same range as the Pearson product moment correlation, that is, from -1.00 to $+1.00$. The result of this analysis, one hopes, will be something like that reported in Table 7.8. There we asked the computer to produce loadings on two factors, so that we could determine whether the items were expressions of none, one, or, possibly, two underlying sets of attitudes.† With this sort of information before him, the researcher can decide whether the items are, in fact, so closely related as to justify treating them as forming a single factor. The task of interpretation is not always easy, for there may be no high loadings at all; there may be a mixture of high and low loadings; or some items may load high on one factor and low on another or high on all factors. Moreover, the problem of distinguishing strong from not-so-strong associations remains.

The message in Table 7.8 is clear, however. Even by rigorous standards the items are all closely associated and form one factor. The lowest loading

---

* See Philip E. Converse, "The Nature of Belief Systems in Mass Publics," in David E. Apter (ed.), *Ideology and Discontent* (New York: Free Press, 1964); Converse, "Attitudes and Non-Attitudes: Continuation of a Dialogue," in Edward R. Tufte (ed.), *The Quantitative Analysis of Social Problems* (Reading, Mass.: Addison-Wesley, 1970); and Herbert McClosky, Paul J. Hoffman, and Rosemary O'Hara, "Issue Conflict and Consensus among Party Leaders and Followers," 54 *American Political Science Review* 406 (1960).

† We would not have been surprised if some respondents had been "liberal" on economic and welfare issues and quite "conservative" on racial problems. While the strength of the associations on Factor 1 distracts attention from Factor 2, that second factor does indicate that such a relationship exists for many respondents.

TABLE 7.8

Factor loadings of administrative assistants

Item: opinion about	Factor 1	Factor 2	Communality*
1. Power of federal government	.83	.15	.71
2. School desegregation	.79	−.31	.72
3. School prayers	.73	.07	.54
4. Action of civil rights leaders	.69	−.45	.68
5. Racial intermarriage	.75	−.39	.72
6. Increased federal aid to education	.76	.31	.67
7. Broadened Medicare	.72	.46	.72
8. Governmental regulation of the economy	.69	.16	.50

* Communality is the squared multiple correlation between the item and the two factors. The higher the communality, the greater the proportion of variance in the item accounted for by the two factors.

is .69. Thus we have good reason to try to construct a single measure to express the views registered in the answers of the administrative assistants and, insofar as our questions actually tapped an underlying attitude of liberalism-conservatism, to use liberalism-conservatism as the name of the single factor.

Standard computer programs for factor analysis calculate just such a measure by assigning a composite score to each respondent. The researcher can then use those scores to try to explain his problem—in this instance, the amount of variation in support for the Supreme Court that can be accounted for by general political ideology. Figure 7.3 provides a scatterplot of the liberalism-conservatism scores run against the diffuse-support scores—also obtained by means of factor analysis—for the administrative assistants. The pattern of dispersion among the scores, the resulting slope of the regression line, and the strength of the correlation (.80) show a very close relation between an administrative assistant's general ideology and his overall support for the Court as an institution.

We have stressed the utility of factor analysis in testing the strength of the relationships among a number of items and in producing a common index. We should also mention two properties of that index. First, the kind of Likert scale we initially described assigns each of the items equal weight. This is an assumption, and a potentially significant one. In our illustration, several of the questions may have been far more important than others in expressing an underlying ideology. One can, to be sure, construct an index with different weightings for each item, but it is sometimes difficult a priori to justify this sort of ranking. The index that factor analysis produces gives different weights to the various items and does so according to the strength of the correlations of each variable with the other items, a criterion that, although arbitrary, has some intuitive justification.

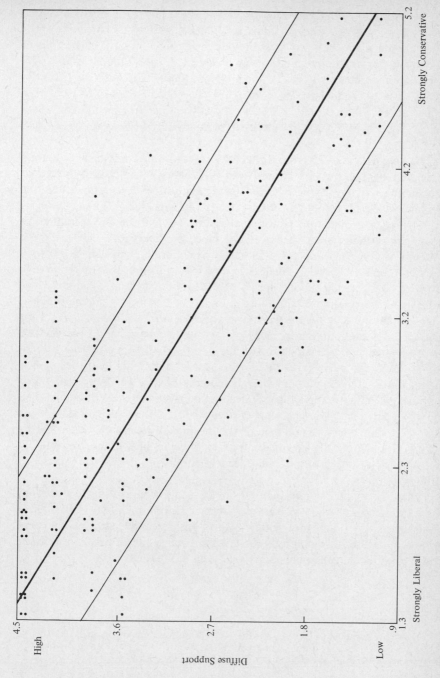

FIGURE 7.3 Administrative assistants; diffuse support versus liberalism

Second, factor analysis usually yields a much larger number of unique scores than do other kinds of indices. Thus if one wants to see how the data fall on a scatterplot—such as the one in Figure 7.3 or the earlier one in 7.1, which portrayed the relationship between diffuse support and Court knowledge for blacks—he gets a much clearer picture, because each respondent is more likely to have his own point on the plot than to share a glob with a dozen other people. This second advantage is only one of visual clarity, but visual clarity in this kind of analysis can lead to conceptual clarity.

As long as a scholar relies on factor analysis to test associations among items that he believes are related and to create indices based on those associations—as long as he relies on factor analysis to test hypotheses—the problems involved, although formidable, are manageable. When, however, the researcher tries to use factor analysis as a substitute for thinking, he encounters serious risks that are all the more grave because they are often hidden. Merely throwing a host of handy items into a computer in the hope that the Great JuJu will make sense out of a mishmash is a dangerous business. The principal, but hardly the sole, peril is that of spurious or meaningless correlations. One might find, for instance, that the times of judges' grandmothers' deaths were strongly associated with judges' votes for criminal defendants or that the day of the month when a case was decided was associated with decisions for or against asserted claims to free speech. The absurdity of these relations is obvious, and they are figments of our imaginations. Other relations may be equally bizarre yet quite real. For example, it is a fact in the United States that a driver's chances of being killed in an accident rise when he enters a state with less than seven letters in its name or a state that was not one of the original thirteen colonies. Factor analysis would dutifully produce a high loading on such items, and blindly following the resulting output could lead to confusion, despair, or ridicule—perhaps all three.

These sorts of dangers increase as an analyst inserts more and more disparate items into the correlation matrix. The moral is that although a scholar should use any tool within his—or his research assistant's—reach, he should never trust factor analysis unless he has a substantively important reason to think that the items being analyzed are related.

NOTES

1. We are indebted to Prof. Edward R. Tufte, whose comments on an earlier version of this chapter led us to revise it drastically. However, we do not wish to imply that this revision carries his nihil obstat.

2. See, for example, Joseph Tanenhaus *et al.*, "The Supreme Court's Certiorari Jurisdiction: Cue Theory," in Glendon A. Schubert (ed.), *Judicial Decision-Making* (New York: Free Press, 1963), p. 111; Stuart S. Nagel, "Political Party Affiliation and Judges'

Decisions," 55 *American Political Science Review* 843 (1961); John H. Kessel, "Public Perceptions of the Supreme Court," 10 *Midwest Journal of Political Science* 167 (1966); Kenneth M. Dolbeare, "The Public Views the Supreme Court," in Herbert Jacob (ed.), *Law, Politics, and the Federal Courts* (Boston: Little, Brown, 1967), p. 194; Dolbeare and Phillip E. Hammond, "The Political Party Basis of Attitudes Toward the Supreme Court," 32 *Public Opinion Quarterly* 16 (1968); Walter F. Murphy and Tanenhaus, "Public Opinion and the United States Supreme Court: A Preliminary Mapping of Some Prerequisites for Court Legitimation of Regime Changes," in Joel B. Grossman and J. Tanenhaus (eds.), *Frontiers of Judicial Research* (New York: Wiley, 1969), p. 273; Harrell R. Rodgers, Jr., *Community Conflict, Public Opinion, and the Law: The Amish Dispute in Iowa* (Columbus: Charles E. Merrill, 1969); and Herbert Jacob, *Debtors in Court: The Consumption of Government Services* (Chicago: Rand McNally, 1969).

3. For an important scholarly treatment of sampling, see Frederick F. Stephan and Philip J. McCarthy, *Sampling Opinions* (New York: Wiley, 1958); a less learned but still useful treatment can be found in Morris James Slonim, *Sampling: A Quick Reliable Guide to Practical Statistics* (New York: Simon and Schuster, 1960).

4. See the important analysis by William H. Kruskal, "Significance, Tests of," *International Encyclopedia of the Social Sciences* (New York: Macmillan, 1968), XIV, 239, and the references cited there. The discussion in M. J. Monroney, *Facts from Figures* 3rd ed. (Baltimore: Penguin Books, 1956), chaps. 13 and 15, is particularly lucid.

5. Two textbooks frequently relied on by public law scholars are Hubert M. Blalock, Jr., *Social Statistics* (New York: McGraw-Hill, 1960), and J. P. Guilford, *Fundamental Statistics in Psychology and Education* 3d ed. (New York: McGraw-Hill, 1960). The totally uninitiated will profit from William Buchanan's *Understanding Political Variables* (New York: Charles Scribner's Sons, 1969). Buchanan's book is less a statistics text than a workbook intended for supplementary use in political science courses in which some knowledge of quantitative methods would be helpful. His presentation is very elementary, wonderfully clear, and witty. Moreover, he includes some illustrative material drawn from the literature of public law.

6. For an unusually full discussion of the phi coefficient, see Guilford supra note 5, pp. 311–316.

7. See, for example, Glendon A. Schubert, *The Judicial Mind: Attitudes and Ideologies of Supreme Court Justices, 1946–1963* (Evanston, Ill.: Northwestern University Press, 1965); David J. Danelski, "The Supreme Court of Japan: An Exploratory Study," in Schubert and Danelski (eds.), *Comparative Judicial Behavior: Cross-Cultural Studies of Political Decision-Making in the East and West* (New York: Oxford University Press, 1969), p. 121; George H. Gadbois, Jr., "Selection, Background Characteristics, and Voting Behavior of Indian Supreme Court Judges, 1950–1959," in Schubert and Danelski, p. 221; Vilhelm Aubert, "Conscientious Objectors Before Norwegian Military Courts," in Schubert supra note 2, p. 201; Tanenhaus *et al.* supra note 2.

8. The data for the 1962 Term of the U.S. Supreme Court, on which Table 7.5 and the discussion related to it are based, have been adapted from Schubert, *The Judicial Mind*, supra note 7, p. 66.

9. We substantially revised an early version of this section after the appearance of Edward R. Tufte's "Improving Data Analysis in Political Science," 21 *World Politics* 641 (1969).

10. For a useful introduction to the advantages and disadvantages of Likert-type scales, see Claire Selltiz *et al.*, *Research Methods in Social Relations* (New York: Holt, 1959), pp. 366–370.

11. An especially effective introduction to regression analysis can be found in Blalock supra note 5, pp. 273–358.

12. The statistics books cited in note 5 deal with the first three multivariate tools referred to in this section, partial correlation, multiple correlation, and multiple regression. For references to literature on the analysis of residuals, see Tufte supra note 9.

13. Walter F. Murphy and Joseph Tanenhaus, "Public Opinion and the Supreme Court: The Goldwater Campaign," 32 *Public Opinion Quarterly* 31 (1968).

14. Applications of all these multivariate statistical techniques can be found in either Grossman and Tanenhaus, supra note 2, or Schubert and Danelski, supra note 7.

15. Factor analysis receives only cursory treatment in the statistics books cited in note 5. For more detailed discussions from the viewpoints of statistics and psychology, as well as for references to some of the more important literature, see A. E. Maxwell, "Factor Analysis: Statistical Aspects," *International Encyclopedia of the Social Sciences*, V, 275, and Lloyd C. Humphreys, "Factor Analysis: Psychological Applications," *ibid.*, 281. Many public law scholars have used factor analysis. See, for example, Richard M. Johnson, *The Dynamics of Compliance: Supreme Court Decision-Making from a New Perspective* (Evanston, Ill.: Northwestern University Press, 1967); Fred Kort, "Content Analysis of Judicial Opinions and Rules of Law," in Schubert, supra note 2, p. 133; Schubert supra note 7; and Murphy and Tanenhaus supra note 2.

8
The Future of
Public Law

We began this book by sketching the development of the study of public law in the United States and silhouetting some of the main targets of past and current research. In subsequent chapters we tried to show, in a substantive way, the important effects that decisions of a constitutional court can have on a political system, how potential litigants can achieve and exploit access to judicial power, and the processes by which judges are selected and trained as well as some of the consequences of existing bases of recruitment. We next turned to problems of decision making—how judges influence each other and are influenced by their personal values and by forces outside the courtroom. At each point we also tried to analyze some of the approaches political scientists have used in attacking these substantive problems. In this chapter we shall outline what seems to us will be the future thrust of public law research. In so doing, we shall deal briefly with " ought " questions, which have typically received short shrift from modern political science.

Changes in Scope and Depth

Among the more salient characteristics of current research in public law is that it is more cosmopolitan in outlook than was work through the early 1960s. We expect that the interests of American political scientists will become even more broadly ranging. The U.S. Supreme Court may continue to hold first place in the hearts of American scholars, but it is more and more becoming a reference point rather than a focus of research. On the one hand, interest is rapidly spreading to a subject we have barely mentioned: the operations of trial and intermediate appellate court judges as important political actors in their own right or as lower-level bureaucrats in a judicial hierarchy. From either point of view, these judges help shape policy. They may do so less dramatically but, in the aggregate, probably no less effectively —and certainly much more frequently—than do Supreme Court justices.

Concomitantly, the interest of American political scientists has spread to judicial subsystems of other nations. One of the purposes of the illustrations used in this book has been to show that although a great deal remains to be done, there is already a large body of useful literature in English devoted to courts in many political systems. As of early 1971 the bulk of this literature dealt with one nation or, if with several, then seriatim.* Accurate, detailed, and widespread dissemination of knowledge about the work of constitutional courts will undoubtedly generate more and more truly comparative research.

A second important feature of future public law scholarship will be

---

* There are, of course, some exceptions. See particularly Glendon A. Schubert, "Judges and Political Leadership," in Lewis J. Edinger (ed.), *Political Leadership in Industrial Societies* (New York: Wiley, 1967) and Victor E. Flango and Schubert, "Two Surveys of Simulated Judicial Decision-Making: Hawaii and the Philippines," in Schubert and David J. Danelski (eds.), *Comparative Judicial Behavior* (New York: Oxford University Press, 1969). The articles, documents, and materials collected by Julius J. Marke and John G. Lexa (eds.), *International Seminar on Constitutional Review*, mimeographed (New York University, 1963), are invaluable. See also Walter F. Murphy and Joseph Tanenhaus, "Constitutional Courts and Political Representation," a paper delivered to the 1967 meeting of the International Political Science Association, reprinted in an abridged form in Michael N. Danielson and Murphy (eds.), *Modern American Democracy* (New York: Holt, Rinehart and Winston, 1969), which is also an effort at comparative analysis. For other studies along more traditional lines of case and doctrinal analysis, see Edward McWhinney, *Judicial Review*, 4th ed. (Toronto: University of Toronto Press, 1969), chaps. 1, 11–13; McWhinney, *Comparative Federalism: States' Rights and National Power* (Toronto: University of Toronto Press, 1962); Victor S. MacKinnon, *Comparative Federalism: A Study in Judicial Interpretation* (The Hague: Martinus Nijhoff, 1964); and Thomas M. Franck, *Comparative Constitutional Process: Cases and Materials* (New York: Frederick A. Praeger, 1968). There is also a large literature on primitive law that is comparative in nature. See especially E. Adamson Hoebel, *The Law of Primitive Man* (Cambridge, Mass.: Harvard University Press, 1954), and Max Gluckman, *Politics, Law, and Ritual in Tribal Society* (Chicago: Aldine Publishing Company, 1965).

increased reliance on quantitative analysis. Those who denigrate numbers as evidence of flashy but unsound scholarship have shrunk to the same minority status as those who equate digital manipulation with erudition and accept it as a worthy substitute for thinking. Most scholars are anxious to see quantitative techniques used with skill and imagination to point the way to new lines of inquiry or to support explanations of political phenomena. Quantification is now not only accepted, it is respected; but as a sign of their maturity, most political scientists are becoming impatient with unsophisticated data analysis and intolerant of quantification for its own sake.[1] As e. e. cummings put it:

> (While you and i have lips and voices which
> are for kissing and to sing with
> who cares if some oneeyed son of a bitch
> invents an instrument to measure spring with?[2]

Measuring spring falls within the jurisdiction of poets, not social scientists. But linking social background characteristics to actual behavior or votes to values, discerning patterns in popular attitudes toward courts, and accounting for differing effects of judicial decisions are all matters of political concern; and in each instance the tools that statisticians have developed can be of some use. It is likely that in the very near future political scientists in public law will routinely use techniques like content analysis, mathematical model building, and computer simulation. Studies utilizing these approaches are becoming quite common in other branches of political science and even now are making an appearance in public law.[3] In the longer run, scholars interested in courts and judges will probably develop more advanced analytical operations as they work closely with statisticians and mathematicians.

As a third feature of future public law scholarship, judicial biographies will probably continue to flourish. These are likely to be of two kinds. One, using traditional opinion analyses and discussions that place the judges and their work in proper historical perspective, will remain alluring to graduate students interested in a manageable dissertation topic. Particularly if the judges under scrutiny are from courts outside the United States or if the analyses tap previously unused sets of private papers, such works are apt to be very useful. It is less likely, however, that this kind of study can add much to the contributions of Swisher, Fairman, Howard, and most especially Mason to the development of biography as an instrument for understanding the judicial process.

A second kind of biography, one relying heavily on psychological analysis, can add a new dimension to public law.[4] Studies of this sort are becoming more frequent in other areas of political science, and the availability of huge collections of private papers of American judges makes the spread of this approach to public law almost inevitable. If well executed, a series of psychological analyses of individual judges would superbly complement the work done by scholars who are more inclined toward psychometric investigations of larger samples of judges.

Theory Building

A fourth mark of a rejuvenated study of public law is that although it will continue to be grounded in hard empirical research, it will also become more theoretical in orientation. When the boundary-defining role of the U.S. Supreme Court was the major focus of investigation, political scientists had little need to indulge in abstract analysis. On the basis of the excellent historical and biographical material available, they could describe in vivid and exhaustive detail what boundaries the Court had set at different time periods. This kind of response is usually not feasible in accounting for the multifarious effects of what courts do in many different countries under many different circumstances. The shortcomings of relying on description and anecdote when assessing a single court in a single country quickly multiply when one begins to discuss two or three levels of courts in five or more countries.

How a scholar should go about building an explanation causes bitter debate among academics.* Deduction in the strict sense leads to obvious problems, not least of which is how one first creates the central proposition or propositions from which explanation is to be drawn. The physical sciences made little progress until they abandoned deduction. In the social sciences sweeping generalizations like "Man is a political animal" or "Men are naturally good; their institutions are corrupt" either are vague, impose heavy burdens on credulity, or admit of too wide a range of exceptions to be useful. Propositions more firmly based on hard empirical data, it might be argued, partake as much of induction as deduction.

Although used with imagination by some writers,[5] the deductive approach has been out of vogue in political science for some years, and it shows little evidence of reincarnation in anything resembling a pure form. On the other hand, recent emphasis in political science on data gathering and analysis can hardly be said to have created an explosion of explanations

---

* Judges suffer from similar difficulties in deciding how they decide. "The power of searching analysis of what it is they are doing," Felix Frankfurter once wrote, "rarely seems to be possessed by judges, either because they are lacking in the art of critical exposition or because they are inhibited from practicing it." Frankfurter, "The Judicial Process and the Supreme Court," in Philip Elman (ed.), *Of Law and Men: Papers and Addresses of Felix Frankfurter, 1939–1956* (New York: Harcourt Brace & World, 1956), p. 32. But compare Judge Joseph Hutcheson's brash but lucid explanation quoted on p. 220.

at a general level. Part of the reason may lie in a misidentification of induction as the method of the physical—the successful—sciences. This notion may have brought about a mistaken, however well-intentioned, effort at emulation.

If one looks at theory building as proceeding inductively from data gathering and description of one event to another and then another and another until a general pattern emerges, empirical research has a burden to bear that it probably cannot lift, much less carry. Physical scientists have long realized this, and the fog is beginning to clear from the eyes of many social scientists as well. Einstein, for example, rejected induction in no uncertain terms. He claimed that "there is no inductive method that could lead to the fundamental concepts of physics . . . in error are those who believe that theory comes inductively from experience."[6]

Newton and Freud would probably have agreed with Einstein. Newton, after all, did not watch thousands of objects fall, measure their velocity and acceleration, and then produce his concepts of motion. As others have pointed out, one of the more interesting aspects about Newton's "law of gravity" is that it could not be induced from observing the behavior of the most numerous of solid falling objects: dust, leaves, and snowflakes. Analogously, Sigmund Freud listened to the troubles and fantasies of a few Viennese, mostly Viennese Jews, and from this limited and unrepresentative sample of humanity created explanations of the emotional stresses that beset all mankind.

Fortunately, there are views of scientific method other than induction and deduction. One, best explained by Norwood R. Hanson, has been saddled with the awkward title of retroduction. According to Hanson, scientific discovery no more proceeds from the particular to the general than it does from the general to the particular. It is the explanation—theory— that imposes order and categorization on data, not the data that create order, categories, and finally, theory.

> Physical theories provide patterns within which data appear intelligible. They constitute a "conceptual Gestalt." A theory is not pieced together from observed phenomena; it is rather what makes it possible to observe phenomena as being of a certain sort, and as related to other phenomena. Theories put phenomena into systems.[7]

The retroductionist model of scientific discovery is much like the following: A scientist encounters a mass of data that he cannot account for in terms of previously developed theory; in short, he confronts a problem. Since the data do not order themselves, the scientist faces the intellectual problem of finding basic relationships that, when uncovered, will make the problematic behavior fall into understandable patterns. The new theory he offers—if he is able to construct one—may borrow from, but will in important respects be different from, existing theories.   Creative imagination, perhaps fermenting slowly through painful trials and errors or exploding in a sudden all-revealing flash, plays a critical role in forming the new explanation. Writing in innocence of the philosophy of science, Joseph C. Hutcheson, Jr., when he was a federal district judge, described his decision making in the following fashion:

> When the case is difficult or involved, and turns upon a hairsbreadth of law or of fact, that is to say, "when there are many bags on one side and on the other" and Judge Bridlegoose would have used his "little small dice," I, after canvassing all the available material at my command, and duly cogitating upon it, give my imagination play, and brooding over the cause, wait for the feeling, the hunch—that intuitive flash of understanding which makes the jump-spark connection between question and decision, and at the point where the path is darkest for the judicial feet, sheds its light along the way.[8]

Retroduction is not deductive in approach, although it may borrow from previously formulated general principles, and from the theories that it produces, broad corollaries as well as specific predictions may be deduced. Neither is retroduction inductive, although it is firmly linked to empirical research: It tries to explain data from the real world, and its explanations are supposed to be phrased in such a form that they or their corollaries and predictions can be subjected to empirical tests and so be proved, modified, or disproved.   The method of retroduction states a problem and tries to offer an explanation that can account for that problem as well as for a more general body of problems.

Of course, no intellectual process proceeds by means of the neat, clearly defined steps of a formal model.   The human mind frequently operates with such subtlety and swiftness that we are unable to reconstruct accurately the individual stages of our analysis.   The germ of doubt about existing theory may have been lurking in a scientist's mind for years although he himself was unaware of it.   His search for data may in part have been directed by vague and perhaps even unconscious notions about a new theory.   As Abraham Kaplan has said, "All observation involves theorizing, and—for science, at any rate—perception is impossible without conceptual processes."[9] Moreover, pure chance—serendipity—may play a role, although, as in sports, chance seems to benefit the most skilled.

In the process of building theory, empirical research can assist in sharply identifying the variety of phenomena for which an explanation must account. Empirical research can tease creative responses from the minds of social scientists.   It can also supply the means by which theories may be tested, although usually not with the precision possible in the physical sciences. In addition, even when it does not rise above the level of description, empirical research can still play an important recruiting function in interesting and stimulating the minds of future scholars.

It seems to us that whether they are doing so consciously or not, more and more political scientists are approaching theory building along the lines of retroduction. Dissatisfaction with the mechanical explanation that judges lay the law and the Constitution side by side and then see if the former equates with the latter led to a search for a more plausible theory of decision making. At first, there were rather naïve general propositions about economic outlook; then, more refined and subtle propositions about the interactions of individual values, considerations of public policy, and conceptions of proper role. At another level political scientists have been developing theories about the influence of judges on each other and the effect on judicial decision making of the reactions—and anticipated reactions—of other officials. Scholars who are more quantitatively oriented have tended to spell out many of these kinds of explanations and, less successfully, some of the assumptions that underlie their analyses. Propositions and theories are embedded in the work of other scholars in public law, but they are more difficult to capture in a clear, testable form.

As attention is broadening to courts of other countries, scholars are considering the same sorts of problems they or their colleagues did in the United States, and they are trying out the explanations developed in the American context. The modifications they will be forced to make in their fledgling theories will probably not only increase knowledge of judicial decision making in general but also permit deeper understanding of that process in particular countries and for individual judges. In other problem areas as well, we believe that scholars will progress more and more systematically in much the same manner: carefully defining a problem, evaluating old explanations, attempting to fashion more satisfactory explanations, modifying the new explanations—perhaps even revising them to the extent of constructing a totally new set of propositions—and then retesting the fresh theories. The process is not likely to be any smoother or neater than it has been in the past, nor is it likely to have any end, since we are never likely to achieve final truth.

Jurisprudence

Theory building in public law will occur, of course, in a particular framework. During most of this century political scientists have almost universally accepted, often without thinking much about it, the general notions of sociological jurisprudence. Sociological jurisprudence, developed by Roscoe Pound in the early 1900s from both American and German ideas, tried to merge law into the social sciences.[10] It replaced both a normative Thomistic concept of law as the embodiment of social justice and an amoral Austinian concept of law as a command of the sovereign with a notion of law as a means of social control—the end result of a series of efforts to accommodate a congeries of interests in society and to shape behavior of individual citizens. Sociological jurisprudence thus pictured a statute or a judicial decision less as a carefully reasoned deduction from general principles than as a practical attempt to solve a particular problem. Lawmakers—judges and legislators —were social engineers, not high priests or logicians. "The life of the law," the sociological jurisprudent might have said, paraphrasing Oliver Wendell Holmes, "is not abstract logic but wisdom informed by experience." Legal rules represent efforts to cope "with the felt necessities of the time." This general orientation, stressing as it did the power of interest groups and the discretion of lawmakers, has obviously been quite compatible with much of what political scientists have been saying in public law and elsewhere in the discipline.

The resurgence of interest in theorizing about the work of judges and their place in the political system will undoubtedly continue to be, for the immediate future, roughly shaped by the notions of the sociological school and heavily colored by the Realism that has permeated political science since World War I. This does not mean, however, that the emerging jurisprudence would have met with the approval of Pound, Corwin, Cushman, Haines, Powell, Llewellyn, or Frank, but only that it will be forged out of a debate that has begun in the language and concepts of sociological jurisprudence and in the skeptical mood of Realism. Indeed, in the long run, the sociological paradigm will very likely be cast aside and replaced with a different or at least thoroughly revised set of ideas.[11]

The approach of the new jurisprudence will differ from the old in several ways. It will certainly be less optimistic than the approach of the earlier commentators in their predictions that law would be melded with the social sciences and in their evaluation of the power of judges to operate efficiently as social engineers. Concern with the possible, with the limits of power, runs deep in political science and generally carries with it a somewhat pessimistic outlook. More importantly, the new jurisprudence will be, as Martin Shapiro has emphasized, a political jurisprudence.[12] It will center, as we have implied, on the political system—on law as a product of political interaction and on the relevance of law and lawmakers for maintaining or changing that system. Although neither the technical nature of legal rules nor the relationships of those rules to the larger social system can be intelligently neglected, the focal point is likely to be the structure and processes of the political system.

Much of the empirical work for such a political jurisprudence has already been done. We described some of it in earlier chapters of this book. What remains to be accomplished is not merely more empirical investigation, although we still have great gaps in our knowledge, but a conceptual linking of the various relations we have been discovering by looking at judges as one species of political actor and their work as one kind of policy output in a governmental system. The questions on which attention in the immediate future is likely to be concentrated will probably be very much like those we listed in chapter 1. The next step will be of an even more general theoretical character, tying in the new jurisprudence with similarly rigorous studies of other aspects of politics and then relating the political system to the broader social structure. The accomplishment of this last set of aims remains, we fear, far in the future.

Science and Values

"Jurisprudence" has several connotations.[13] It can mean an ordered way of looking at a body of legal rules. For example, "medical jurisprudence" would refer to regulations and decisions regarding the rights and duties of doctors, nurses, hospital corporations, and patients. In a second sense "jurisprudence" can mean, as we used the word in the previous section of this chapter, a theoretical framework for the analysis of law and lawmakers. In this sense, a "sociological jurisprudence," for instance, would refer to a study of law as a means of social and political control. "Jurisprudence" also can have a normative connotation, referring to a justification for a particular set of principles or, more broadly, a certain kind of legal-political order. We believe that although development is less certain here than in other areas, political science is approaching a renaissance of serious work in normative as well as theoretical jurisprudence.

In contrast to philosophers and academic lawyers,[14] political scientists have in the last few decades produced only a small trickle of research in public law that has been deliberately and systematically value oriented. Alpheus T. Mason, for instance, developed into an interrelated set of normative concepts Chief Justice Stone's somewhat inchoate notions about the representative role of the Supreme Court in American politics.[15] Walter Berns has published several provocative—to some people, aggravating—studies about the relationships among law, freedom, and the good life.[16] In addition, one could cite dozens of other works that have been value oriented in the sense of criticizing or praising specific policies, statutes, and decisions. On the whole, however, political scientists have made remarkably few efforts to order coherently and then justify a broad set of goals and values that society, and judges in particular, should be fostering.

The fact-value dichotomy, the belief that one can never logically proceed from the "is" to the "ought," has been partly responsible for the neglect of normative questions by political scientists. It is not so much that political scientists have succeeded in expunging their value judgments from their work, but rather that so many of them wish they could.   On the other hand, if some political scientists have experienced feelings of inadequacy in not being able to analyze the real world of politics with the same dispassion a zoologist achieves in observing the mating habits of chimpanzees, others have suffered remorse that they have been unable to justify, in terms their colleagues would accept as professionally valid, the democratic values they cherish.   Perhaps because we think that the stuff of morality and the play of values are more immediately obvious, though not more important, in the judicial process than in other phases of politics, we believe that a revival of normative jurisprudence is at hand.   We concede that this may be a visceral reaction rather than a cool assessment of the evidence, for the evidence is scarce indeed.*

Somewhat paradoxically, one of the signs we see as hopeful is the increasing excellence of the character of empirical research.   Carl G. Hempel, the noted philosopher of science, has pointed out that scientific method can illuminate problems of moral valuation in several ways.   First, it can provide data needed to arrive at value judgments,

> to ascertain (a) whether a contemplated objective can be attained in a given situation; (b) if it can be attained, by what alternative means and with what probabilities; (c) what side effects and ulterior consequences the choice of any given means may have apart from probably yielding the desired end; (d) whether several proposed ends are jointly realizable, or whether they are incompatible in the sense that the realization of some of them will definitely or probably prevent the realization of others.[17]

Second, Hempel argues, scientific method can broaden analysts' outlooks, making them aware of alternatives that they had not thought of or had not realized were open.   Third, science can shed light on fundamental problems of value judgments by revealing in what sense such judgments are final and in what sense they should be open to reconsideration when additional evidence is available or additional analyses are made.

These kinds of help are important.   They spell the difference between dogmatism based on ignorance, superstition, or sheer stubbornness, on the one hand, and, on the other hand, deep conviction held by those who, nevertheless, are willing to reexamine their conclusions in the light of reason and changing evidence.   And much work in public law lends itself to such value calculations.   Still, what Hempel is talking about is only a conditional kind of value judgment.   Scientific method, at best, yields a statement like

* There is, however, some positive evidence.   See, for example, David J. Danelski, " A Behavioral Conception of Human Rights," 3 *Law in Transition Quarterly* 63 (1966) ; Gerald Garvey, *Constitutional Bricolage* (Princeton, N.J.: Princeton University Press, 1971).

the following: "If you want Value G, you can try to attain it by Alternatives A and B. Alternative A has x probability of success and carries k costs; Alternative B has y probability of success and carries m costs. If x probability is greater than y probability and if k costs are less than m costs, Alternative A is the more rational choice." What this method cannot tell us is whether Value G should be pursued at all, whether k costs are worth Value G, or how to discount x probability by k costs.

Hempel, like most philosophers of science and leading political scientists, concludes that the scientific method can only perform clarifying functions. It cannot lead to "an absolute, or categorical, judgment of value to the effect that a certain state of affairs (which may have been proposed as a goal or end) is good, or that it is better than some specified alternative."[18] This limitation is what Arnold Brecht referred to as the "tragedy" of modern political science.[19]

Given the current state of research, "tragedy" may be too strong a word. It would be no mean achievement to formulate a jurisprudence that specified certain values and explained, on the basis of hard data, what sorts of behavior by political actors would be necessary to achieve those values and how that behavior could be made highly probable. Neither would it be a simple undertaking, for the values that most of us want are often not easily reconciled with each other. A value structure composed of justice, equality, personal freedom, and public peace and order, even if one had specific definitions for these vague terms, would inevitably have certain strong internal tensions, if not contradictions.

A second encouraging sign is that not every serious political thinker accepts the assertion that the chasm between the "is" and the "ought" is unbridgeable. For instance, Thomas L. Thorson, a young political theorist, claims that political scientists as well as political philosophers have been wrestling with a false dilemma in their discussion of a fact-value dichotomy. Thorson makes a distinction between a normative approach that is absolutist and one that is contextual. The first takes as a starting point particular postulates, such as "all men . . . are endowed by the Creator with certain unalienable Rights" or "only the elect of God have a right to rule." These statements are not susceptible of proof, either of a deductive or an inductive nature. Nor have they been arrived at by retroduction. In contrast, the contextual approach that Thorson advocates takes as its starting point an empirical description of a factual reality and from that reality formulates certain "musts." For example, scholars cannot be sure that they know, truly know, in any science that they have achieved final truth. Everywhere one turns there is something new to be discovered or something old to be more accurately explained. Thus "Do not block the road to inquiry" is a "must" of any science that is consistent with its purpose of increasing understanding.

On this basis, Thorson reasons, it is possible to construct in politics rational justifications for fundamental value choices. We can justify democracy, for instance, because in politics, as in science generally, we cannot be absolutely certain that we—or anyone else—have attained final, absolute truth. "Do not block the possibility of change with respect to societal goals"[20] is as much a "must" of any intelligent approach to the study of politics, practical or academic, as "Do not block the road to inquiry" is to science generally. The lesson for public law and jurisprudence is that a contextual approach like Thorson's offers an opportunity to grapple rationally and unself-consciously with the "oughts" of a legal-political system, to examine existing situations, and to formulate principles, perhaps phrased as "musts," that are intellectually defensible.

Perhaps more basic than Thorson's interesting argument is the fact that a commitment to science, to discovery of underlying causes of phenomena and exposition of those causes in a way intelligible to others, even a dedication to the pursuit of truth itself, represents a commitment to a set of values, and a set of values that is not universally shared. In a sense, to talk of a "value-free" science is misleading, for in accepting science and a scientific approach, one is really accepting a particular set of values as dominant over other sets of values. In short, science, whatever else it is, is also an ideology.

As products of a materialistic culture in which "progress" has depended on an explosion of technical knowledge in the physical and mathematical sciences, many scholars find it easy to accept science as an unmitigated good. Yet they might experience difficulty in persuading a deeply religious man who believed that the Deity spoke to men in many different ways to prepare him for a life after death that modern science's values and approach to life were desirable, much less natural. Scientists might also have difficulty in explaining to an intelligent being from another planet that fallouts from atomic bombs, nerve gases, air pollution, jet-plane accidents, and motor-vehicle crashes are worth the cost either in this world or some other. Certainly, a large segment of today's youth is implicitly and explicitly rejecting the pursuit of objective truth in favor of subjective experiences and immediate gratification, for thinking as well as doing one's own thing.

We are not advocating a renunciation of efforts to understand reality, nor do we deny that knowledge can be meaningfully communicated. Neither are we suggesting that scholars should forgo scientific research for polemical broadsides for or against the values of modern science or society. We are, however, saying that, at the very least, political scientists, if they so desire and if they have the talent, can map out many of the costs and benefits that are likely to flow from changing or maintaining the status quo. At best, political scientists, again assuming they have the desire and talent, can legitimately and intelligently order their own values, justify them in a professionally respectable manner—though not "prove" them as one can test formulas like $F = MA$ or $E = MC^2$—and, informed by empirical research, formulate broad and specific policies likely to achieve those goals.

The best political philosophers specified a set of goals for society and, using the information available to them, explained how to achieve those ends. Given the masses of data they have accumulated and the theories they are beginning to construct, it seems to us that political scientists will soon have an unmatched opportunity to build normative structures around which future societies can grow.

Law, like most political decisions, inevitably fosters some values and stifles others. The presence or absence of these values—including the values of modern science—can shape the nature of the entire political system for generations. Certainly, it would be a frustrated and frustrating discipline that limited itself to foreseeing but not forestalling human disaster, to envisioning but not justifying a better way of life. To know and to understand, after all, are merely the first, not the final, objectives of human activity.

NOTES

1. See Hugh Donald Forbes and Edward R. Tufte, "A Note of Caution in Causal Modelling," 62 *American Political Science Review* 1258 (1968), and Tufte, "Improving Data Analysis in Political Science," 21 *World Politics* 641 (1969), reprinted in Tufte (ed.), *The Quantitative Analysis of Social Problems* (Reading, Mass.: Addison-Wesley, 1970).

2. From e. e. cummings, "voices to voices, lip to lip," *Poems, 1923–54* (New York: Harcourt Brace Jovanovich, Inc., 1954), pp.189–190. Reprinted by permission of the publisher.

3. For example, Werner F. Grunbaum, "Analytical and Simulation Models for Explaining Judicial Decision-Making," in Joel B. Grossman and Joseph Tanenhaus (eds.), *Frontiers of Judicial Research* (New York: Wiley, 1969); Edward J. Weissman, "Mathematical Theory and Dynamic Models," in Glendon A. Schubert and David J. Danelski (eds.), *Comparative Judicial Behavior* (New York: Oxford University Press, 1969); Jay A. Sigler, "A Cybernetic Model of the Judicial System," 41 *Temple Law Quarterly* 398 (1968). See also Alan Sager, "The Use of Simulation in the Study of the Judicial Process," (mimeographed, 1970), 38 pp.; and Norman Jacknis, "Theory and Methods for Analyzing Processes of Political Influence and Policy Making" (unpublished Ph.D. dissertation, Princeton University), chap. 8.

4. See the literature cited in chapter 4, notes 29, 44–48.

5. Anthony Downs' books, *An Economic Theory of Democracy* (New York: Harper & Row, 1957) and to a lesser extent *Inside Bureaucracy* (Boston: Little, Brown, 1967), might be viewed as deductive analyses, but if so they offer a deduction of a peculiar—and most useful—sort.

6. Albert Einstein, *The Method of Theoretical Physics* (New York: Oxford University Press, 1933), quoted by Norwood R. Hanson, *Patterns of Discovery* (Cambridge: Cambridge University Press, 1958), p. 119. More generally see Morris R. Cohen, *Reason and Nature: An Essay on the Meaning of Scientific Method* (New York: Harcourt, Brace & World, 1931), and Cohen and Ernest Nagel, *An Introduction to the Logic of Scientific Method* (New York: Harcourt, Brace & World, 1934).

7. Hanson, supra note 6, p. 90.

8. Joseph C. Hutcheson, Jr., "The Judgment Intuitive: The Function of the 'Hunch' in Judicial Decision," 14 *Cornell Law Quarterly* 274, 278 (1929). © copyright 1929 by Cornell University.

9. Abraham Kaplan, *The Conduct of Inquiry* (San Francisco: Chandler, 1964), p. 131.

10. Among the better discussions of and bibliographies on sociological jurisprudence is Julius Stone, *Social Dimensions of Law and Justice* (Stanford: Stanford University Press, 1966).

11. See Thomas S. Kuhn, *The Structure of Scientific Revolutions* (Chicago: University of Chicago Press, 1962).

12. Martin Shapiro, *Law and Politics in the Supreme Court: New Approaches to Political Jurisprudence* (New York: Free Press, 1964), especially chap. 1. See also Theodore L. Becker, *Political Behavioralism and Modern Jurisprudence* (Chicago: Rand McNally, 1965).

13. See Thomas A. Cowan, "Jurisprudence," *International Encyclopedia of the Social Sciences* (New York: Macmillan, 1968), VIII, 332.

14. See, for instance, Morris R. Cohen, *Reason and Law* (New York: Free Press, 1950); Lon L. Fuller, *The Morality of Law* (New Haven, Conn.: Yale University Press, 1964); H. L. A. Hart, *Law, Liberty, and Morality* (Stanford: Stanford University Press, 1963); and Hart, *Punishment and Responsibility: Essays in the Philosophy of Law* (New York: Oxford University Press, 1968).

15. Alpheus T. Mason developed this concept in *Harlan Fiske Stone: Pillar of the Law* (New York: Viking, 1956), and more explicitly in *The Supreme Court from Taft to Warren* 2d ed. (Baton Rouge: Louisiana State University Press, 1968).

16. Walter Berns, *Freedom, Virtue and the First Amendment* (Baton Rouge: Louisiana State University Press, 1957), and "*Buck v. Bell.* Due Process of Law?" 6 *Western Political Quarterly* 764 (1953). See also David J. Danelski, "Values as Variables in Judicial Decision-Making: Notes Toward a Theory," 19 *Vanderbilt Law Review* 721 (1966).

17. Carl G. Hempel, "Science and Human Values," in his *Aspects of Scientific Explanation and Other Essays in the Philosophy of Science* (New York: Free Press, 1965), pp. 93–94. Copyright © 1965 by The Free Press, a Division of The Macmillan Company.

18. *Ibid.*, p. 85. (Italics in original omitted.)

19. Arnold Brecht, *Political Theory: The Foundations of Twentieth-Century Political Thought* (Princeton, N.J.: Princeton University Press, 1959).

20. Thomas L. Thorson, *The Logic of Democracy* (New York: Holt, Rinehart and Winston, 1962), p. 141.

NAME INDEX

Abbott, Douglas C., 162–167, 172n
Abe, Hakaru, 98n
Abel-Smith, Brian, 113n
Abelson, Robert P., 112n
Abraham, Henry J., 6n
Adamany, David W., 106–107, 115n
Adenauer, Konrad, 75
Alexander, Paul, 64n
Ali, Fazl, 102
Alsop, Joseph, 85, 91n
Andrews, William G., 63n
Apter, David E., 209n
Aquinas, Thomas, 221–222
Aristotle, 8, 19n, 26n, 47
Arnold, Thurmond, 64n
Atkinson, David N., 176n, 177n
Aubert, Vilhelm, 213n
Austin, Granville, 114n
Austin, John, 222

Baade, Hans W., 90n
Barton, Edmund, 104
Batailler, Francine, 88n
Beaney, William M., 47, 61n, 62n, 63n, 64n
Beard, Charles, 13
Beatty, Jerry K., 106, 114n
Becker, Theodore, 62n, 63n, 64n, 89n, 143, 149n, 228n
Beiser, Edward N., 63n, 64n
Berman, Harold J., 31n
Bernard, Jessie, 127, 148n
Berns, Walter, 25n, 177n, 223, 228n
Beth, Loren P., 62n
Beveridge, Albert J., 85, 91n, 121, 147
Bickel, Alexander, 79n, 177n
Biddle, Bruce J., 149n
Birkby, Robert H., 58n, 63n
Black, Charles L., 60n

Black, Hugo L., 33, 87n, 99, 102, 122–125,
    130–137, 141–143, 147, 161, 166–168,
    170–171, 174–175, 190–193
Blake, Edward, 60n
Blalock, Hubert M., 213n
Bogardus, E. S., 127, 148n
Borkin, Joseph, 28n, 90n
Bowen, D. R., 107, 115n
Brandeis, Louis D., 25, 32, 79n, 80, 88,
    96n, 99, 102, 104–105, 155, 177n
Brecht, Arnold, 225, 228n
Brennan, William J., 87n, 96n, 101, 171,
    174–175, 191–193
Browne, G. P., 61n
Bryce, James, 13
Buchanan, William, 140n, 213n
Bullitt, William C., 115n, 119n
Bunn, Ronald F., 63n
Burton, Harold H., 99, 124–125, 130–137,
    142, 174–175
Bushoven, Cornelius, 177n
Butler, Pierce, 94, 115n, 153, 176n
Buxton, C. Lee, 69
Byrnes, James F., 99

Cahn, Edmond, 90n, 147n
Cappelletti, Mauro, 63n, 114n
Cardozo, Benjamin N., 17, 80, 90n, 96n,
    117, 146, 177n
Carp, Robert A., 114n
Carr, Robert K., 16
Carswell, G. Harrold, 37n
Cartwright, John R., 162–167, 174
Catledge, Turner, 85, 91n
Chapman, Brian, 88n
Chase, Harold W., 94, 113n
Chase, Salmon P., 99n
Chave, E. J., 148n
Christman, Henry M., 26n
Clark, Charles, 91n, 122
Clark, Tom C., 99, 130–137, 142, 174–175,
    191–193
Cleaver, Eldridge, 38, 60n
Cohen, Morris R., 227n, 228n
Converse, Philip E., 209n
Coolidge, Calvin, 101
Coombs, Clyde H., 149n
Corbett, Edward M., 61n
Corwin, Edward S., 4, 13–14, 20, 23, 27n,
    36, 47, 61n, 77n, 117n, 146n, 222
Cowan, Thomas A., 228n

Crisp, L. F., 26n, 59n
cummings, e. e., 217, 227n
Cushman, Robert E., 13–15, 20, 23, 27n,
    36, 47, 48n, 61n, 90n, 222

Dahl, Robert A., 59n, 60n
Danelski, David J., 6n, 20, 24n, 25n, 61n,
    80, 90n–91n, 94, 113n, 115n, 146n,
    147n, 148n, 152n, 154, 159, 172n,
    176n, 213n, 214n, 216n, 224n, 227n,
    228n
Danielson, Michael N., 28n, 60n, 216n
Darrow, Clarence, 105
Daugherty, Harry, 115n
Dawson, R. MacGregor, 113n
Degan, J. W., 148n
Dennis, Jack, 60n
Dewey, John, 15
Dietz, Gottfried, 146n
Dilliard, Irving, 60n
Dimock, Marshall E., 27n
Dixon, Owen, 9–10, 159
Dixon, Robert G., 64n
Dolbeare, Kenneth M., 6n, 28n, 58n, 63n,
    213n
Douglas, William O., 87n, 97, 102, 104,
    124–125, 130–137, 141–143, 161,
    166–168, 170–171, 174–175, 190–193
Downing, Ronald G., 113n
Downs, Anthony, 227n
Duncan, Otis D., 203
Dunham, Allison, 146n

Easton, David, 60n
Edelman, Murray, 64n
Edinger, Lewis J., 177n, 216n
Einstein, Albert, 219, 227n
Eisenhower, Dwight D., 55, 101
Elman, Philip, 149n, 218n
Etherington, Edwin D., 89n
Eulau, Heinz, 26n, 140n
Evers, Tilman Tonnies, 60n
Everson, David H., 63n
Ewing, Cortez A. M., 18, 27n

Fair, Daryl R., 6n
Fairman, Charles, 16, 121, 217
Faulkner, Robert K., 29n, 58n
Fauteux, J. H. G., 162–167, 172n
Fazal, M. A., 63n
Fellman, David, 47, 61n–62n
Ferguson, LeRoy C., 140n

Field, Stephen J., 25, 85, 121, 147n
Flango, Victor E., 216n
Foner, Philip S., 60n
Forbes, Hugh Donald, 227n
Forrestal, James, 108, 115n
Fortas, Abe, 85, 96n, 99
Fouts, Donald E., 148n, 172n
Franck, Thomas M., 62n, 216n
Frank, Jerome, 25n, 26n, 117, 146n, 222
Frank, John P., 28n, 146n
Frankfurter, Felix, 11, 26n, 28n, 90n, 99, 111, 122, 126, 130–137, 141–143, 149n, 157–158, 166–168, 170, 173–175, 177n, 218n
Freddi, Giorgio, 60n, 63n
Freedman, Max, 61n
Freud, Sigmund, 115n, 119n, 219
Fujita, H., 146, 160–161, 165, 174
Fuller, Lon L., 108, 115n, 228n
Fuller, Melville W., 87n

Gadbois, George H., 97, 113n, 148n, 153, 176n, 213n
Gagliano, Felix V., 26n
Garfinkel, Herbert, 90n
Garvey, Gerald, 61n, 146n, 224n
Gaudet, Frederick J., 18, 26n, 27n–28n
George, Alexander L., 115n, 119n
George, Juliette L., 115n, 119n
Gibbs, Robert W., 89n
Glad, Betty, 115n
Glick, Henry R., 6n, 149n
Gluckman, Max, 216n
Goldberg, Arthur, 97, 191–193
Goldman, Sheldon, 6n, 105, 114n, 178n
Goldwater, Barry M., 205
Graham, Hugh D., 28n
Grant, U. S., 56, 99n
Greenberg, Jack, 90n
Greenstein, Fred I., 114n, 115n, 119n
Grey, David C., 60n
Grier, Robert, 85
Griffith, Samuel, 104
Grodzins, Morton, 59n
Gross, Neal, 34n, 149n
Grossman, Joel B., 6n, 24n, 28n, 40n, 59n, 89n, 94, 99, 110–111, 113n, 114n, 115n, 143, 149n, 177n, 178n, 213n, 214n, 227n
Grunbaum, Werner, 24n, 119, 146n, 177n, 227n

Guilford, J. P., 213n
Gurr, Ted R., 28n
Guttman, Louis, 127, 148n

Haines, Charles G., 13–14, 17–18, 26n, 27n, 36, 47, 61n, 85, 91n, 117, 124, 147n, 222
Haldane, Richard D., 159
Hall, Arnold Bennett, 27n
Hall, Emmett M., 162–167, 174
Hammond, Phillip E., 63n, 213n
Hand, Learned, 44, 60n, 91n
Hanson, Norwood R., 219–220, 227n, 228n
Harding, Warren G., 115n
Harlan, John Marshall (the younger), 174–175, 191–193
Harper, Fowler V., 89n, 146n
Harris, George S., 27n–28n
Harris, Robert J., 47, 61n–62n
Hart, H. L. A., 228n
Hashimoto, Kiminobu, 63n
Hattori, Takaaki, 98n
Hayakawa, Takeo, 138, 146n, 148n, 161n
Hempel, Carl G., 224–225, 228
Henderson, D. F., 39n, 59n
Hensley, Thomas R., 26n
Herndon, James F., 106–107, 115n
Hess, Robert D., 60n
Heuss, Theodor, 81–82
Higgins, H. B., 104
Hoebel, E. Adamson, 216n
Hoffman, Paul J., 209n
Holmes, Oliver Wendell, Jr., 17, 32, 56–57, 79n, 85, 88, 102, 104, 116, 119–120, 140–141, 146n, 222
Hoover, Herbert, 101
Howard, J. Woodford, Jr., 61n, 90n, 115n, 119n, 147n, 154, 176n, 177n, 217
Howell, Ronald F., 11n
Hruska, Roman L., 37n
Hughes, Charles Evans, 27n, 99, 102, 115n, 154, 166, 169–170, 172, 177n
Huitt, Ralph K., 149n
Hurst, Willard P., 62n
Hutcheson, Joseph, 218n, 220, 228n

Ike, Nobutaka, 176n
Ikeda, K., 146
Irie, T., 146, 160–161, 165
Isaacs, Isaac, 104

Jacknis, Norman, 24*n*, 177*n*, 227*n*
Jackson, Andrew, 56
Jackson, Robert H., 44, 88, 99, 118–119, 130–137, 142, 146*n*, 168–169
Jacob, Herbert, 6*n*, 20, 28*n*, 213*n*
Jacobs, Clyde E., 26*n*, 90*n*
Jaffe, Louis L., 146*n*
Jahnige, Thomas P., 6*n*, 178*n*
Jaros, Dean, 26*n*
Jay, John, 99
Jefferson, Thomas, 39, 60*n*, 84, 104, 147*n*
Johnson, Lyndon B., 31, 55, 94, 110
Johnson, Richard M., 63*n*, 214*n*
Johnson, William, 153, 176*n*
Jordan, Gerald I., 90*n*
Judson, Wilfred, 162–167

Kalven, Harry, Jr., 117*n*
Kaplan, Abraham, 220, 228*n*
Kaufman, Herbert, 31, 58*n*, 113*n*
Kawamura, M., 146, 160–161, 165, 174
Kawashima, Takeyoshi, 114*n*, 176*n*
Kelly, John M., 59*n*, 91*n*
Kemp, Edward G., 90*n*
Kennedy, John F., 55, 94
Kessel, John R., 28*n*, 213*n*
Keynes, John Maynard, 79, 80, 90*n*
Kobayashi, S., 160–161, 165, 174
Kommers, Donald P., 50, 59*n*, 63*n*, 89*n*, 94, 97, 100, 113*n*, 159
Konefsky, Samuel J., 79*n*
Konvitz, Milton, 90*n*
Kort, Fred, 20, 146*n*, 213*n*
Kotani, K., 146, 160–161, 165, 174
Kruskal, William H., 213*n*
Kuhn, Thomas S., 228*n*
Kurland, Philip, 61*n*, 62*n*, 146*n*

LaFave, Wayne R., 31*n*
Lane, John C., 59, 64*n*, 89*n*
Laskin, Bora, 59*n*
Lasswell, Harold D., 18, 27*n*, 108*n*, 114*n*, 115*n*, 119, 147*n*
LaViolette, Forrest E., 60*n*
Lederman, W. R., 59*n*, 60*n*, 88*n*
Lexa, John G., 6*n*, 147*n*, 216*n*
Likert, Rensis, 127, 148*n*, 196*n*, 209, 210
Lincoln, Abraham, 76, 99, 99*n*
Lipscomb, Andrew A., 147*n*
Litchfield, E. H., 59*n*
Llewellyn, Karl, 26*n*, 90*n*, 117, 146*n*, 222

Loeb, Isidore, 17
Loeber, Dietrich A., 31*n*
Loewenstein, Karl, 32, 59*n*, 91*n*
Lowell, A. Lawrence, 13

MacArthur, Douglas, 71
MacBride, Sean, 74
McCarthy, Philip J., 213*n*
McCloskey, Robert G., 27*n*, 47, 62*n*
McClosky, Herbert, 209*n*
McEachern, A. W., 34*n*, 149*n*
McKenna, Joseph, 85, 96*n*, 99
MacKinnon, Victor S., 216*n*
MacLeish, A., 26*n*
McRae, Duncan, 194*n*
McReynolds, James C., 99, 104, 154, 166, 169, 172*n*
McWhinney, Edward, 6*n*, 89*n*, 90*n*, 91*n*, 176*n*, 216*n*
Maki, John, 32*n*, 59*n*, 89*n*, 176*n*
Mano, Tsuyoshi, 32
Manwaring, David R., 63*n*
Marke, Julius J., 6*n*, 147*n*, 216*n*
Marradi, Alberto, 60*n*
Marshall, John, 9, 14–15, 24, 29*n*, 30, 32, 40, 44, 56, 58*n*, 85, 99, 102, 121, 147*n*, 153
Marshall, Thurgood, 37*n*
Martland, Ronald, 162–167
Mason, Alpheus T., 16, 47, 61*n*, 62*n*, 85, 87*n*, 90*n*, 91*n*, 121–122, 125, 147*n*, 154, 172, 176*n*, 177*n*, 217, 223, 228*n*
Mason, Ward S., 34*n*, 149*n*
Maxwell, A. E., 214*n*
Medalie, Richard J., 64*n*
Mendelsohn, Robert I., 26*n*
Mendelson, Wallace, 147*n*
Merillat, H. C. L., 83*n*
Mermin, Samuel, 63*n*
Merryman, J. H., 63*n*, 114*n*
Messick, Samuel, 149*n*
Michels, Roberto, 114*n*
Miller, Arthur S., 11*n*, 59*n*
Miller, Charles A., 61*n*
Miller, Samuel, 25, 28*n*, 121
Minton, Sherman, 99, 122, 130–137, 142
Mitchell, Stephen R., 163*n*, 164*n*, 165*n*
Monroe, Alan H., 63*n*
Monroney, M. J., 213*n*
Moore, John Basset, 90*n*
Morgan, Donald G., 176*n*

Morrison, Fred L., 89*n*, 113, 159, 177*n*
Mott, Rodney, 6*n*, 17–18, 27*n*
Muir, William K., Jr., 57, 63*n*, 64*n*
Murphy, Frank, 44, 60*n*, 87*n*, 90*n*, 96*n*, 99, 121–125, 130–137, 141–143, 147, 154, 156–158, 166–171, 176*n*, 177*n*
Murphy, Walter F., 6*n*, 28*n*, 29*n*, 40*n*, 60*n*, 62*n*, 63*n*, 79*n*, 85, 89*n*, 90*n*, 91*n*, 114*n*, 115*n*, 147*n*, 154, 176*n*, 177*n*, 213*n*, 214*n*, 216*n*
Myrdal, Gunnar, 79, 90*n*

Nader, Ralph, 105
Nagel, Ernest, 227*n*
Nagel, Stuart, 20, 26*n*, 105, 108*n*, 114*n*, 212*n*
Narain, Jagat, 83*n*, 91*n*
Nelson, Samuel, 106
Neuman, Dale E., 176*n*, 177*n*
Neustadt, Richard E., 58, 64*n*
Newcomb, T. M., 34*n*
Newland, Chester, 60*n*, 90*n*
Newton, Isaac, 219
Nixon, Richard M., 52, 55
North, Robert C., 146*n*

O'Brien, F. W., 59*n*
O'Connor, Richard, 104
O'Dalaigh, Cearbhall, 40
O'Donovan, John, 73–74, 74*n*
O'Hara, Rosemary, 209*n*
Orfield, Gary, 63*n*–64*n*

Parris, Henry, 88*n*
Paschal, Joel Francis, 146*n*
Paterson, William, 99
Patric, Gordon, 63*n*
Paul, Arnold M., 26*n*
Paul, Cedar, 114*n*
Paul, Eden, 114*n*
Pearson, Karl, 189, 203–204, 209
Peck, Sidney R., 148*n*
Pedersen, Mogens N., 26*n*
Peltason, Jack W., 6*n*, 20, 28*n*, 29*n*, 61*n*, 63*n*, 146*n*
Perillo, J. M., 63*n*, 114*n*
Pitkin, Hannah, F., 60*n*
Pollock, James K., 59*n*, 64*n*, 89*n*
Pound, Roscoe, 15, 221–222
Powell, Thomas Reed, 13, 15–16, 27*n*, 36, 47, 61*n*, 117–118, 146*n*, 222

Pratt, George C., 89*n*
Pritchard, E. F., Jr., 26*n*
Pritchett, C. Herman, 19–20, 28*n*, 47–48, 62*n*, 63*n*, 85, 89, 90*n*, 91*n*, 118, 124–126, 130, 132, 134, 137, 141–142, 147*n*, 148*n*, 149*n*, 166*n*, 168*n*, 169, 176*n*, 177*n*

Rand, Ivan, 102, 104
Ratner, Sidney, 99*n*
Reed, Stanley, 124–125, 130–137, 142, 166–168
Rinfret, Thibaudeau, 172*n*
Ritchie, Roland A., 162–167
Roane, Spencer, 104
Roazen, Paul, 114*n*
Roberts, Owen J., 83, 124–125, 157, 166–167, 169
Rodgers, Harrell R., 63*n*, 213*n*
Rogow, Arnold A., 115*n*
Roosevelt, Franklin D., 14, 83, 85, 99, 154, 172
Rosenthal, Alan S., 89*n*
Rossiter, Clinton, 90*n*
Rostow, Eugene V., 61*n*
Rubin, Gerald, 60*n*, 62*n*, 88*n*
Rumble, Wilfred E., Jr., 26*n*
Russell, Peter H., 59*n*, 100, 114*n*, 155, 171, 172*n*, 177*n*, 178*n*
Rutledge, Wiley, 124–125, 137, 141–143, 168–171
Ryan, Richie, 74*n*

Sager, Alan M., 24*n*, 177*n*, 227*n*
St. John, Charles W., 27–28*n*
Saito, Y., 146, 160–161, 165
Samonte, Abelardo G., 148*n*
Sato, Isao, 59*n*
Sawer, Geoffrey, 59*n*, 104, 114*n*
Sayre, Wallace, 31, 58*n*, 113*n*
Schick, Marvin, 6*n*, 91*n*
Schlesinger, Joseph A., 26*n*
Schmidhauser, John, 97, 106, 113*n*, 114*n*, 146*n*, 148*n*
Schoenbaum, David, 63*n*
Schroeder, Theodore, 119, 147*n*
Schubert, Glendon A., 6*n*, 20, 24, 26*n*, 28*n*, 47, 62*n*, 88*n*, 91*n*, 106–107, 113*n*, 114*n*, 115*n*, 118–119, 146*n*, 147*n*, 148*n*, 152*n*, 161*n*, 163–164,

Schubert, Glendon A. *(Cont'd)*
172*n*, 176*n*, 177*n*, 212*n*, 213*n*, 214*n*,
216*n*, 227*n*
Schwartz, Mildred A., 61*n*
Seervai, H. M., 83*n*, 88*n*
Selltiz, Claire, 213*n*
Shapiro, Martin, 222, 228*n*
Sherwood, Foster H., 25*n*, 91*n*
Shima, T., 146, 160–161, 165
Sigler, Jay A., 227*n*
Sills, David L., 61*n*
Silver, David M., 114*n*
Slonim, Morris J., 213*n*
Smith, M. Brewster, 115*n*
Snyder, Eloise, 176*n*
Sobel, Nathan, 54, 64*n*
Somit, Albert, 6*n*, 26*n*, 27*n*, 28*n*, 147*n*
Sorauf, Frank J., 63*n*
Spaeth, Harold, 20, 148*n*
Spence, Wishart F., 162–167, 174
Sprague, John D., 26*n*, 106, 115*n*, 162–
164, 166–169, 171, 172*n*, 174–175,
177*n*, 178*n*, 191*n*
Stephan, Frederic F., 213*n*
Stevens, Robert, 113*n*
Stewart, Potter, 191–193
Stone, Harlan F., 25, 38, 80, 87*n*, 90*n*, 99,
101, 121–123, 125, 141, 149*n*, 153,
156–157, 161, 166–170, 172, 176*n*,
177*n*, 223, 228*n*
Stone, Julius, 61*n*, 228*n*
Stouffer, Samuel, 148*n*
Strayer, B. L., 59*n*, 67*n*, 71*n*, 88*n*
Sutherland, George, 99, 104, 141, 149*n*,
177*n*
Swenson, Rinehart, 17
Swisher, Carl B., 16, 121, 147*n*, 217

Taft, William Howard, 6*n*, 27*n*, 88, 95,
101, 111, 115*n*, 121–122, 147, 153–
155, 176*n*, 228*n*
Tanaka, Kotaro, 40, 120, 146, 147*n*
Tanenhaus, Joseph, 6*n*, 24*n*, 26*n*, 27*n*,
28*n*, 29*n*, 40*n*, 59*n*, 60*n*, 88*n*, 89*n*,
90*n*, 113*n*, 115*n*, 147*n*, 148*n*, 149*n*,
177*n*, 212*n*, 213*n*, 214*n*, 216*n*, 227*n*
Taney, Roger B., 99, 102, 121, 147*n*
Tarumi, K., 146
Tascherau, Robert, 104, 162–167, 172*n*
Thomas, Edwin J., 149*n*
Thorson, Thomas L., 225–226, 228*n*

Thurstone, Louis, 127, 148*n*
Torgersen, Ulf, 97, 113*n*
Torney, Judith V., 60*n*
Trudeau, Pierre Elliott, 61*n*
Truman, Harry S, 96*n*
Tucker, Ledyard R., 149*n*
Tucker, Robert C., 114*n*
Tufte, Edward R., 112*n*, 209*n*, 212*n*,
213*n*, 227*n*
Tukey, John W., 112*n*
Twiss, Benjamin, 26*n*

Ulmer, S. Sidney, 20, 106–107, 115, 148*n*,
149*n*, 177*n*, 178*n*, 194*n*

Vines, Kenneth N., 6*n*, 28*n*, 143–144,
149*n*
Vinson, Fred M., 99, 124–125, 130–137,
142
von Mehren, A. T., 63*n*, 98*n*
von Schmertzing, Wolfgang P., 59*n*
Vose, Clement E., 73, 89*n*

Wahlke, John, 140*n*, 149*n*
Walsh, Brian, 71*n*
Ward, Norman, 113*n*
Warren, Charles, 63*n*, 85, 90*n*, 91*n*
Warren, Earl, 12, 44, 99, 102, 171, 174–
175, 191–193, 228*n*
Wasby, Stephen L., 57, 63*n*, 64*n*
Watson, Lord, 159*n*
Watson, Richard A., 113*n*
Way, H. Frank, Jr., 63*n*
Wayne, James M., 106
Weissman, Edward J., 24*n*, 177*n*, 227*n*
Westin, Alan F., 48, 62*n*, 63*n*
White, Byron, 191–193
White, Edward D., 77*n*, 96*n*, 99
Whittaker, Charles, 174–175
Wildenmann, Rudolph, 43, 80*n*
Wilkie, Walter, 26*n*
Wilson, T. Woodrow, 13, 108, 115*n*, 119*n*
Wolfenstein, E. Victor, 114*n*
Woodbury, Levi, 99

Yokota, Kisaburo, 59*n*
Young, Roland, 25*n*

Zeisel, Hans, 117*n*
Zeitz, Leonard, 64*n*
ZoBell, Karl M., 176*n*

CASE INDEX

Abbatte and Falcone v. United States, 177*n*

Adams v. Tanner, 77*n*

Adkins v. Children's Hospital, 77*n*

Article 26 and Electoral Amendment Bill, 1961, *In re*, 74*n*, 91*n*

Attorney General for Prince Edward Island v. Attorney General for Canada, 59*n*

Baker v. Carr, 28*n*, 54–55, 64*n*

Baldwin v. Missouri, 149*n*

Bank of New South Wales v. Commonwealth, 90*n*

Barr v. Columbia, 147*n*

Barrows v. Jackson, 89*n*

Bell v. Maryland, 147*n*

Bouie v. Columbia, 147*n*

Bridges v. Wixon, 156–157, 177*n*

Brown v. Board, 38, 44, 52, 60*n*, 90*n*

Communist Party Case (West Germany), 59*n*

Cooperative Committee on Japanese Canadians v. Attorney General, 60*n*

Dartmouth College v. Woodward, 15, 27*n*

Dissolution Case (Japan), 31, 59*n*, 72, 89*n*

Duncan v. Kahanamoku, 90*n*

East Donegal Cooperative Livestock Mart v. Attorney General, 71*n*

Educational Co. of Ireland v. Fitzpatrick, 91*n*

Endo, *Ex parte*, 59*n*

Erie Railroad v. Tompkins, 90*n*

European Defense Community Case (West Germany), 67–68, 81–82

Falbo v. United States, 149*n*
Flast v. Cohen, 89*n*
Frothingham v. Mellon, 89*n*

Gibbons v. Ogden, 15, 27*n*, 56, 64*n*
Golak Nath v. Punjab, 83*n*, 91*n*, 114*n*,
    153, 176*n*
Griswold v. Connecticut, 69, 89*n*
Guinn v. United States, 58*n*

Harper v. Virginia, 58*n*
Hepburn v. Griswold, 99*n*
Hill v. Massachusetts, 87*n*
Hirabayashi v. United States, 33, 59*n*,
    157–158, 177*n*
Home Building & Loan Association v.
    Blaisdell, 177*n*
Hurd v. Hodge, 89*n*

James v. Commonwealth, 26*n*
Johnson v. Stevenson, 58*n*
Jones v. Opelika, 87*n*

Kerala Education Bill, *In re*, 88*n*
Korematsu v. United States, 33, 59*n*, 161,
    177*n*

Lane v. Wilson, 58*n*
Leisy v. Hardin, 87*n*
Lochner v. New York, 149*n*

McArthur Ltd. v. Queensland, 26*n*
McCardle, *Ex parte*, 84, 91*n*
McCulloch v. Maryland, 56, 64*n*
Malcolm Baxter, The, 176*n*
Manitoba Education Reference, 88*n*
Martin v. Struthers, 122–123, 147*n*
Melbourne v. Commonwealth, 10*n*
Milkwagon Drivers Union v.
    Meadowmoor Dairies, 147*n*
Milligan, *Ex parte*, 87*n*
Miranda v. Arizona, 48, 53–54, 62*n*, 64*n*
Missouri, Kansas, & Texas Railway v.
    May, 149*n*

National Union of Railwaymen v.
    Sullivan, 91*n*
New York Times v. Sullivan, 147*n*

O'Donovan v. Attorney General, 59, 73–
    74, 89*n*, 91*n*
Osborn v. Bank of the United States, 26*n*

Party Finance Cases (West Germany),
    75, 89*n*

Pierce v. Society of Sisters, 89*n*
Poe v. Ullman, 89*n*

Reapportionment Cases:
    Canada. *See* Attorney General for
        Prince Edward Island v. Attorney
        General for Canada
    Ireland. *See* Article 26 and the Elec-
        toral Amendment Bill, 1961, *In re;*
        O'Donovan v. Attorney General
    Japan, 31, 59*n*
    United States. *See* Baker v. Carr; Rey-
        nolds v. Sims
Reynolds v. Sims, 54–55, 64*n*
Russell v. the Queen, 45
Ryan v. Attorney General, 90*n*

Saumur v. Quebec, 90*n*
Scott v. Sandford, 40, 60*n*
Screws v. United States, 177*n*
Segregation Cases. *See* Brown v. Board
Shelley v. Kraemer, 73, 89*n*
Sit-in Cases. *See* Barr v. Columbia; Bell
    v. Maryland; Bouie v. Columbia
Slaughterhouse Cases, The, 15, 27*n*
Smith v. Allwright, 58*n*
Socialist Reichs Party Case (West
    Germany), 57, 64*n*
Sonzinsky v. United States, 154, 176*n*
South Carolina v. Katzenbach, 58*n*
State (Quinn) v. Ryan, 48
St. Catherine's Milling and Lumber Co.
    v. the Queen, 61*n*
Sunakawa Case (Japan), 69, 89*n*, 153,
    176*n*
Suzuki Case (Japan), 72, 89*n*

Television Case (West Germany), 75
Terminiello v. Chicago, 149*n*
Terry v. Adams, 58*n*
Tileston v. Ullman, 89*n*
Toronto Electric Commissioners v.
    Snider, 45, 61*n*

United States v. Butler, 149*n*
United States v. Carolene Products, 38,
    60*n*
United States v. Lee, 28*n*
Uverges v. Pennsylvania, 149*n*

West Coast Hotel v. Parrish, 149*n*
West Virginia v. Barnettee, 60*n*

SUBJECT INDEX

Access to constitutional courts, 65–75
  by government officials, 34–35, 65–68, 73
  by private citizens, 34–35, 65–72, 73
  informal rules, 72
  standing to sue, 70–72
  strategies to obtain, 72–75
Advisory opinions, 49, 66–68, 81–82, 158
Amicus curiae, 35
Argentina:
  constitutional court (Supreme Court)
    judges
      recruitment and selection, 93
      tenure, 23, 76, 84, 101–102
    power, 23, 33, 76
    procedures and processes, 120, 150
  political system, 23
Australia:
  constitution, 11, 36
  constitutional court (High Court)
    access to, 68, 70
    blocs, 171, 173
    judges
      backgrounds, 98, 99, 100

      recruitment and selection, 93, 96
      tenure, 84, 102–103
      values, 24–25, 80
      voting data, 137
    judicial review
      federalism, 32
      free speech and press, 32
      political association, 32
    jurisdiction, 36, 70, 84
    political roles, 9–10, 36
    procedures and processes, 21, 49, 76n, 77, 78, 81, 117, 120, 137, 150–151, 153, 155, 159
    standing rules, 71
  judicial system, 36, 81
  political system, 23

Backgrounds of judges
  impact on decision making, 16–18, 103–112, 171
  political, 17–18, 92, 99–101
  professional, 17–18, 80, 98–99
  social, 17–18, 37–38, 96–98, 121
Bargaining among judges, 155

Belief systems, judicial impact on, 32–33,
    38, 40, 44, 56–57
Bloc analysis
    advantages of, 167–172, 175–176
    limitations of, 173–176, 190–194
    procedures, 160–167, 190–194
Briefs, 77

Canada:
    constitution, 45
    constitutional court (Supreme Court)
        access to, 66–67, 70
        blocs, 162–167, 171–172, 173, 174
        judges
            backgrounds, 37–38, 96, 98, 100
            recruitment and selection, 93, 95–
                96
            tenure, 84, 102–103
            values, 171–172
            voting data, 137, 162–167
        judicial review, 39
            districting and reapportionment, 31
            federalism, 32, 45–46
            free speech and press, 32, 38
            political association, 32
            voting rights, 38
        jurisdiction, 36, 46, 49, 70
        political roles, 36, 46, 49, 70, 84
        power, 83, 84
        procedures and processes, 76n, 77,
            78, 81, 120, 137, 150–151, 153, 155
        public perceptions of, 43
        standing rules, 70
    judicial system, 36, 81, 84
    political system, 23, 37, 38, 45–46, 83,
        84, 95
Capability analysis, 22–24
Certiorari, 72
Chi square, 181–188
Colombia, access to constitutional court
    in, 69–70
Compliance with judicial decisions, 57–58
Consensus among judges, 155
Constitutional courts:
    definition of, 4
    general surveys of literature, 6n
    political roles, 33–44
        defining boundaries, 34–35
        educating, 40–44
        legislating, 36–37
        representing, 37–38
        rule interpreting and application, 34

    stabilizing, 39–40
    supervising, 36
    See also Argentina; Australia; Canada;
        India; Ireland; Italy; Japan; Nor-
        way; Privy Council; Switzerland;
        United States; West Germany
Correlation analysis
    bivariate, 203–204
    multiple, 206
    partial, 205–206
Corruption, judicial, 76
Content analysis, 18, 118–119, 120, 121,
    217–218
Court packing, 84
Crime Control Act of 1968, 54–55
Cumulative scaling. *See* Scalogram
    analysis

Decision making, judicial:
    data for study of
        interviews with judges, 158
        judicial opinions, 46–51, 104, 118,
            120, 121, 123, 151–154
        private papers, 85, 111, 121–123,
            153–159, 167–169, 170
        votes, 51, 110–112, 119, 120, 123–
            126, 129–140, 141–143, 160–176,
            190–194
    group phase, 117, 120, 122, 150–178
    interaction, importance of, 154–159,
        221
    individual phase, 87–88, 110–111, 116–
        149, 160, 221
    methods for analyzing
        aligning judges, 124–125, 150
        bloc analysis, 160–176, 190–194
        capability analysis, 22–24
        case studies, 20
        content analysis, 18, 118–119, 120,
            121, 159
        game theory, 160
        judicial biography, 85, 121–123
        legal case analysis, 46–51, 118, 159
        models, 108–112, 176n, 220
        psychological techniques, 108, 119,
            120, 121, 217–218
        role analysis, 19, 140–144
        scalogram analysis, 126–140, 160, 170
        statistical techniques, 118, 127, 160,
            179–214
Decision making, juries, 117

Decisions, judicial
  correcting, 83–87
  factors influencing, 13–18, 21, 103–112
  impact studies, 51–57
  measuring influence of, 44–58
  methods of influencing, 76–82, 110–111
  political consequences of, 14–17, 22,
    30–64, 151
  symbolic value of, 56–57
Declaratory judgments, 69–70, 74
Democracy, and judicial review, 33–44
Discretion, exercise of by judges, 9–12,
  21, 49, 87–88, 108–112, 116–117, 120–
  121, 142, 151–152

Factor analysis, 196*n*, 208–212
Federalism, 32, 37–38, 45–46, 51, 55–56,
  81, 106, 124–125
Fictions, 47
Forum shopping, 80–81
France, Constitutional Council, 66–67

Great Britain
  judges, 80, 98
  judicial system, 36
  See also Privy Council
Greece, judges coerced in, 76

Honduras, tenure of judges in, 102

Impeachment, 23, 84–85
India:
  constitution, 83*n*, 86, 95
  constitutional court (Supreme Court)
    access to, 67
    blocs, 173
    judges
      backgrounds, 97–98, 100–101
      recruitment and selection, 49, 93,
        95, 97
      tenure, 84, 102–103
      voting data, 137
    judicial review
      economic regulation, 86–87
    jurisdiction, 36, 84
    political roles, 36
    power, 83*n*, 86–87
    procedures and processes, 137, 150–
      151, 153
  judicial system, 36, 84, 100–101
  political system, 83*n*, 84, 86–87, 153
Ireland:
  constitution, 10–11, 74
  constitutional court (Supreme Court)

    access to, 66–67, 70, 73–74
    blocs, 173
    judges
      backgrounds, 37, 80, 97, 98, 99–100
      recruitment and selection, 93, 95,
        96, 97
      tenure, 84, 102–103
      values, 80
      voting data, 123, 137
    judicial review
      criminal justice, 48
      districting and reapportionment,
        31, 73–74
      free speech and press, 38
      labor relations, 86
      voting rights, 38
    jurisdiction, 36, 49, 70, 84
    political roles, 36, 37, 43–44, 50
    power, 83, 86
    procedures and processes, 77, 78, 81,
      120, 137, 150–151, 158
    public perceptions of, 40, 44
    standing rules, 71
  judicial system, 36, 39
  political system, 23, 83, 86, 95
Italy:
  constitutional court (Supreme Court)
    access to, 68, 69*n*
    judges
      backgrounds, 97, 98
      recruitment and selection, 97
      tenure, 101–102
      voting data, 120, 123
    judicial review, 39–40
    political roles, 50
    procedures and processes, 150, 152,
      158
  judicial system, 50

Japan:
  constitution, 10, 69, 71, 152
  constitutional court (Supreme Court)
    access to, 68, 69, 71–72
    blocs, 160–161, 173, 174
    judges
      backgrounds, 80, 98, 100
      recruitment and selection, 49, 93,
        95, 96
      tenure, 84, 102–103
      values, 80
      voting data, 123, 137–138, 145,
        160–161

Japan *(Cont'd)*
  judicial review, 39
    criminal justice, 32
    districting and reapportionment, 31
    electoral disputes, 31, 72
    free speech and press, 32
    legislative-executive relations, 31,
        72
    military affairs, 32, 69, 71–72
    travel, 32
  jurisdiction, 36, 71–72, 84
  political roles, 36
  power, 76
  procedures and processes, 81, 120,
        137, 150–151, 152–153
  public opinion and, 40
  standing rules, 71–72
  judicial system, 36, 96
  political system, 23, 95
Japanese Americans in World War II, 33
Jehovah's Witnesses, 38
Judges
  backgrounds, 16–18, 37–38, 80, 92, 96–
        112, 121
  neutrality, 10–11
  discretion, 9–12, 21, 49, 87–88, 108–
        112, 116–117, 120–121, 142, 151–
        152
  policy choices, 87–88, 151–152
  role, 9–12, 19, 21, 108–110, 125, 140–
        144, 152, 173
  selection and recruitment, 49, 92–97
  socialization, 98–99
  tenure, 23, 76, 84–85
  training, 98–105
Judicial myth, 9–12
Judicial power, 9, 22–24, 36–37, 86–87,
        92, 99
Judicial review, 4, 35, 39
  substantive exercise in cases relating to
    birth control, 69, 71
    church-state relations, 15, 32, 43, 52
    criminal justice, 32–33, 43, 48, 53–54
    districting and reapportionment, 31,
        54–55, 73–74
    economic regulation, 15, 32, 36, 43,
        46–47, 79–80, 86–87
    electoral disputes, 31, 32, 72
    federalism, 32, 45–46, 55–56
    foreign affairs, 32, 81–82
    free speech and press, 15, 32, 38, 75
    labor relations, 36, 86

    legislative-executive relations, 31,
        46–47, 72
    military affairs, 32, 69, 71–72, 81–82
    political association, 32
    race relations, 15, 31–32, 36, 38, 40,
        46–47, 52, 55, 71
    travel rights, 32
    voting rights, 31, 38
Jurisprudence, 15, 221–223

Knowledge of publics about
  constitutional courts, 40–42
  U.S. Supreme Court, 41–43, 195–208

Lawyers, 7–9
Leadership in collegial courts, 155
Legal reasoning, 47
Legitimation by constitutional courts, 39–
        40, 46
Lower courts, 4, 6*n*, 17, 20, 21, 31, 36, 37,
        48–50, 66, 69, 81, 92–93, 105–110,
        117, 124, 137, 143–144, 150

Mexico, constitutional court procedures
        in, 155
Models of judicial decision making, 108–
        110, 176*n*

National Conferences on the Science of
        Politics, 17–18
Neutrality of judges, 10–11
Nicaragua, tenure of judges in, 102
Nigeria, judges coerced in, 76
Norway:
  constitutional court (Supreme Court)
    access to, 66
    blocs, 173
    judges
      backgrounds, 97, 98, 100
      recruitment and selection, 93, 96
      tenure, 84, 102
      voting data, 123
    political roles, 43–44
    public perceptions of, 44
  political system, 23

Oral advocacy, 76–77, 78

Perceptions of U.S. Supreme Court
        held by
  administrative assistants to U.S.
        Senators and Representatives, 208–
        212
  attentive public, 42
  blacks, 197–207

Perceptions, U.S. Supreme Court *(Cont'd)*
college graduates, 42, 186–187
national cross sections, 41–43, 180–189
Princeton undergraduates, 42
southern whites, 203–208
Phi coefficient, 160, 188–194
Policy choices by judges, 87–88, 151–152
Political culture, 44, 79–80, 87, 152–153
Pragmatism, 15
Presumption rule, 76
Preview by constitutional courts, 66–68
Pritchett, C. Herman, contributions to the
study of public law, 18–20, 124–126,
141–143
Privy Council as a constitutional court,
39, 45–46, 76n, 84, 153, 158–159
Public law:
definition of, viii
study of
interdisciplinary character of, 4
political science and, 46–47
behavioral impact, 5, 18–20, 124–
126, 141
current interests, 20–25, 30–214,
216
future of, 215–228
realist impact, 13–18, 117, 141
relevance for
lawyers, 7–9
political scientists, 3–5, 12, 30–64
practicing politicians, 8–9
social scientists, 7, 9–12
Public opinion, and constitutional courts,
15, 25, 28n, 32, 37, 40–44, 54–60
See also Belief systems; Knowledge of
publics; Perceptions of U.S.
Supreme Court; Support, public

Quantitative methods, 5, 14, 17–18, 19,
20, 124–140, 160–214, 216–217

Realism in study of public law, 13–18, 51
Recruitment and selection of judges, 49,
92–97
Regression analysis
bivariate, 199–204
multiple, 206–207
outliers, 201–203
residuals, 207–208
Role
definitions of, 34n, 140
judges, 9–12, 19, 21, 108–110, 125, 140–
144, 152, 173

lawyers, 7–9
Role analysis, 19, 140–144
Roles, political, of constitutional courts,
9–10, 14–17, 36–44, 46, 49, 50, 57, 70,
84
Roosevelt Court, The, 18–20

Scaling, Likert, 127, 196
Scaling, multidimensional, 139–140
Scalogram analysis, 126–140
advantages, 135–138
assumptions, 126–135
criticisms, 138–139
procedures, 129–135
Scatterplot, 197–199, 201–202, 205
Socialization, judicial, 98–99
See also Training of judges
Socialization, political, 41
Social science evidence, use by judges,
77–78
Soviet Union, 31n, 105
Standing to sue, 70–72
Stare decisis, 67
Statistical methods, 179–214
measuring association, the phi
coefficient, 189–194
numbered data, multivariate analysis,
205–212
numbered data, two variables, 194–204
testing statistical significance, chi
square, 181–188
See also Correlation analysis; Factor
analysis; Regression analysis;
Scatterplot
Support, public
for constitutional courts, 40–44
for U.S. Supreme Court, 41–43, 180–189,
195–212
Switzerland:
constitutional court (Federal Tribunal)
access to, 70
judges
backgrounds, 37–38, 97
recruitment and selection, 94, 97
tenure, 84, 101–102
voting data, 120
judicial review
districting and reapportionment,
31
political roles, 37–38
procedures and processes, 77, 150,
152, 155–156

Switzerland *(Cont'd)*
  political system, 37
Systems analysis, 34

Tenure of judges, 23, 76, 84–85, 101–103
Training of judges, 98–105

United States:
  constitution, 14–16, 45, 83
  constitutional court (Supreme Court)
    access to, 66, 68, 69, 70, 71, 72, 73
    blocs, 19, 166–170, 171–172, 173,
      174–175, 190–194
    decisions, impact of, 15, 20, 52–56,
      105–112
    judges
      backgrounds, 17, 18, 37, 79–80, 96,
        97, 98, 99, 101
      recruitment and selection, 94, 95,
        96
      tenure, 84–85, 102–103
      values, 14–16, 17, 79–80, 104–106,
        110–111, 118–119, 121–123,
        124–125, 129–137, 140–143,
        171–172
      voting data, 110, 123, 124–125,
        129–137, 141–143, 166–170,
        190–194
  judicial review, 39
    birth control, 69, 71
    church state relations, 15, 32, 43,
      52
    criminal justice, 32–33, 43, 48, 53–
      54
    districting and reapportionment,
      31, 54–55
    economic regulation, 15, 32, 36,
      43, 46–47, 79–80
    electoral disputes, 31
    federalism, 55–56
    free speech and press, 15, 32, 38
    labor relations, 36
    legislative-executive relations, 46–
      47
    military affairs, 32
    race relations, 15, 31–32, 36, 38,
      40, 46–47, 52, 55, 71
    voting rights, 31, 38
  jurisdiction, 36, 66, 70, 71, 72, 83, 84
  political roles, 14–17, 36–44, 50, 56
  power, 16, 22–24, 32, 33, 36, 51, 84–
    86, 87
  procedures and processes, 20, 21–22,
    77, 79–80, 110–111, 117, 120,
    150, 153–155, 156–159, 167–169,
    172
  public opinion and, 15, 25, 28, 37,
    54*n*, 56–57
  public perceptions of, 40–43, 179–
    190, 194–212
  standing rules, 70–72
  judicial system, 20, 36, 49–50, 93
  political system, 15–16, 23, 37, 38, 46,
    51, 55–56, 83, 85, 87, 95

Values, and science, 223–226
Values, judicial, 13–16, 17, 18, 21, 24–25,
  49, 56–57, 99, 101, 103–112, 116–117,
  119–120, 121–123, 124–126, 129–137,
  140–144, 151–152, 153–154, 156–159,
  171–172, 173, 221
Venezuela, tenure of judges, 102

West Germany:
  constitution, 10, 75
  constitutional court (Federal
    Constitutional Court)
    access to, 67–68, 70, 74–75
    decisions, impact of, 57
    judges
      backgrounds, 37, 80, 96–97, 98,
        100
      recruitment and selection, 93, 94,
        95, 96–97
      tenure, 84, 101, 102–103
      values, 80
      voting data, 120, 123
    judicial review
      electoral disputes, 31, 32, 75
      federalism, 32
      foreign affairs, 32, 81–82
      free speech and press, 32, 38, 75
      military affairs, 32, 81–82
      political association, 32
      voting rights, 38
    jurisdiction, 32, 70, 74–75, 81–82, 84
    political roles, 37, 43–44, 50, 57
    power, 32, 38, 50, 81–82, 83
    procedures and processes, 77–78, 81–
      82, 150, 152, 158–159
    public perceptions of, 43–44
    standing rules, 70–72
  judicial system, 50
  political system, 23, 37, 83, 94, 95

ABOUT THE AUTHORS

WALTER F. MURPHY, McCormick Professor of Jurisprudence at Princeton University, has been with the Princeton faculty since 1958. He is a member of the editorial board of *American Political Science Review*, the New Jersey Commission on Civil Rights, and the Committee on Legal and Governmental Processes of the Social Science Research Council.

In addition to numerous contributions to professional journals, his published works include *Congress and the Court* (1962), *Elements of Judicial Strategy* (1964), and *Wiretapping on Trial* (1965).

JOSEPH TANENHAUS is Professor and Chairman of the Department of Political Science at the State University of New York at Stony Brook. He has served on the advisory boards of the *International Encyclopedia of Social Science* and the Law and Society Program of the Northwestern University School of Law and as Council Chairman of the Inter-University Consortium for Political Research.

A frequent contributor to professional journals, he is also coauthor of *American Political Science: A Profile of a Discipline* (1963) and *The Development of American Political Science: From Burgess to Behavioralism* (1967); and he is coeditor of *Frontiers of Judicial Research* (1969).